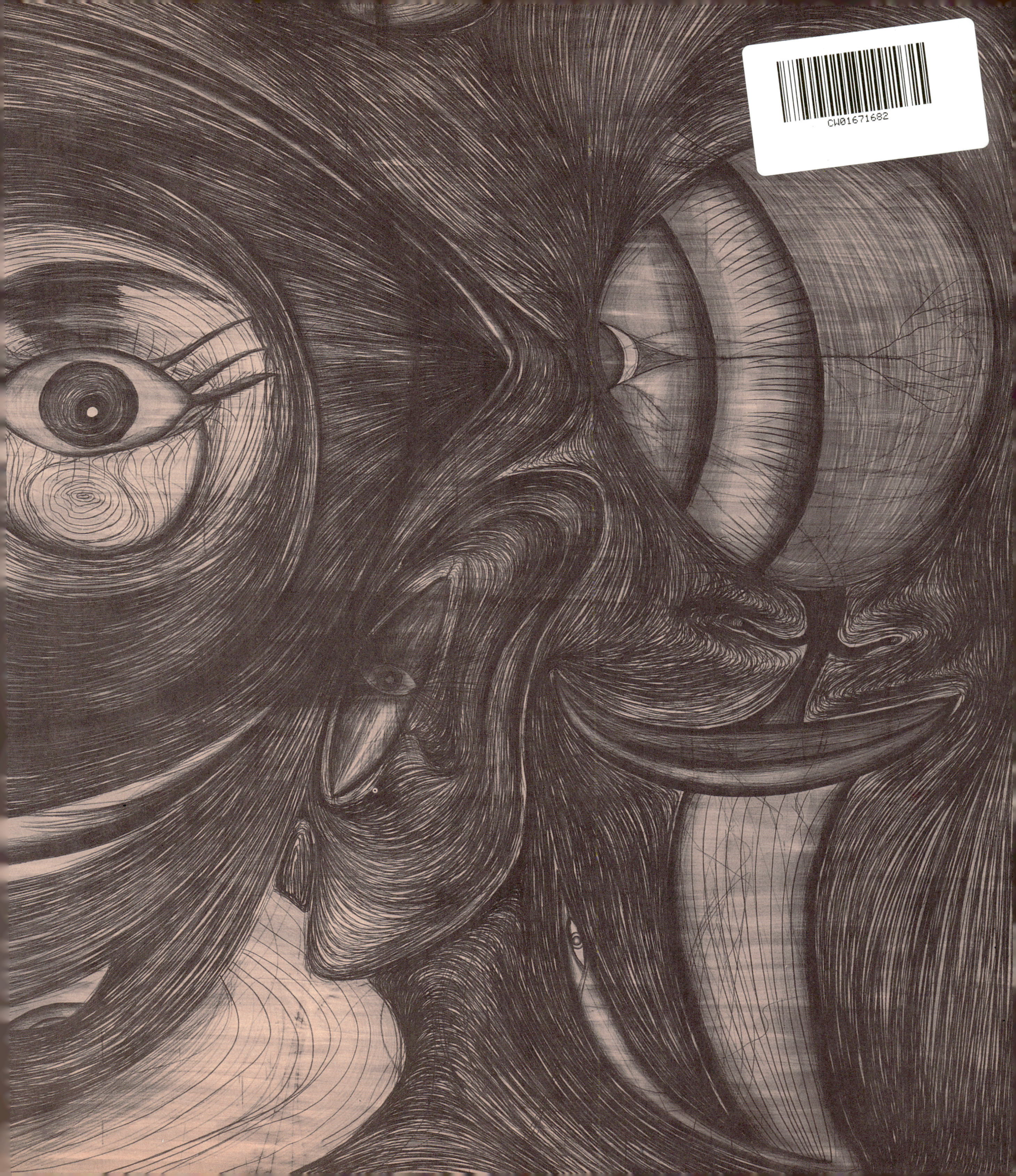

E. NICHOLAS.   39.00   / 14.95

DALE FRANK

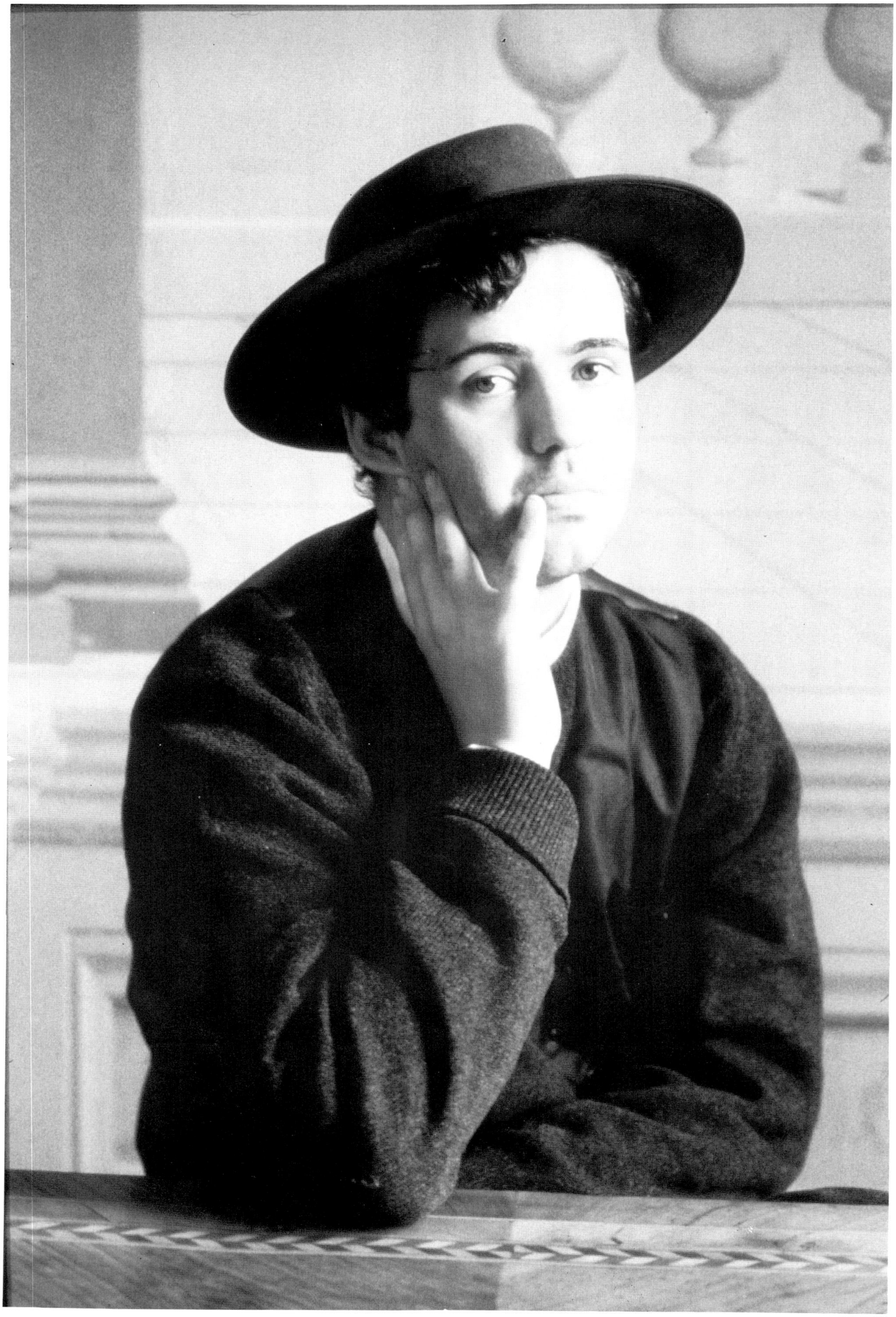

DALE FRANK

Jane Magon

CH

CRAFTSMAN HOUSE

First published in 1992 by Craftsman House BVI Ltd., Tortola, BVI
Distributed in Australia by Craftsman House,
20 Barcoo Street,
East Roseville, NSW 2069, Australia

Distributed internationally through the following offices:

USA
STBS Ltd.
PO Box 786
Cooper Station
New York
NY 10276

UK
STBS Ltd.
5th Floor, Reading Bridge House
Reading Bridge Approach
Reading RGI 8PP
England

ASIA
STBS (Singapore) Pte Ltd.
No. 25 Tannery Road
Singapore 1334
Republic of Singapore

ISBN 976 8097 31 0

Design *Sue Edmonds*
Typesetter *Craftsman House, Sydney*
Printer *Kyodo, Singapore*

Opposite title page
The Artist
Villa Rosa, Lucca, Italy, Summer 1986

This book is dedicated to
Napoleon, Iris-Ophelia and Hieronymus
Dale Frank

This book is dedicated to my parents,
Mick and Naomi Scott
and my husband Richard
Jane Magon

Contents

Acknowledgments

I would like to thank Hugh Jamieson for continuing to follow his excitement; Chroma Acrylics; Roslyn and Tony Oxley for the loan of their transparencies; Jane Magon for her parallels and insights and her reading; Paul Groot for being the 'Stephen King' that will always haunt my friendship; and to Kim Machan for all her support and strength to enable me to be able to deal with all these people I have mentioned; and finally to the people on my good list.

Dale Frank

I am grateful to and would like to thank Louise Martin-Chew who drew the publisher's attention to my work on Dale Frank. I also owe thanks to my husband Richard Magon for all his practical help and encouragement. I need to thank my thesis supervisor Dr Nicholas Zurbrugg for his support, reading and editing and Associate Professor Tony Bennett, Dean of Humanities at Griffith University. I am also grateful to Dr Wayne Hudson who has always been generous with time spent on discussion and with his encouragement of my work. I would also like to thank Graham Coulter-Smith and Associate Professor Richard Hutch and Nicholas Tsentas for reading and commenting on my text. I also appreciate the assistance from Naomi Scott, Dr Margaret Cameron and Heather Eastwood, who checked my 'proofs'. I would also like thank other people who had a positive impact on my art education such as Betty Churcher, David Jaffé and Dr Urszula Sz. Thanks must also go to Dale Frank and Kim Machan, for their co-operation and assistance and to my four children, Nicholas, Luke, Alexis and Camille for their patience and understanding.

Jane Magon

FOREWORD

The art of Dale Frank offers more than his paintings reveal. His paintings are so important because they can be read as a type of palimpsest, reflecting not only his own artistic development but also his own cultural period. The aspirations of this *oeuvre* show us the shadowing and the searching aspects of his work in relation to the art which has inspired him. These elements are both paradoxical and personal and have provided his work with a sense of extremism. Sometimes it can be hyper-serious, at other times sentimental, triumphant or self-doubting. In short, it provides a mirror of his most extreme feelings, expectations and disappointments.

Sometimes these paintings seem to be enshrouded by a secret. You have to know the password to fully understand the layers of meaning in his work. I think I do know some of the levels in his art. One of the passwords is, of course, 'baroque'.

It is the baroque which connects Dale Frank with the European mainstream, with the tradition of Rubens and Rembrandt, Soutine and Fautrier — and finally with the end of modern baroque art represented by Andy Warhol. Frank's paintings are intrinsically baroque. They do not represent what we used to call 'beaux-art'. In a sense, they do not even represent 'modern art'. It is Frank's devilish attempt to *shadow* the arts, to revive the old material that producers of 'fine art' thought unfit for use, that makes Dale Frank so subversive. These paintings of Dale Frank's play a game of hide and seek — they offer the viewer an alternative to standard Classical principles. Frank evokes the baroque way of re-arranging the world of good taste. His world is one where the old criteria of the arts no longer apply, where the old standards are ridiculed.

To understand these elements in Frank's paintings, one must avoid looking at the tradition of painting in general. Better, perhaps to explore the decadent Romanticism of the late 19th century. But beware — here is a reflection of the dark and bleak atmosphere summoned by Edgar Allan Poe, but in full colour! Here the light of Rationalism that usually pervades the fine arts has been eclipsed by the shadow of hidden things. Here the character of the world has taken on a mask of artificiality, reflecting less the qualities of Nature, more the dominance of Culture.

Baroque art was originally suspect because it was associated with the asceticism of the Reformation and the decadence of the Old Church. The Jesuits took the example of Michelangelo as a starting point for an entirely new concept of Art. No longer was it an instrument in the search for truth and beauty. Now it became a tool in the missionary zeal of the Church of Rome. The baroque was overrun as the Church attacked the very foundation of Art itself.

Another password which might apply in understanding Dale Frank's art, is the world 'critic'. It is intriguing to see how an artist not only plays first violin but at the same time offers a comment on the works of others similarly engaged in the orchestra of modern art. Everywhere we feel, see or suspect some kind of trap, or just a funny comment. We know this artist has something to say. He knows what he wants from his public. He doesn't expect our sympathy, but he does provoke our empathy. You cannot remain on the outside: you either embrace the work or fail to understand it.

The world 'Australian' is another of these key passwords. In the huge Australian sub-continent the exchange between the new and original cultures is still developing. But Frank's work is not the cliché we might perhaps suspect. Frank himself may suffer from existential and artistic doubts but he has never endeavoured to incorporate Aboriginal influences within his work. I think he knows that the essence of multiculturalism involves respecting the Other, and not trying to imitate it. It is only by trying to discover and understand the Other in your own personality that enables you, finally, to develop mutual understanding. Frank gives words to silent doubts — his personal ones. Only in retrospect can we discover the different aspects of the society and civilisation an artist lives in. Only with the perspectives of time can we find a mirror of his creative sensibility. When Dale Frank came to Europe he was confronted by the reverse process of his Artistic Dream for here he faced an over-civilised culture. Frank's extensive contacts with European traditions have helped him understand the many parts of himself and of the Australian civilisation as a whole. Here the Dreams and Dreaming are interwoven.

My favourite password for Dale Frank, however, is 'Napoleon'. This is the name of his son. The works he has created with young Napoleon are quite exceptional.

One sunny morning I discovered Napoleon taking revenge for those many occasions when he would have liked to be involved in Dale's art but was not allowed to. While his father wasn't looking, Napoleon took the pencils and paint and began working in the same way that he had seen his father painting. In the end he used his whole body as an instrument for an exclusive painting! As I watched him, I saw — minute by minute — a whole painting emerge. Jackson Pollock would have understood what Napoleon had brought to fruition. So did his father, who showed this work in an exhibition as a collaborative effort. The more structural details and formatting were Dale's but the freehand work was Napoleon's. I am waiting for the continuation of this collaboration — particularly for that moment when it becomes impossible to know who painted what, and who inspired whom.

Dale Frank's creativity has led him to many places without ever forcing him to betray his own Self, nor the Other within him. He understands the different artistic perspectives but this multi-talented artist — who is far more than just a performer or a painter — never shows any doubts about his own position.

When I first met Dale Frank, I could sense something of the electricity Verlaine must have felt when he met Arthur Rimbaud. I am not a pair to Verlaine, but Frank is a kind of

20th century Rimbaud. Look at his portraits: he could pass easily for Rimbaud. In fact, I pasted a photograph of Frank on my copy of the *Livres des Poche* edition of Rimbaud's collected poems. Later I added a portrait of Titus, son of Rembrandt van Rijn. Good company.

Dale Frank used to be a talented youngster. Now he has become a classical master. This is the perfect time to present the body of his work. Some of his paintings I already know by heart, others I have had to discover. But I know that in the end, just when I am beginning to understand him, he will escape me again.

That is why I call him a baroque master.

Paul Groot

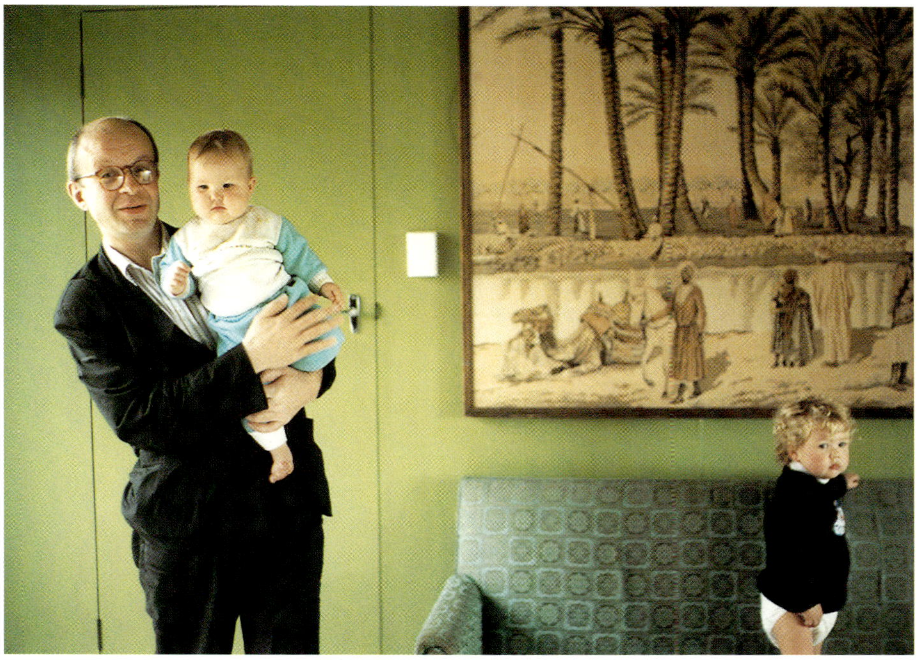

Paul Groot, Iris-Ophelia and Napoleon — Scone, April 1990.

ONE

Early Work, Shamanism, Symbols and Mythology

The art of Dale Frank is often found to be complex in the extreme and difficult to analyse. He has been generally accused of not being consistent and it has been argued that neither structure nor developmental phases are present in his work. On the contrary, his work evokes considerable structure and consistent development but frequently these come from an angle one least expects. Critics usually try to analyse his work only from the traditional angle of artistic 'style'. This has not been entirely successful for his work has remained elusive to categorisation. His line, his direction, his thematic concerns originate from those of a visionary, religious and mythological structure rather than from art alone, although he does engage and draw in other contemporary styles.

This chapter will discuss Frank's apparent affinity with the role of the shaman in his early work, to his later self-identification with Christ and other leaders. Repeatedly, Frank's early work displays many correspondences with shamanic traditions and in this respect his work can be interpreted in terms of its correspondences with the phases, rituals and symbols of the shamanic process. This chapter will outline some of the key phases in the shaman's life, particularly in terms of Mircea Eliade's classic work, *Shamanism: Archaic Techniques of Ecstasy*, 1972, and will attempt to indicate how Frank's work consistently evokes corresponding images and concerns.

Eliade describes the traditions of 'shamanism' as techniques for attaining ecstasy, found among Indo-Europeans and many other ethnic or cultural groups.[1] Sickness, dreams and ecstasies, are some of the means of reaching a shamanic state, as they 'constitute an initiation; that is they transform the profane pre-"choice" individual into a technician of the sacred'.[2]

Frank's content and working methods are usually expressed simultaneously on both the macro and micro levels. His work is most easily understood when considered in terms of three successive phases. The first chapter of this book introduces the shamanic symbols which are particularly obvious in the earlier works, but are also scattered throughout all his works. The second chapter introduces the extraordinary ideology which appears to form the central core of his content, directions and process. Chapter Three looks at Frank's work on the metacritical level, in terms of its critique or parody of artistic styles and in terms of his place in the international context of Post-modern art.

As I have suggested, while Frank is an artist of international contemporary repute, he might also be considered in terms of ancient shamanic traditions. As Dr Michael Harner points out, shamans have existed since prehistoric times around the world and are at the nucleus of many world religions. And while 'shamanic methods are strikingly similar the world over'[3], I.M. Lewis reminds us that shamanism 'is obviously subject to historical development and change'. Frank's work similarly develops from concerns with primal religion, in the early work, to a vision that also incorporates and integrates with Christianity.[4] In many ways Frank's works reveal him to be a shaman. Repeatedly, his work evokes the myths and symbols of the shaman's cosmic drama — of the Primordial Beginning. In this way, aspects of Frank's work overlap with shamanic beliefs. Repeatedly, his work evolves the dimension of 'the symbol as a primordial sign of the sacred'.[5]

These myths recreate Frank's metabiography,[6] his conflict between the forces of good (light) and the forces of evil (darkness), and like the shaman's practice, Frank's art advocates life, health and fertility in opposition to the forces of death, disease and sterility.[7] Considered in such terms, Frank's painting evokes a quest for a better world; for utopia, heaven, salvation and the ultimate prize of immortality, or if it fails, catastrophe. Put another way, his shamanic vision celebrates the tensions between the worlds of 'light' and 'darkness' and evokes a collective religious experience crystallising around the imminence of the eradication of the present world and the emergence of a new 'beginning'.[8] Frank's mystical visions conflates eschatology and cosmology, for 'those who have visited the nether worlds and paradise in ecstasy' have 'nourished the multimillenary visionary literature of the entire world'.[9] Yet, as Eliade points out, the problems addressed by shamanism are 'far from being solved'.[10]

Frank's endeavours fall into an extensive tradition that goes back to graphic fusions of shamanism and Christianity on cylinder seals and amulets of the third century AD. There is, as Guthrie notes, also the adoption of Orphism by the Jews[11] and an extensive tradition linking Christ and Orpheus: 'Just as Christ is to be seen in Christian monuments with the attributes of Orpheus, so here ... Orpheus is represented in the attitude of Christ'; an overlap due to the fact that 'crucified representations of the Crucifixion in art do not go back beyond the fifth or sixth century.'[12] Guthrie also notes the 'similarity' between 'the myth of Dionysus (the central story in Orphism) and the story of Christ,' observing that both Christ and Dionysus were sons of God, suffered, died and were resurrected.[13] Harner, meanwhile, tells of a famous North American Indian shaman, Essie Parish, who was both prophet and shaman and who integrated Christian concepts into her shamanism.[14]

I shall suggest that Frank might often be seen as both a shaman and a Chiliastic prophet, in terms of his use of mystical, anarchistic language. In this respect Frank's paintings are set apart from the 'profane' space insofar as they share the same status that Warden equates with art which is 'the last refuge of the shaman'.[15]

As I shall suggest, Eliade's summary of shamanic 'concepts' in *Shamanism: Archaic Techniques of Ecstasy*, helps to clarify the general concerns of much of Frank's art. Growing up outside Singleton, a small country town in New South Wales, Australia, Frank's variants of shamanism emerged of their own accord — gradually merging with Christian concepts.

Eliade describes shamans as religious leaders or prophet-priests, medicine men, sorcerers and magicians, who are found in all nomadic 'primitive' societies.[16] Shamans usually evolve from pre-literate cultures associated with hunter-gathering societies and having undergone physical illness or a psychological crisis, cure themselves and ultimately attain great personal power.[17] As Joseph Campbell suggests, shamans provide the first type of religious leadership, prefiguring priests and prophets. Priests are subsequently associated with planting and breeding societies that have more ritualised ways and a more regulated existence than the hunter-gathering societies of the shaman.[18] Planting and breeding societies ensure a plentiful supply of food and a more peaceful lifestyle with emphasis placed on group conformity rather than individuality, while the accent of hunter-gathering societies is on individual performance. The shaman offers an even more extreme and exclusive example of this type of individual performer.[19]

As Campbell observes, this insecure lifestyle of hunter-gathering groups often leads the shaman to act as something of a 'jack-of-all-trades', a magician and a 'trickster',[20] and a 'patcher' of problems in society. This aspect of the shaman as trickster is not given emphasis in Eliade's study although it is in Joseph Campbell's. The shaman becomes an innovator who combats the precariousness of existence through his own force of will, assuring his people's well-being by the power of his personality. According to Campbell the priest follows a more planned ritual so that the impact of his personality is of little importance. In this way the role of shaman and priest is governed by the economy and lifestyle of the immediate environment in each instance. Several parallels can be drawn between these patterns and the events in Frank's early life.

Frank's childhood was financially secure until he was six years old. His maternal grandparents were financially well-off, well established and well connected socially. His own parents lived a fairly comfortable farming life but in 1965, when Frank was six, they experienced the worst drought in one hundred years. Many people suffered, losing properties and business. At this time the government in New South Wales passed legislation which meant that valuable farming and grazing land was taken from his parents and grandparents for State projects, in return for a pittance. Other legislation was passed and Frank's parents were ultimately excluded from earning an income altogether. The government progressively took more and more land from three generations of his family estates for national parks and forestry.

From the ages of six to nine years his family lived a precarious existence, being forced to leave their successive homes. For several years this family of six children struggled to survive, and only began to manage financially by the time Frank was in his mid-teens. By then his powerful personality had been forged, both through economic ordeals and the personal trauma experienced by a difficult relationship with his father. Considered very generally, both his nervous, highly-strung personality and his unstable early life had much in common with the insecure lifestyle that Campbell associates with hunter-gatherers. Discussing the harshness of these times, Frank remembers walking home five kilometres from the school house in bitter cold or unbearable heat, faced with the constant threat of lurking snakes, as he passed stagnant waters and dead and decaying animals killed by the drought. These memories almost certainly provide a source for many of his later images.

In his mid-teens the family's life improved but by this time his growing sense of isolation became even more marked. At home and at school he was always the outsider, the 'other'. After leaving school he attended various art schools, leaving quickly in frustration after only a few weeks. From the age of seventeen he lived for many months in a Spartan environment in a cold, dark basement in virtual isolation, under the Experimental Art Foundation in Adelaide. This experience seems to have had much in common with the periods of fasting and seclusion so characteristic of the early stage of a shaman's behaviour and initiation.[21] At this time Frank lived exclusively on apples and cold, tinned vegetable soup and at the time of his leaving for overseas in October, 1979, weighed only six stone. His performance art included a ritual entombment and resurrection and a 'public initiation'[22] — two other traditional symbols of shamanic initiation. In this respect, then, the experience of Frank from the ages of six to nineteen overlap in many fascinating ways with the more formalised initiation ceremonies of the shaman.

As Eliade observes, a shaman becomes a shaman only after he has been transformed by ecstatic dreams or 'instruction'.[23] Many shamans apparently inherit a nervous disposition or receive 'calls' from ancestors, as the shamanic gift which 'descends from generation to generation'.[24] Frank interestingly mentions past and present relatives who were popularly considered to be 'evil'. He also relates how his great-grandfather built his migrant Scottish family a large, comfortable house and then proceeded to live in a remote shack on the same property, anticipating Frank's own subsequent hermetic seclusion in Adelaide.

Another critical, important phase in the shaman's development is the process of encountering a divine being in a dream or trance who identifies the initiate as the 'chosen' one. Mythological instruction by a master usually follows the initiatory dreams and visions. While Frank was not 'instructed' by another in this sense, the process of his early works seems to have afforded him independent awareness of such shamanic concerns as mastering the techniques of ecstasy: the aspiration to undergo a mystical journey to the sky to recover the lost paradisial condition, to descend to the underworld and to converse with Gods, semi-divine beings and dead souls.[25] It seems that Frank has 'instructed' himself through his early art making.

As Campbell indicates, the shamanic path usually entails a process of healing oneself of either a physical illness or a mental crisis that resembles a nervous breakdown. On occasion the 'healing of the shaman is achieved through art'[26] a process which, as I shall suggest in more detail in this book, offers the perfect paradigm for much of Frank's career. By going through initiatory ordeals such as illness, emotional sufferings, ritual death and resurrection, the shaman gains a powerful personality that he believes enables him to cure the ills of the world. Frank's artistic career seems to embody a similar search for this kind of shamanic power.

Considered more specifically, the shaman's ecstatic experience occurs only during a celestial or underworld journey. As Eliade points out the shaman believes that he will ascend to heaven on the *axis mundi* — the post, Pole Star, Cosmic tree, liana, rope, mountain or rainbow[27] or riding on the shaman's drum, horse or bird. Many shamans also believe that they journey into the sky and converse with the Divine God, often on the behalf of others. Here they undergo what Eliade terms 'the ecstatic experience of illumination' and are filled with a glorious light in the presence of God.[28]

Novice shamans must go through initiatory ordeals which can be presented either in a dream or public ritual. It is often believed that a Supreme God instructs the future shaman through dreams and visions and that they are expected to pass through difficult and painful initiatory ordeals.[29] Such ecstatic experiences involve the schema of symbolic death in initiation ceremonies and rituals of suffering, death and resurrection.[30] These initiations involve dismemberment, renewal of organs, trial by fire, cutting and opening, acquiring a new skin, becoming an animal and so on. The early and middle work of Frank reflects many of these shamanic myths, including fears that Murray associates with imminent annihilation by a monster, subterranean journeys of 'descent', metamorphoses, flight, being invisible and invulnerable and 'murder, crime and punishment, death and resurrection'.[31]

Considered in these thematic terms, Frank's art could be said to reflect a quest for immortality, for resurrection, for ecstasy and for 'light'. Murray describes these quests as being 'engendered during periods of excessive strain, anxiety, resentment, or despair' providing a 'psychic source of the important death and resurrection myth', conditions which certainly have many counterparts in Frank's family conflict and his early troubled years.[32]

Shamans have also been described as 'quarrelsome', 'excited or raised', and at times the shaman's 'combativeness sometimes becomes an aggressive mania',[33] descriptions which all at times apply to Frank's passionate creativity. Alternatively, the shaman symbolically combats the powers of evil or death, a process suggested in Frank's drawings *The Devil May Care Ingrained Ears, Portraits 1–3* (1982). While many shamans mime the journey of the soul in dramatic form,[34] Frank mimes this process through his painting. Eliade suggests that shamans 'feel drawn to a kind of life that gives them intimate contact with the supernatural world and allows them to expend their nervous force freely' and psychologists in turn might describe the developing shaman as having a 'psyche in crisis', often characterised by a sudden, rapid transition from irritability to normality or from melancholia to agitation: shamans are vulnerable to morbid dreams.[35] Frank's 'initiatory' dreams described in his paintings frequently evoke specific, recognisable aspects of what we might think of as the shamanic journey.

Repeatedly Frank's dreams evoke the experience of one who ascends to the heavens as a psychic traveller through the visionary world. As Eliade notes, this phenomenon happens mostly when the psyche is most active when the body is asleep or 'when it lies at the point of death'. Works which employ the symbolism of magic flight[36] in sleep, dreams and fantasies, include the painting *The Sleeping Artist and the Mind's Eye in the Sour Ear,* 1984, and *The Sleeper with a Strange Perspective on Life (The Abstracted Liver Eye),* 1985. Here Frank seems to be portraying himself in a shamanic state of sleep and psychic travel, as his soul leaves his body in a trance to cross the mythical dimensions of inner space. Frank's dreams include aerial views of his psychic travel through the landscape of the vagina, an experience depicted in his painting *An Aerial View of the Hidden Valley in the Dentata Mountains,* 1983.

According to Eliade, shamanic elevation is achieved through encountering a divine being, or spiritual guide. *The Saints Koln 1* and *2*, 1981, evoke swirling faces in knotted woodgrain which might seem to symbolise souls of shamans hiding in the knots of trees,[37] and — according to Eliade's account — announce that the viewer has been 'chosen' to follow a new rule of life.[38] In this respect Frank's dream-paintings chronicle his quest for celestial knowledge and for the process of becoming one with the Divine God. But, as Eliade and other commentators specify, the Way to the Divine God can be terrifying, and the initiate may encounter many horrifying dreams that are just the first of a continuing series of 'trials'.

Initiations and Themes

Dismemberment

Frank's pictorial account of 'initiation' seems to follow several pre-determined patterns. According to shamanic literature, one of the first ecstatic experiences almost always includes 'dismemberment of the body, followed by a renewal of the internal organs and viscera'.[39] A number of works by Frank from 1982 onwards depict internal organs, and refer to them quite specifically in titles such as: *Being Just a Liver the Virgo, Portrait,* 1982*;* or *Portrait, and Memories of Arms and Fingers Double Self-Portrait,* 1983. In the painting *A Track to Medieval Artist and Fountains,* 1982 one finds 'artery-fountains', two kidneys and a liver which form a face. Disturbingly disconnected and reassembled, Frank's drawings of internal organs seem very likely to refer to his shamanic 'renewal' of his internal organs and his life.

Seas of blood

Another of Frank's initiatory experiences involves a sea of blood, an image with strong correspondences with the way in which evil spirits are described by shamans as ' blood waters rising' and which test the initiate's 'psychic force'.[40] This 'sea of blood' is most evident in such paintings as *The Fleshy Islands and the Red Tide*, 1983, *The Wake*, 1984, *The Tired Salt*, 1984, and *The Flooded Studio: The Studio and the Stain from Memory*, 1984 — a title which perhaps alludes to the 'blood' of his nightmares.

Renewal of organs

Discussing *The Fleshy Islands and the Red Tide* during an interview in 1991, Frank interestingly refers to it as 'a portrait made of pieces of meat and a red tide of blood'.[41] Eliade uses much the same terminology when he points out that 'dismemberment of the neophyte's body and renewal of his organs' is a 'ritual death followed by resurrection'.[42] Images of internal organs can also be found in many of Frank's early works,[43] which also seem to record monstrous dreams. For example, *The Sleeper with a Strange Perspective on Life (The Abstract Liver Eye)* of 1985 refers to Frank's vision witnessing the decapitation of his own head; an image which in turn recalls the myth of the dismembered shaman, Orpheus, who became a 'prophesying trunkless head'.[44]

Eyes, Multiple Eyes, the bleeding eye and the distended eye

Sometimes Frank's blood red seas are strangely scattered with many eyes. According to Harner, shamans similarly discuss their visions of 'a thousand eyes' which 'search the night for enemies'.[45] Such eyes floating in blood can also be seen in Frank's paintings of *The Wake*, 1984, and *The Flooded Studio — The Studio and the Stain*, 1984.

In some of his early drawings such as *The Artist with no Excuse*, 1984, Frank also depicts small, multiple eyes attached to large eyes. Multiple and bodiless eyes are also prominent in *The Demon Artist's Portrait with a Question of Siamese Success*, 1984. Here, large, single eyes portray what Harner might term the shaman's 'strong eye', or the eye of knowledge 'visualising' or 'imaging' in 'an altered state of consciousness'.[46] This kind of 'strong eye' appears elsewhere in works like *The Demon Artist's Portrait with a Question of Siamese Success (Green Portrait)*, 1984. A bleeding eye in Frank's *The Beached Sperm Whale and his Affection to the Disinfected Onlooker, an Art Moral*, 1985, also seems to suggest a shamanic vision that Paul Foss associates with a 'pagan', 'feminine ecstasy' which can be related to the 'bleeding eye' of God.[47]

According to Eliade, the shaman's eyes are also sometimes 'strong' in the sense that they test the initiate by appearing as disembodied 'eyes ripped from their sockets', witnessing their own dismemberment.[48] Frank similarly confronts the point, described by Foss, at which 'horror becomes fascinating'.[49] Some shamans can see inside their own and other people's bodies. Their eyes become virtually extended from their body — an experience that Nevill Drury associates with eyes, distended 'like a sort of thread made of gum' like a lobster's or 'snail's antennae'.[50] Frank's drawing *Self-Portrait to the Peered at the Yellow Sea,* 1984, grippingly portrays a view from the inside of the head, detailing optic nerves and cords reflecting the 'inner self', or what he described in an interview as 'the gap between the surface of the face and the mind'.[51]

The double

Frank's notion of a 'gap between' might extend from the 'inner self' and 'outer self' to 'self' and 'other self', creating what Frank frequently refers to as the importance of the theme of doubles in his work.[52] Double images are present in a large body of Frank's work, for example *The Two Moons,* 1984. While his double image may suggest a schizoid self it might also refer to the battle that Eliade identifies between the shaman's double and the sorcerer on which a cure for the shaman's patient depends.[53] The shaman's double is described as having 'a ghost with you always — another self'[54] and is perhaps symbolised in later works such as *Classicism,* 1990, in images such as the two tigers. Frank's work also frequently depicts the unmistakable presence of mutated male and female sexual motifs that seem to correspond to the shamanic initiation that Eliade associates with 'ritual androgynisation'.[55]

Ritual androgynisation

Frank has merged and androgynised male and female sexual organs in his drawings and paintings of 1982–83, somewhat as shamans draw human sexual organs on their costumes to 'sanctify' them.[56] Ritual androgynisation can also be seen in Frank's early performances of 1979 where he dressed as a female in a pale blue ball gown in *People never tell you, if, is up,* 1979. Ritual androgynisation is used perhaps to symbolise a divine bi-unity, and to abolish opposites[57] — an impulse which might explain Frank's evocations of confused sexual identity.[58] Further counterparts to the shaman's initiatory 'change of sex' can also be seen in his painting *Self-Portrait as a Woman and an Artist,* 1983, and in his drawing *The Three Heads,* 1982. *Self-Portrait: The Full of Fear Soldier in View of the Trench and Gases,* 1983, offers another vision of the subject matter that he describes in an interview as 'the female within the male'.[59]

The shaman's theory of illness

The shaman's theory of illness entails the curing of their own physical or psychological crises. A similar ritual seems apparent in drawings such as Frank's *A Cruxing Moral, Lonely Boys with Wide Hips Lead to Only Breast Cancer and Empty Cradles,* 1981, *The Making Of Oral and Loin Cancer,* 1981, and *The Hierophant's Cancerous Oats,* 1982. All of these works refer to spreading cancerous tumours and present expressive 'anatomical' drawings of intestinal organs and tumours. Later works with black blotches, simultaneously refer to Black Holes, Black Death and Syphilis. In the shaman's role as healer, magical darts are supposedly 'extracted' from the victim's body.[60] 'Magical darts'[61] can be found in some of Frank's more recent paintings with nails literally embedded in the surface, such as in the painting *The Cosmology of the Recurring Reactionary*, 1990.

As Eliade notes, the shaman's 'healing' of his patients takes place when the shaman puts his hand in, or makes a 'wound', that will 'close of itself'.[62] Frank similarly places his hand into the 'wounds' he makes in his own paintings and has referred to Anton Jean Gros' painting *Napoleon Putting his Hand Through the Wounds at Jaffa*, 1804. Wounds are depicted in Frank's *The Wounded Painting that Tempted to Look into the Mirror behind the Artist's Back — Why Women are not Artists*, 1985, and in *The Two Saints*, 1985 (which refers to St Bartholomew and St Sebastian). In the latter work a hole has been burnt into the surface, and almost certainly represents Frank's existential suffering. Frank's tendency to make cuts in his painting also suggests the shamanic initiation ceremony of 'opening'.[63] Sometimes the 'wounds' in his paintings are stitched together in a garish child-like way, reminiscent of the shaman's ritualised wounding that implies 'death and rebirth'.[64] Collectively the caves, graves, wounds and vagina symbols in Frank's work all seem to evoke suffering, death, entombment and rebirth.

The new skin and ritual nudity

The shaman's initiation is continued in the 'new skin', visible only to initiates, and appearing only after a symbolic death.[65] Frank interestingly describes *And the Painting of the Painting that was Justly so Afraid, it Stuck to the Frame of the Inner Light and the Guiding Light of the Virgin Painting (The Studio Eye)*, 1984 as a work in which the surface has 'fallen away into the corner through fear to reveal the virgin painting' below. This concept seems to correspond to what Eliade defines as the shaman's notion of a 'new skin', visible only to initiates after symbolic death. Skin and ritual nudity are described by Eliade when the shaman bares his torso, which he says probably has some religious significance.[66] 'Ritual nudity' is also seen in Frank's painting of a man's torso in *Self-Portrait of St Bartholomew, The Torso— 1985* a portrait of himself as St. Bartholomew.

Mastery of fire

Another of the shaman's consecration festivals concerns 'mastery of fire', where he must either touch burning flame or 'tread on fire'.[67] Frank's performance *Parted — Walking On*, 1979 where he walked on flames on oil-covered water, appears to offer a direct counterpart to this ritual. More importantly Frank uses the 'mastery of fire' as part of his painting techniques in his later works of 1985 and 1986.

The obstacle wall and the sacred waterfall

Frank's imagery also has counterparts to the shaman's journey which takes him to the remote and 'sacred' waterfall of 'liquefied quartz', to acquire a guardian spirit.[68] The waterfall or the wall can also obstruct the shaman's quest. Works such as *The Falls from Memory*, 1984, and *The Studio Falls (The Sleeping after the Light)*, 1984, are described by Frank in terms of 'a tiring journey to get knowledge or gain insight'.[69] Initiatory exhaustion in gaining insight in the face of the obstacle or adversity is clearly evident in this statement.

The cave

Entering a cave is also important as a 'passage into another world', in order for the shaman to gain insight. Eliade notes that many shamans have their initiation in caves where they 'meet their helping spirits'.[70] Frank's *The Evil Seepage and the Caveman*, 1983, and *The Deep and Cavernous Sea*, 1983, associate the vagina with an initiatory cave feared both as a scene of death and as an image of the Void.

In some shamanic journeys the cave or tunnel may have a stream or river, that[71] can be seen in *The Evil Seepage and the Caveman*, 1983, which also probably refers to Frank's childhood memory of vaults, death and water. At the age of seven he was trapped in a large water tank that had only a tiny opening and running water. He felt entombed and that he was experiencing death at that very time. The conviction of experiencing death is a crucial occurrence in the developmental experience of a shaman. This feeling of terror — voids, tunnels, water, entombment and death — seems to permeate a large section of Frank's oeuvre. *The Cave Cleaner in the Storms*, 1981, depicts a face of 'caves' or underground tombs where a figure 'cleans up' the place of death, evoking what Frank terms as 'trauma and anxiety' — the shaman's 'classic initiatory ordeal'.[72]

Eliade further describes how the shaman must become an animal, by putting on an animal mask to prepare himself for the Underground journey. In this way the shaman is carried into the beyond by an animal, or is swallowed, killed and resurrected.[73] Once again, Frank's work presents images of such shamanic processes. Mask-like images such as a 'flayed face' with sexual organs as facial features appear in Frank's *The Head and Blood Their, a State of Mind*, 1982. Through the mask-faces in his work and titles which involve animals, Frank evokes metamorphosis into a superhuman condition.[74] Here the shaman re-establishes a lost paradisial state,[75] just as his rituals attempt to inaugurate ecstatic descent to the underworld and ascension to the sky.[76] At times this descent can be a fearful journey to a place of spiders, snakes and dead souls. The spider in *Self-Portrait with the Spider's Itch in the Mind's Eye for the Baboon's Dinner where the I's have it (Self-Portrait with the Future)*, 1985 seem to refer to this kind of fearful underworld landscape.

Shamanic descent can also be made through a process of engulfment or swallowing by human or animal entities, or alternatively through a tunnel. These rituals are reflected in Frank's work *The Miner's Rich Vein and a Double Portrait of the Possible Miner from the Front Triple Portrait,* 1983, where three portraits are 'swallowed' one inside the other, resembling apocalyptic images of the swallowing 'mouth of the beast or dragon'[77]. Frank's painting *The Fearful Soldier and his Hound Self-Portrait with the Drowning Hound Poodle,* 1983, offers a transverse section of his own head as it 'swallows' male and female genitalia.

The experience of engulfment and descent into the underworld is also evoked in Frank's drawing *Self-Portrait at 21 with Milk Maids,* 1983 — a pictorial equivalent of the shaman's discovery of the 'mysterious labyrinthine cave', and a 'world of pain'.[78]

Frank has declared that he had 'a sense of urgency to find the Beast'.[79] It seems many shamans have a method for regaining lost guardian spirits. The shamanic method of 'Calling the Beasts' provides a way of getting in touch with one's 'animal aspects' by mentally welcoming a spirit animal into one's body. In this way the shaman metamorphoses himself into other forms of life in order to travel to the underworld or the depths of the ocean in order to retrieve a lost 'power animal'. Frank in turn seems to undergo a human, penis-whale metamorphosis for a potentially ecstatic journey to the underworld or oceanic lower-world, in the drawing *The Beached Sperm Whale and his Affection to the Disinfected Onlooker, an Art Moral,* 1985. Here, life and death and animal and human parts separate and merge.[80]

The shaman's descent to the Underworld can be undertaken by entry into a tunnel, often symbolised by concentric motifs. Joan Vastokas notes that:

> *the concentric motif seems characteristic of the visionary experience itself and stands for the aperture through which the shaman penetrates the Underworld or sky, by means of which he transcends the physical universe.*[81]

Like many shamanic masks with their 'concentric circles radiating from a central void',[82] Frank's earliest known drawings, 1981–1982, such as the portraits *Cave Cleaner in the Storms,* 1981, *Judgement, The World, The Fool,* 1982 and *Devil May Care,* 1982, are built up of concentric circles. In shaman's terms these apertures allow Frank to enter tunnels and undertake journeys into the visionary world, above or below. Frank's *The Inland Sea (New Moon to the Warren),* 1984, interestingly evokes an entrance to the underground world — a zone which many shamans describe as a hole which has been made by a burrowing animal,[83] and thus a sort of 'warren'.

Other paintings refer to the journey of Frank's friends in the world beyond the grave. *Dorian's Eye to the Painter's Yellow Sea and Winter Willow (Therese's Pretty View in View of the Rocky Palette),* 1984, for example commemorates Therese, one of Frank's friends who shot herself with a ship's flare gun. This work depicts a view from Therese's grave, looking up to the sky. Eliade notes that some shamans who wish to become medicine men 'lie by graves'[84] adding that having 'contact with the souls of the dead signifies *being dead oneself*'.[85] In this way these works partially evoke Frank's sense that one might rescue others and avoid death by confronting its mysteries.

The Stagnant Sea, a 'mirror image of rotting green',[86] associated with death and decomposition, has more general resemblances with the miasma. This muddy, encrusted, noxious landform has had connotations of 'pollution', 'curse' and 'sin' from very early times.[87] In the Orphic world such rivers and marshes constituted the gathering place for the souls of the dead.[88] Frank's later works are often burnt, chemically treated and corroded so that they look like stagnant places of death, toxicity and dissolution. These images might also refer to his childhood recollections of the stagnant water that he passed by on his long walks home from school. Frank's paint flows also recall the visionary's imagined Underworld places, suggestive of Plutarch's vision of 'a basin into which flowed rivers of various colours,'[89] — a description reminiscent of Frank's working method.

These 'ecstatic experiences' involve the traditional schema of almost all initiation ceremonies: suffering, death, resurrection.[90] If Frank's paintings evoke places and processes of death and immortality, some of his works also have much in common with the shamanic process of resurrection. For example, in an early performance *Closet: Entombed, Burial and Resurrection,* 1979, Frank lay on the ground as if entombed in loosely-laid fire bricks which gradually shook and fell off with his increased breathing. In this performance Frank virtually created his own initiatory ritual of resurrection, somewhat as the shaman's ritual of rebirth allows him to return to the Earth and the Heavens on bridges which link the three cosmic planes, Underworld, Earth and Sky.[91]

'Bridges' are seen in his later works, such as the painting *Sour Love and the Ad of Buffalo Never Set an Easel — View from the Window,* 1988. In this work Frank's multicoloured threads — the shaman's bridge — symbolises 'the passage to the beyond', where the guilty cannot cross and are 'precipitated into the abyss'.[92] Frank suggests that, 'My art is like a bridge over a chasm of boredom and emptiness. All you need are one or two images that don't support the bridge and the whole thing collapses.'[93] For the shaman, the process of crossing the bridge 'as thin as a hair' and connecting two cosmic regions signifies the passage from one mode of being to the other. It represents the transition from neophyte to initiate, from living to dead, and the ability to pass from one cosmic plane to another: Underworld, Earth and Sky.[94] By crossing bridges 'narrow as a razor's edge', the shaman proves he is no longer merely a human being.[95] Frank's stitched webs and nets suggest the place where the gods and demons of death might capture vagabond souls.[96]

Shamanic accounts also mention that the gods used meteors to open what is often called the 'tent' of the sky to survey the Earth. Similarly, it is suggested the Pole Star makes a hole in the celestial vault, thereby connecting the three worlds: Underworld, Earth and Sky. 'Meteors' made of coloured ashtrays are to be seen in Frank's two paintings *Red Trees And Yellow Trees with Meteors,* both produced in 1984. Through such images Frank evokes an ascent to the paradise that shamans associate with their 'pastoral' cultures.[97] Discussing this painting, Frank confirmed that such images might be compared with the shamanic theme of mystical ascent to paradise. Such ascents are attained via the *axis mundi* in the form of a bridge, tower, mountain, tree, or vine. The shaman may ride on a bird or horse, utilising his ceremonial drum-beat to attain a state of ecstasy.

As Eliade and Harner note, the shaman's drum is crucial to the shamanic process. The drum allows the shaman to break through the planes of time and space to 'the world above and the world below' and to attain ecstasy through its 'musical magic', which makes possible his ecstasy.[98] While Frank's early drawing, *They saw a Cave Cleaner and Hindu Drums on the Autobahn*, 1982 evokes such magical dreams, there are few other images of drums in Frank's work. But as Eliade also specifies, the drum is often called the 'sea'[99] an image elaborated by Frank in works such as *The Sea and the Sore Eye*, 1984, which seems to depict a remarkable image of an 'exploding' water fountain, an *axis mundi* connecting sea and heaven in an ecstatic vision of ascension. Frank suggests that his eye is sore 'because it is tired of seeing its own vision'.[100]

Eliade suggests that most shamanic 'paradise myths' centre around the 'idea of immortality', and the aspiration for higher revelations[101] obtained by journeying up the cosmic tree, vine, ladder, rope or mountain which unite the shaman with the Supreme God in Paradise.[102] All these symbols are to be found in Frank's early work from 1981, particularly the vine around the fountain in works such as *The Delusions of the Studio Fountain*, 1985, and *The Fountain and the Trellis, The Trellis and the Delusions of the Studio Fountain*, 1985, and *All at Least a Mountain Tradition*, 1982. The shaman's symbol of the tree or inverted tree — 'a mythical image of the cosmos'[103] — can be seen in his drawing *The Intrusion and Facial Shock of the Tree*, 1982. Other symbols such as the tower, drum, sea, mirror, rope, cord and woollen threads can be found across the spectrum of Frank's works and in a sense represent shamanic 'tools' for ascending into his paradise.[104] Discussing the image of tangled rope, Frank initially suggested the image functioned as a symbol of chaos. Reflecting upon his use of sections of rope and wool threaded across holes in his paintings, Frank hinted at their other connotations, including their spiritual significance.

In this respect Frank's images of mirrors, 'drums', rope and sea all correspond potentially to sources of shamanic flights of ecstasy which cannot be performed without a mirror.[105] Harner notes that a mirror is said to help the shaman to 'see the world' and to locate the souls of the dead. In the mirror the shaman becomes aware of two realities — the heavenly self and the earthly self.[106] Precisely this sort of distinction seems present in *The Painting of a Painting at Low Tide (The Painting at Low Tide and the Beaching)*, 1985, and images of the mirror are also found in *The Wounded Painting that Tempted to Look into the Mirror behind the Artist's Back — Why Women are not Artists*, 1985, a painting Frank describes as attempting to 'create or encounter its own sense of self'[107]. As Frank himself has noted in a recent interview, his painting *And the Painting of the Painting that was Justly so Afraid, it Stuck to the Frame of the Inner Light and the Guiding Light of the Virgin Painting (The Studio Eye)*,1984, suggestively 'reveals a shimmering primeval swamp', reflected in the framed and luminous 'mirror' which he has integrated into this painting.[108]

According to shamanic lore, it is during ecstatic journeys to the sky that the shaman can 'abolish the present fallen state of the universe and humanity and re-establish the primordial situation, when heaven was easily accessible to all men'.[109] It is to this 'fallen state' that some of Frank's later work refers: to his task of healing the cosmic wound represented by black blotches or cuts in the canvas. Frank's *It's my party — To Johnny and Mickey — He's left Home*, 1990, is even more suggestive of a 'fallen', exploded planet. *Sour Love and the Ad of Buffalo Never Set an Easel — View from the Window*, 1988, features a beautiful blue galaxy with holes and similarly evokes what Frank describes as cosmic wounds,[110] both in terms of the numerous holes in the picture's surface and the coloured wool stitches which hold these wounds together. In this way the shaman heals not only himself and others but also the wounded cosmos.

Howitt, one of the many scholars quoted by Eliade, explains that in order to get to paradise, the shaman has guardian, helper — spirits who mysteriously travel through rock crystals which in turn are regarded as magical 'solidified' light. When the initiate swallows these crystals he is able to ascend to the sky.[111] Images of crystals can be found in *The Island Structure and the Sugar Recollections*, 1983, where sugar is an example of something 'sweet and crystalline'.[112] A number of his early self-portraits and other drawings, such as *Self-Portraits as Floating Prisms*, 1982, depict crystalline prisms as in the delicately coloured *Intrusions and Facial Shock of the Tree*, 1982, where the prisms are crystals. Similar images are used in *Self-Portrait with Lockjaw and Crystal*, 1984. Frank's subsequent works of 1985–86, have chemically derived crystals growing on the surface of the canvas, a process causing considerable alarm to museum curators and considerable satisfaction to Frank. Frank's crystalline surfaces and images typify the ecstatic and spiritual impulse of these paintings and drawings.

In his book *Ecstatic Religion*, I.M. Lewis explains that 'the shaman is an inspired priest who in ecstatic trance, ascends to the heavens on "trips".'[113] Detailing the further progress of the shaman, Eliade notes that once in paradise the shaman finds himself in the presence of a celestial deity who signals that he has transcended the profane condition of humanity through becoming one with God's light. As they approach paradise shamans feel a celestial light in both their brain and body which, 'lifts them up', inaugurating a powerful vision.[114] Frank's drawing *The Gentle Touch*, 1982, which he terms an image of the 'usually hidden' Messiah's face and his drawing *The Miracle and God the Father, Portrait*, 1982, seems to offer a similarly beatific vision, while Frank's ultimate ecstatic experience portrayed in *The Painting (The Vicious Conspiracy)*, 1984, depicts Frank himself as a light shining out of the darkest void. Here he takes on the characteristics of the Great God and represents himself as the prophet of the next century. This image suggests that Frank himself obtains his quest for God, who confirms his special nature, transports himself into mythical time and like a shaman experiences visions of Creation and the Apocalyptic End as the revelation of aspects of production and creation.

We can see that there seems to be a religious impulse fuelling the production of Frank's painting and that it can be identified in the history of religion, and the study of shamanism in particular. It would seem that Frank's shamanism, like some others, ultimately gravitates towards, and becomes integrated with Christian concepts as it is 'obviously subject to historical development and change'.[119]

As this chapter has attempted to suggest, there are many significant correspondences between the symbols and rituals of shamanism and the more autobiographical symbols and thematic rituals in Frank's painting. Frank's obvious sympathy and enthusiasm for Future Time.[115] This painting seems highly important as it is one of Frank's most explicit references to his own attainment of what one might think of as a contemporary shamanic experience.

Frank's shamanic cosmology re-creates the Universe through the medium of flowing paint and Heraclitan notions of universal flux — a concept which he has mentioned in conversation — and in this way evokes the movement and creation of the cosmos as a whole.[116] For example *The Cosmos with Ornamentation (The Spotted Sailor)*, 1987, virtually acts out his own mythical account of a Universe created from chaos, through the pouring of paints in his later works and scenes of the primordial waters and moons in earlier works. Such viscous flows pertain to Chaos Theory; order in chaos and chaos in order, the apparently accidental nevertheless conforming to certain laws. Chaos is often symbolised elsewhere in many of Frank's works — for example, as a scribbly line or a meandering rope or woollen thread in *The Secret and Desire of Siamese Twins,* 1983, and *Self- Portrait. Candles to Pity Perceptions*, 1983. Here the candle illuminates Frank like a prophet, who emerges from darkness and chaos and, according to Frank, from a process in which all forms are 'confounded in the marine abyss of the beginning'. While the images of sea in Frank's works at times may connote the shaman's drum and ecstatic ascent, they sometimes also represent the creational waters, the creation of the cosmos and rebirth and the salvation of man.[117]

In two early paintings, both titled *The Two Moons* and produced in 1984, the viewer's confusion at contemplating two moons suggests a doubling of time and a time zone beyond the present. Depicting the sea in lurid colours (red, yellow, green and blue), suggests an unnatural and disturbing order which, perhaps, is also Frank's metaphor for social and political confusion.[118] Another of Frank's primordial visions, *The Swimmer in the Flooded Studio and the Drowning at the End of the Peer*, 1984, suggests both stagnation and creation — key images in both shamanic lore and Frank's pictorial imagery. *The Stagnant Sea*, 1984, a 'mirror image of rotting green', is assembled from cut palettes of dried paint that mirror the stagnant shamanic values suggests this area offers valuable points of comparison and helps indicate the consistent metaphysical preoccupations of his work. The following chapter will discuss further correspondences between Frank's vision and that of Chiliasm and its related apocalyptic expectations.

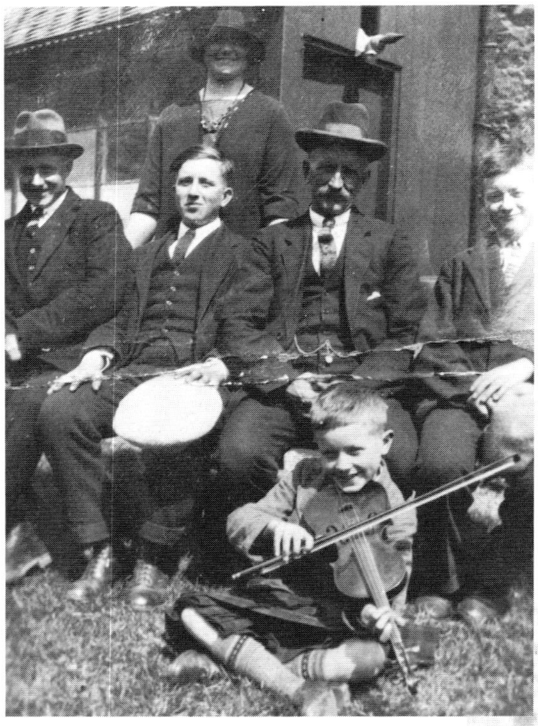

Informal country photograph in Scotland, just after the turn of this century. Frank's grandfather, Arthur Sinclair, is the child with the violin.

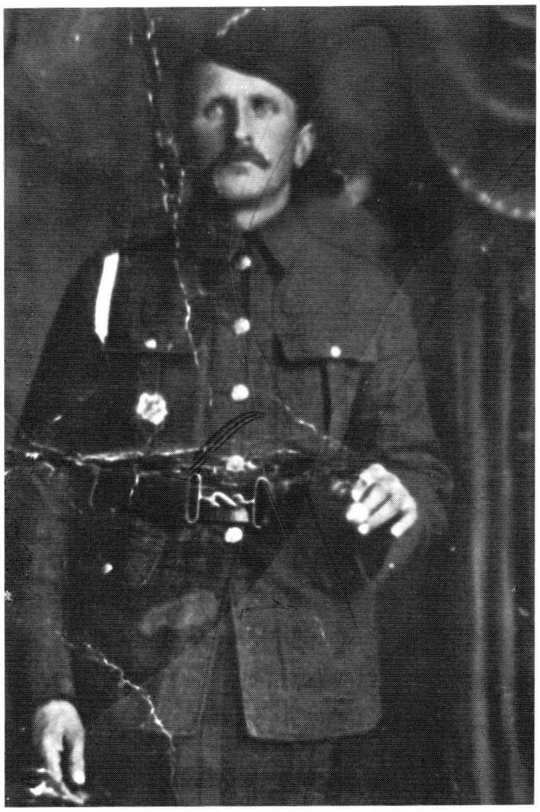

Arthur Sinclair was about eight years old at this time. His father spent the latter half of his life living in a hand built shack at 'Mirannie', having turned his back on everything.

Arthur Sinclair's mother. Her death, after many years of being bedridden with arthritis (but still managing to give birth to the youngest of five), led her husband with the five young children, to leave their family home, for Australia.

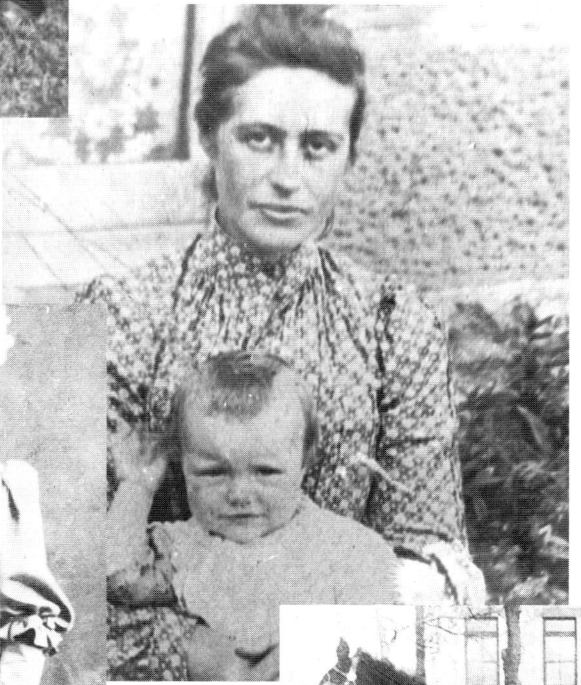

1906 photograph, shortly after their marriage, Alexandrina and Alfred Ogilvey-Moonlight. Frank's maternal great-grandparents.

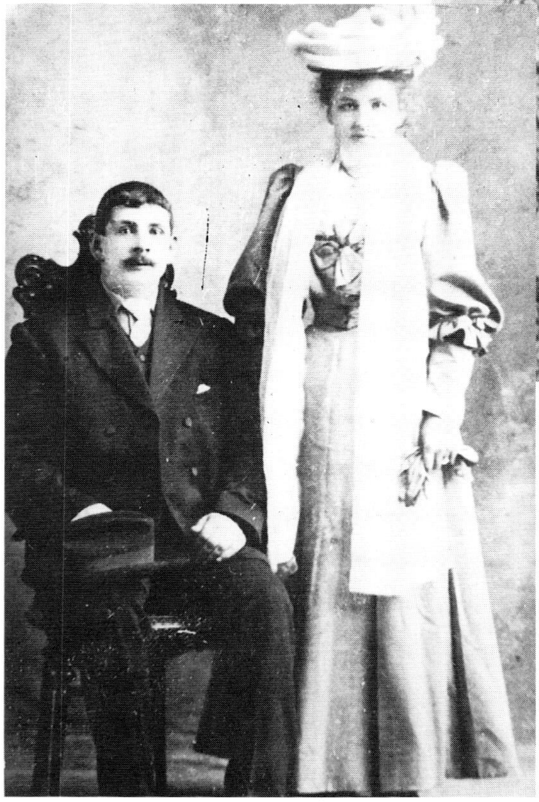

Frank's great-grandfather, Alfred Moonlight at his home in Winnapeg, Canada, in 1906. After spending the time of World War I back at home in Scotland, they moved to Australia.

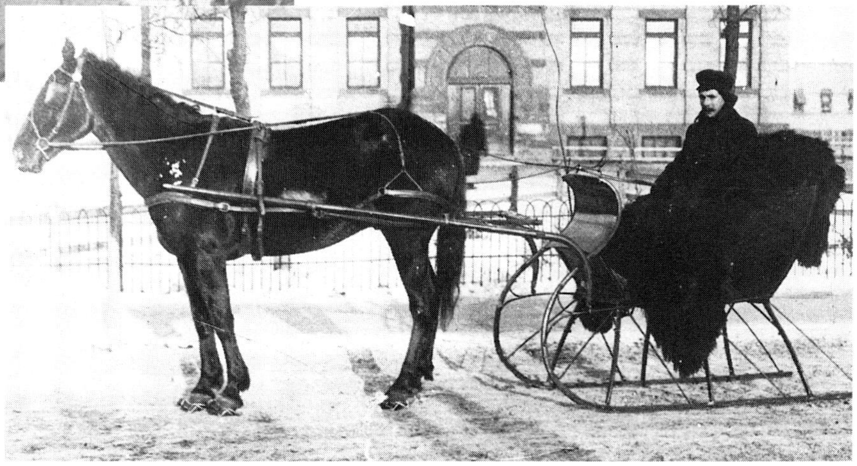

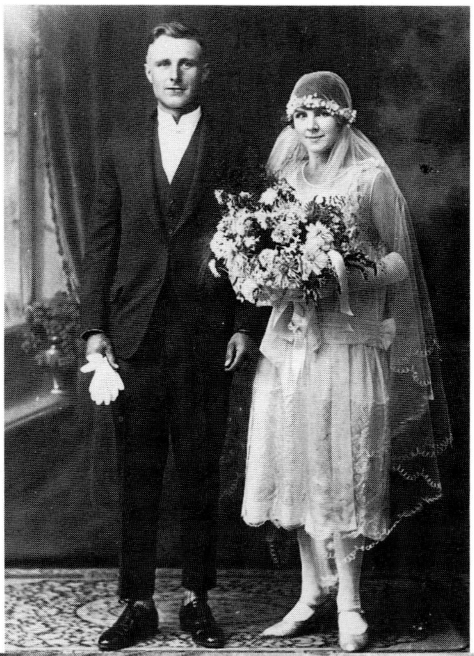

The Moonlight family struggled for many years building a home and family at 'Mirannie', and in the Singleton area, raising four daughters.

A 1928 photograph of the marriage of their eldest daughter at 'Mirannie', Jean Moonlight to Arthur Sinclair (Frank's grandparents).

A 1931 photograph of the Moonlight family's 25th wedding anniversary at 'Mirannie'. To the far left are Frank's grandparents.

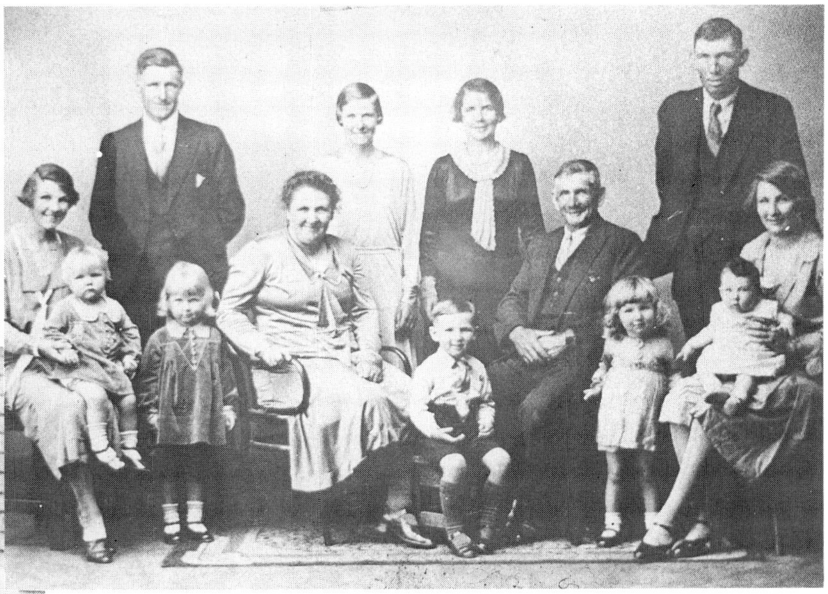

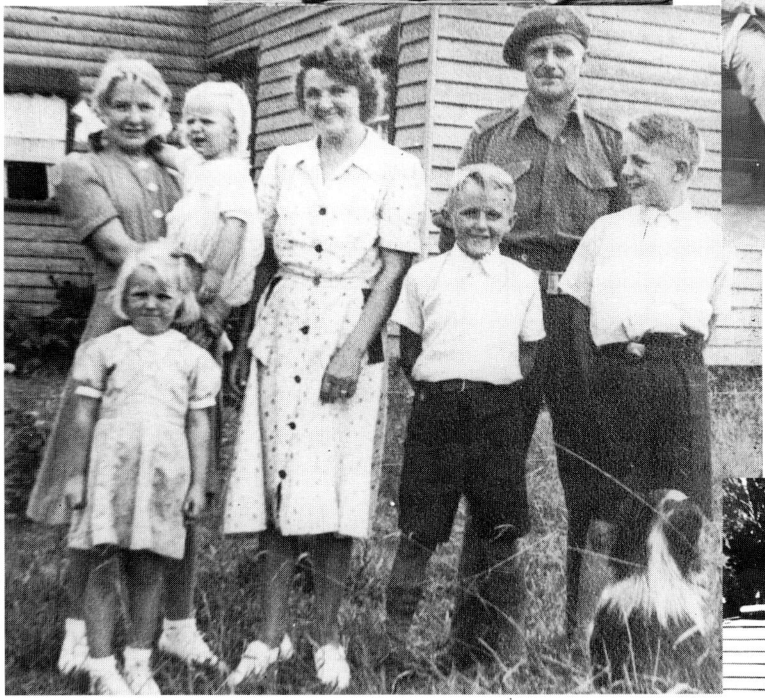

A 1942 photograph of Jean and Arthur Sinclair with five of their six children all born and raised at Number 3, 'Mirannie'. Frank's mother is the smallest standing child.

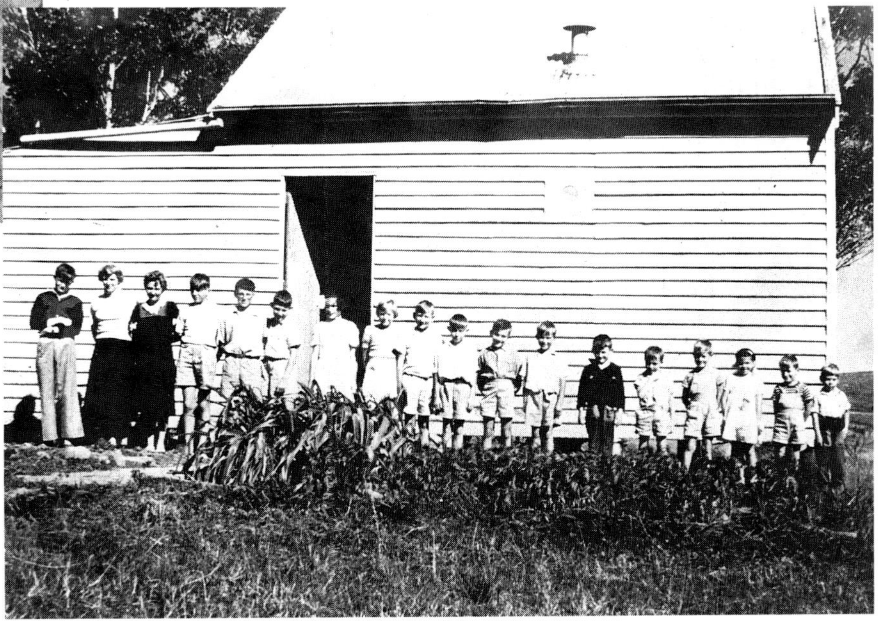

The school attended by Dale Frank from 1964 to 1969, at 'Mirannie'. The school was for infants and primary (to age 12). His mother, Diana Sinclair, can be seen, second from the tallest end, during her days at the school. The school was attended by several generations of the same family, and their relatives. Although these photographs are from the early 1940s, the school had not changed at all by the time Frank was attending.

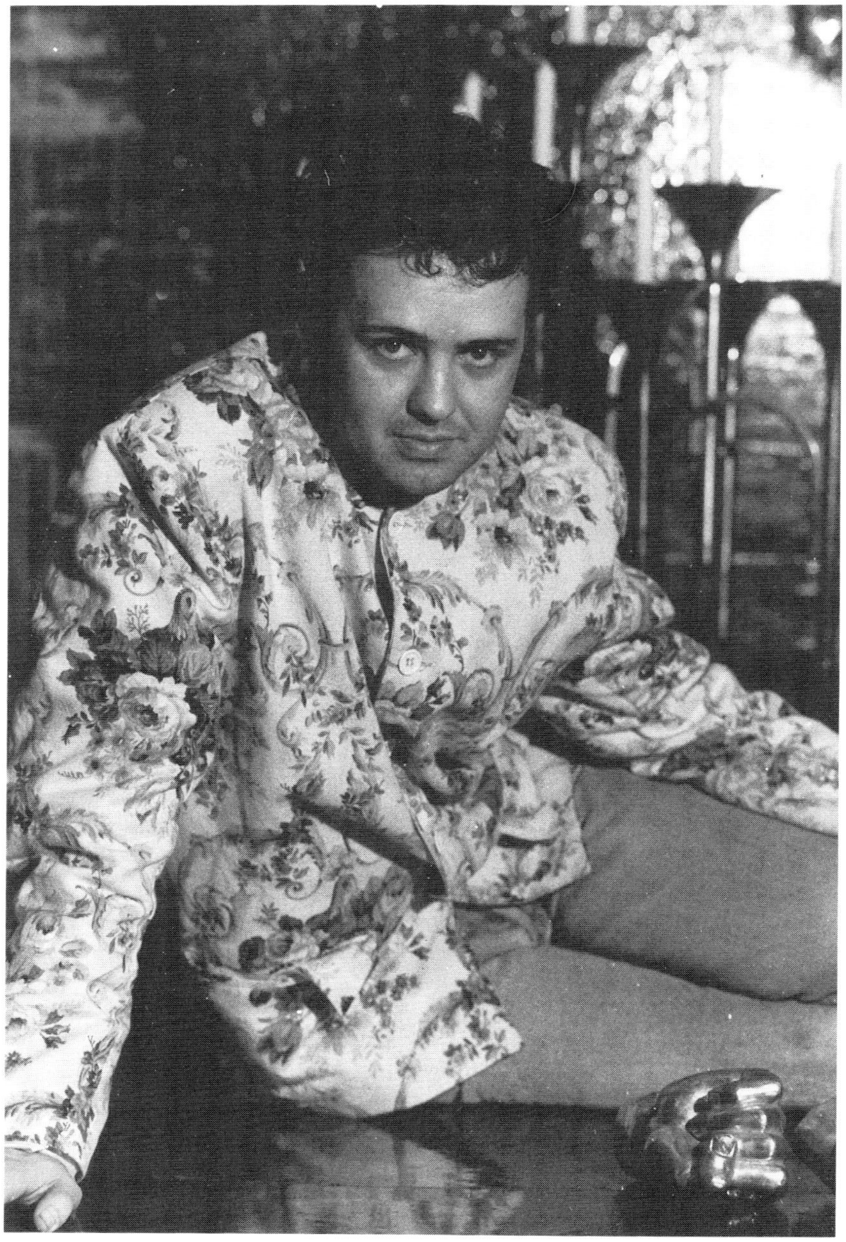

The artist — Milan Studio, 1986

TWO

Chiliasm, Rage and Apocalypse Now: The Ideology of Dale Frank

It seems that there is a link between traditional shamanism and the prophetic, millennarian movements that arose in the 19th century. The Ghost Dance movement of 1890, for example, developed from a shamanic religious heritage.[120] Turning from various correspondences between shamanic mythology and the more specific thematic and symbolic implications of Dale Frank's painting, his art reveals apocalyptic concerns over and beyond those usually associated with shamanic lore. Normally shamanism and such apocalyptic thought as millennarianism are seldom found together. While shamanism is concerned with the mythic processes of creation and resurrection, the millennarianist is primarily concerned with destruction: Apocalypse, Revelation and Resurrection. However, both concerns could well arise from such biographical experience as Frank's memories of having family land taken from him engendering a Chiliastic condition and then being forced to live precariously in a state of uncertainty: experiences often associated very generally with the preconditions of the shamanic hunter-gatherer lifestyle. Considered in this way, Frank's early experience falls into personal (shamanic) and social (Chiliastic) modes of suffering which, taken to extremes, lead either to what one might think of as the shamanic triumph over personal suffering or the state of Chiliastic anger which, in Schwartz's terms, fuels the chiliastic temper, insofar as the charismatic chiliastic prophet 'processes the raw stuff of frustration'.[121] Overcoming suffering forms the personal psychology of shamanism, while deprivation (and frustration) forms the social psychology of Chiliasm. The charismatic prophet uses his raw anger and frustration.

In Frank's case, notions of the millennarian 'Apocalypse' suggest anarchic destruction at the level of the personal, the political and the universal. Like those before him, Frank relates cosmic change to social disturbance and the overturning of the entire historical and social order. As Eliade explains, the impulse towards 'the cosmogonic victory' justifies Messianism and the Apocalypse, and 'lays the foundations for a philosophy of history'.[122]

Frank is evoking the creation of the Universe through the medium of flowing paint, with its suggestion that such fluxes and flows are inherent in creation itself. To this extent

Frank explores the same traditions as the Australian abstractionist, Ralph Balson. Frank associates the rhythm of the universe with the rhythm of painting as in *The Cosmos with Ornamentation (The Spotted Sailor)*, 1987. In Thomas's terms, Frank — like Balson — is the 'enemy of the static ... and a poet of a universal, shifting flux'.[123] Such surging flows and rivers — described by Frank as 'just a flow of sensations'[124] — create taches (colour blotches) and cosmic 'sunspots' through a semi-automatic pouring of paint as in *I Knew the Mandlebrot before it was a Superstar*, 1990. Frank's motifs might also refer to the Micro and Macro worlds, the cosmic, apocalyptic and the microscopic, intertwining a concern for the pure physicality of paint and the metaphysical infinity of the cosmos, within the language of abstraction.

Images of Formalist circles or planets can be found in many of Frank's works. Obviously such motifs are rich in connotation. For example, the circles of the sun and moon, one each side of the cross, are a regular feature of medieval crucifixions. They are also of very ancient, pagan origin and were increasingly reduced to 'two plain discs'[125] as in the manner employed by Dale Frank. While Frank uses moon imagery in the drawing *Revenge of the Records*, 1983, later works such as *The Inland Sea (New Moon to the Warren)*, 1984, have circular plastic records, representing black moons, embedded into their surface. As Stone specifies, images of black moons and black suns comprise an 'apocalyptic vision' which stands 'at the centre of the revelatory experience'.[126] The black planets in Frank's *Cosmos with Ornamentation (The Spotted Sailor)*, 1987, also had their precursors in apocalyptic descriptions from the following lines of St John's *The Book of Revelation*:

> *... there was a violent earthquake and the sun went as black as coarse sackcloth, the moon turned red as blood all over, and the stars of the sky fell on to the earth.*[127]

Against a background of swirling, brilliant, golden colours in *Cosmos with Ornamentation (The Spotted Sailor)* are black discs resembling this type of black sun; an image that R.D. Laing, in *The Divided Self*, describes as 'ancient' and 'sinister', and suggestive of a psychological or 'existential death'.[128] Julia Kristeva also equates dead stars with the 'Black Sun' of 'Melancholia', encircling 'an abyss of sorrow'. Similarly Kristeva describes the appearance of this sign as suggestive of 'psychic death'.[129]

Ancient, apocalyptic, mystical writings, such as Enoch's description of his 'journeys through the cosmos'[130] — tours of Paradise and Hell — similarly anticipate the imagery in paintings such as Frank's *The Road Sign and the Spatial Constellation in Green Harmony Abstraction (Bus Stop at the End of the Universe)*, 1987, a work in which the image of bizarre red traffic lights and planets suggests some sort of cosmic travel. Frank's *The Possible Self-Portrait that was like a Space Shuttle*, 1986, and *It's my party — to Johnny and Mickey — He's left Home*, 1990, also evokes visionary journeys into space and his hope that 'we might all travel there'.[131] As Himmelfarb suggests, the 'sights that the visionary sees in the course of a journey through the cosmos'[132] are often also apocalyptic 'Tours of Paradise or Hell' revealing 'cosmological phenomena'.[133] In this way 'the tour apocalypse emerges as the earliest form of apocalypse' and takes a central place in the discussion of the development of the apocalypse as a literary genre.[134] Kristeva suggests in turn that such 'new apocalyptic rhetoric' produces both a 'wealth of images' and 'a holding back of words'[135] — a paradox also reiterated in Frank's concurrent profusion of complex symbols, images, colours and textures and his reluctance to elaborate on his work.

Considered generally, apocalyptic art forms can be defined as an 'unveiling', described by Hillel Schwartz as the 'penultimate battle between the forces of good and the forces of evil' which, according to Biblical tradition, is then followed by a '1,000 year reign of saintly martyrs of Jesus, and the defeat of Satan, the Last Judgement, a new heaven and a new earth'.[136]

Perhaps the key paradox of apocalyptic genre is its dual tendency to both conceal and reveal, as in St John's *Revelations.* Not surprisingly, Frank's hermetic apocalyptic titles simultaneously hint and hide their associations. Titles such as *Cosmos with Ornamentation (The Spotted Sailor)* suggest general cosmic content while at the same time the more mundane *Spotted Sailor,* juxtaposes self-negating references. The components of the title combine the sublime and the ridiculous, cancelling each other out and diverting the viewer's attention. As becomes evident, Frank's titles and paintings frequently evoke such paradoxes.

Zamora's commentaries upon images of the apocalypse include the bottomless pit, the lake of fire and brimstone, space as an index of time, earthquakes, floods, falling stars and an extinguished sun and moon. Apocalyptic seas and lakes are similarly described in the following lines from St John's *The Book Of Revelation*:

> *This burning lake is the second death; and anybody whose name could not be found written in the book of life was thrown into the burning lake.*[137]

It is perhaps this sort of lake that Frank depicts in the title such as *Dorian's Eye to the Painter's Yellow Sea and Winter Willow (Therese's Pretty View in View of the Rocky Palette,* 1984 and *The Sea and the Sore Eye,* 1984. The painter's yellow sea can also resemble St John's lake of 'sulphur' yellow. The painter (Frank) and St John share a mystical, apocalyptic vision. Extraordinary apocalyptic colours also feature strongly in *The Book of Revelation*:

> *In my vision I saw the horses, and the riders with their breastplates of flame colour, hyacinth blue and sulphur yellow; the horses had lions' heads, and fire, smoke and sulphur were coming out of their mouths.*[138]

Here one perceives a world of heightened and fluorescent colour reminiscent of much of Frank's work.

Perhaps the most apocalyptic of all Frank's images is the extraordinary painting *Dorian's Eye to the Painter's Yellow Sea and Winter Willow (Therese's Pretty View of the Rocky Palette)* where the serrated edges around the painting's perimeter depict a view from Therese's grave up into the swirling Heavens. What is strange about this painting is that the viewer inevitably realises that the grave's edges are not neatly dug and rectangular as in a freshly dug grave. In other words, Frank seems to offer an apocalyptic world view from the grave that opens on Judgement Day. The serrated edges of Therese's grave also resemble the time at the death of Jesus when the 'earth quaked; the rocks were split; the tombs were opened'[139], where we view the apocalyptic grave from inside rather than from without. Here we see simultaneously Frank's association with graves, voids and death.

Death is a notion which is of the utmost importance to Frank. As Zamora points out in *Writing The Apocalypse*, 1989, 'apocalyptic fictions address the very nature of finality'[140], where the death of the individual and the end of the world coincide, and personal and communal social goals become inextricably bound.[141] Frank in turn rather ambiguously proposes that he is iconoclastically 'ending art', even as one senses his mocking that very proposition. In *The Immaculate Crucifixion to Forgive all Art Sinners*, 1990, the word 'Immaculate' mocks the word 'Crucifixion' because it really refers to the Madonna's 'immaculate conception', yet in this case glorifies a hideous death. Here the artist might also be heretically mocking the notion of Christianity. Frank is able to mock the concept of immortality despite his own ideology which is directed towards it. The mocking continues because one might forgive sinners but how does one act towards an 'Art Sinner'? In *The Big Painting Factory in the Sky with a Mother's Paintings Love Reaction*, 1986, the notion of heaven or life after death is mocked by Frank's reference to it as the *Big Painting Factory in the Sky*. Frank's term offers:

> *... a joke about death and the illusion of it being better up there than here ... it's a joke on the idea that Redemption is better.*[142]

The traditional apocalyptist encodes his own version of history although Zamora identifies an important conflict between self-promotion and self-deprecation inherent in apocalyptic forms.[143] In Zamora's terms Frank constantly 'encodes' his own history in titles such as *Self-Portrait as Pitiful Light and Mountain Peaks*, 1982 — a self-portrait of a prophet 'who's gone pretty sour' — where 'Pitiful Light' is his code for 'Prophet' or 'Messiah'. 'Mountain Peaks'[144] implies the hermit's place of enlightenment in the wilderness. This is also noticeable in the previous painting where Frank promotes himself as a 'Prophet' or 'Messiah' and deprecates himself for being 'pitiful' and 'pretty sour'.[145] At these times we see Frank clearly defining his mysticism in Christian terms.

Zamora also suggests that modern visions of apocalypse are less religious than historical, and Frank's work often certainly seems to have a politico-religious base which is not as secular as one might initially believe.[146] This might be seen in his mixing of references to the Cosmos, Creation and Apocalypse, to God, Jesus, the Devil, Hitler and Saddam Hussein.

The idea of the Apocalypse appeals to those with deep psychological needs[147] and is in direct relation to its sociological and political context. Zamora also comments:

> *The resurgence of apocalyptic modes of thought and expression is a predictable reaction to social disruption and temporal uncertainty, and explains in part its currency in our own popular vocabulary.*[148]

There are several reasons for suggesting that Frank's formative experiences as a child provoked his subsequent use of an apocalyptic genre. As the eldest child of six children, a harsh father and from the age of six years, desperate financial circumstances, his environment engendered within him an angry personal and political response that Zamora associates with the 'militantly destructive'[149] personality who dreams 'of heaven' to 'create hell.'[150] Frank, in turn will say that 'to create is to destroy'.[151]

Novelists and artists who use apocalyptic elements, like the biblical apocalyptists, are often critical of present political, social and spiritual practices.[152] While Frank's work criticises society, it is more usually directed to a criticism of the Australian art world and art-making in general, as in the painting *Did the Parrot have Something to do with It?*, 1990. Exasperation with the social and political art scene in Australia prompted the work, which utilises a complete but dismembered issue of *Tension* magazine, January 1990, and is centred around the history of Australian Art in the '80s 'with all its absences and indulgences'.

As I shall suggest, Frank's work envisages a new utopian order which he associates publicly with the art world rather than with society in general. He emphatically states that he wants to 'create a new art by breaking down what has come before'.[153] His apocalyptic, iconoclastic thinking is applied to his art practice rather than social revolution. Apocalyptic thinking has been identified as one form whereby 'religion gives voice to revolutionary stirrings'[154] and characterises what might best be defined as the Chiliastic dimension of Frank's work.

Considered very generally, Chiliasm may be described as a state of mind, an a-historical 'system of thought'[155] or a temporal wish. The most characteristic features of Chiliasm are extreme rage and an ideology of war. The early Chiliastic thinkers of European history, the Anabaptists (1500s), Joachim of Fiore (1145–1202) and the Taborites (1419–1420), all had ideas of a millennial revolutionary kingdom which they transformed into activist movements of a specific social strata.

Karl Mannheim suggests that modern socialism dates its origins from the time of the Anabaptists, where Thomas Muntzer (born 1488) is to be regarded as an initiator in the direction of modern revolutionary movements. Mannheim calls this 'the spiritualisation of politics', which he believes affected all currents of politics at the time. He attributes this spiritual tension to the utopian mentality (which Frank has in his Paradisial longings) originating in the oppressed strata of society and which at this point forms the origins of politics in the modern sense of the word.

The terms 'millennium' or 'millennarianism' come from *mille*, the Latin word for a 'thousand'. In this way millennarianists believe that Christ would come again to reign with the saints on earth for 1,000 years before the Last Judgement and the end of the world.[156] 'Chiliasm' comes from the Greek *chiliad*, which also means a 'thousand',[157] although in general usage there seem to be some subtle differences. Millennarianism is more concerned about external factors and external signs of the end in the future, while Chiliasm is more internal and more about the end in the immediate present world. The Apocalypse and Millennarianism refer to *The Apocalypse of St John* or *The Book of Revelation.*

Schwartz suggests that within contemporary society 'apocalypse has lost its reference to millennium; it has become simply a synonym for disaster'. We can trace the growth of a secular catastrophic mood over the world from World War One, the gas chambers of World War Two and the atomic bomb[158] to current wars and the 'Greenhouse Effect' in the 1990s. However, in the case of Dale Frank the notion of 'apocalypse' retains the original, religious meaning — particularly if one considers Frank's ideas and images in terms of a number of the more specific features that characterise the Chiliastic mode of thought.

According to Schwartz, vengeance is a key characteristic of chiliastic thinking, since the millennarian's ethos:

> ... *is initially retributive, seeking to balance an unfortunate past against an unfortunate future. Few millennarians remain entirely passive ... most conflate the restorative and the retributive.*[159]

The Chiliast's desire for revenge can be seen even in letters from the early 1400s where a prophet exhorts his readers to 'break with not only the existing social order but also the whole past tradition of the Hussite movement' and to 'gather in the time of vengeance and greatest suffering'.[160] Frank, like the Medieval Chiliast prophet, also proposes an ideology of vengeance. He has said in conversation, 'I don't get angry, I get even.' His four drawings, *Three Pools Leading to the Hanged Man Maybe*, 1982, which refer to Frank's vision of himself being deceived, tried and wrongly judged in a psychological landscape, typify his association of water, death, judgement and revenge. This fascination for revenge can also be seen in titles such as *Revenge of the Records*, 1983, and *Judgement, The World, The Fool*, 1982. Discussing this drawing Frank comments that he 'likes the idea of judgement very much, of everyone being punished but himself'. He also suggests that this work refers to ways in which the world judges himself to be a fool, prompting his wish to judge and punish them in order to obtain his revenge.[161] *Art 1 (The Responding Reason Really Rectified Running Raunchily Randy 'early Rancid) (Under the Tank Stand)*, 1989, is apparently a bad spell of revenge 'worked' on another contemporary artist.

For Karl Mannheim, the experience of suffering is part of the Chiliast's experience of oppression and deprivation. For, Mannheim, the decisive turning point in modern history was the moment when '"chiliasms" joined forces with the active demands of the oppressed strata of society', and advocated a millennial kingdom on earth with a revolutionising tendency.[162]

Hillel Schwartz further posits that millennarianism is the religion of both the oppressed and the oppressor and may be both the cause and the result of migration.[163] Frank's identification with the suffering of the persecuted can be seen in his self-portraits of saints, such as *Self-Portrait of St Bartholomew, The Torso,* 1985. Here Frank identifies with the pain and suffering of St Bartholomew, (who was flayed alive), igniting his paints and cutting his canvases in order to create metaphors of pain.

According to Schwartz, another key feature of Chiliasm — dispossession — may be a result of confusion about landholdings due to shifting settlement, or may result from 'anxieties about inheritance, boundaries and language' where believers are 'imperiled by forces within their society'.[164] Schwartz exemplifies this process with reference to Tabor, the first revolutionary society in Europe, where the peasant or artisan who 'abandoned his land or sold his property', who 'burnt his home and left his friends and family' ... was 'truly passing from one world into another'.[165]

A parallel sense of dispossession can be traced to Frank's childhood experience with the New South Wales State Government resumption of his grandparent's land and a gracious home in the early to mid 1960s. Other family members also had land resumed and were forced to sell the remainder of his family's property in similar circumstances. In consequence, Frank's family lost social status, money, occupation and inheritance, and with these legal and financial disasters, Frank was effectively robbed of his shaman's 'paradise'. This dispossession of rural land seems to be a vital factor in the development of the Chiliastic state of mind. Discussing the concept of deprivation, Hillel Schwartz explains how millennarian movements can develop, and why these movements appear in periods of crisis. According to Schwartz:

> *... the crisis engenders personal fantasies of invulnerability and escape, which are transformed by charismatic individuals who are often members of displaced elites. ... and that these prophets shape public expressions of protest.*[166]

Such childhood experience almost certainly accounts at least in part for Frank's future radical mannerisms. Deprivation can be sensed in the writings of Chiliast prophets of the 1400s who wrote of their 'sorrows and sufferings' of the 'hard, terrible and dangerous time prophesied by Christ'.[167] This experience of oppression, both familial and economic, appears to have played a part in forming the raw material of the young Dale Frank.

The process of migration, both real and imagined, is another central feature of millennarian movements.[168] The millennarian religious exile or wanderer (Buddha, the wandering Jew, Jesus and Muhammad) characteristically experiences nostalgia for lost lands and contradictory moods of exited expectation and deep remorse. Frank has travelled extensively overseas, and some of his paintings, seem to depict 'Cosmic Tours', the visionary's imagined wanderings in the cosmos. Frank's 'tantric' paintings could be interpreted as the result of 'practical mystics, who are intent on making maps of the regions into which they have penetrated'. In these paintings the discs represent the planets and the lines between suggest direct paths for the travelling mystic. Schwartz indicates that Millennarian movements go through two key phases: an expansive phase during which believers move out to a ripening world (corresponding to Frank's extensive travelling overseas), and an astringent phase (corresponding to his rural retreat to Scone, Australia), during which they pull in toward a holy refuge. Expansive or astringent, millennarian movements are inherently political but not inherently reactionary or revolutionary.[169] Frank's own wanderings around the world from late October 1979 through to his return to Australia at the end of 1987 — the beginning of the astringent phase — can be understood in this light.

While Frank's motto might be 'I don't get angry, I get even', in truth he is angry, really angry.[170] An ideology of war and rage are the characteristics that most identify the thinking of the Chiliast and his 'acts of violence'.[171] Discussing the Chiliasts of the 1400s, Kaminsky writes that, to their contemporaries, 'the most striking change was from pacificism to an ideology of warfare'.[172] In an essay written nine years after the Taborite preaching had reached its peak, an anti-Taborite wrote of 'enormous cruelty, unheard of violence, and injustice to man'. Summarising the Taborite's view, this author adds:

> *They said that now was the time of greatest vengeance, the time of destruction of all sinners and the time of God's wrath ... it was no longer the time of mercy, but the time of vengeance ... so that people should strike and kill all sinners.*[173]

The Taborites developed a Chiliastic 'doctrine of unlimited warfare'. According to Kaminsky 'the essentially negative goals of Chiliast warfare made anything short of total destruction unsatisfactory'.[174] These observations remind one of the 'destructive' working methods of Frank's tendency to burn, cut and 'poison' his canvases with chemical reactions. In earlier times the destructive Chiliastic burning of crops, monasteries and killing 'all stemmed from the rejection of the existing world'[175] and was projected publicly as a 'Chiliast ideology of unlimited war against the old world'.[176] It could also be seen as an iconoclastic destruction of cultural values. Mannheim explores this desire for destruction a little further writing, that 'It tends at every moment to turn into hostility towards the world, its culture, and all its works and earthly achievements'.[177]

Likewise, Frank also sustains an ideology of war and destruction which can be seen in his attacking the politics within the Australian art scene and many of the icons of traditional art. Frank seems preoccupied with war for reasons that range from political to the personal love of violent excitement. Frank's sons have names that include Napoleon, Hannibal and

Charlemagne, three of history's military leaders. In one of his latest paintings, tellingly named after his admiration for Saddam Hussein — *Saddam Saddam He's My Man*, 1991 — he has 'bombed' the canvas with very deliberately chosen colours, 'craterising' the paint. While his painting *Art Nazis Must Die*, 1989, refers to the death of Nazis, one suspects it might also reflect a sneaking fascination for the power of the 'bad boys' of world history. In essence, Frank is at 'war' not only with the world but also with his paintings, as can be seen in his series entitled *The Painting of Hate,* numbers 1–5, 1986–87. Frank has also said that he sympathises with the Futurists' obsession with war as 'the unique hygiene'.

According to Mannheim, the Chiliast often proposes a revolutionary doctrine or ideology of 'instilling hope and fortitude during times of disaster'. Mannheim argues that 'Chiliasm has always accompanied revolutionary outbursts and given them their spirit ... Chiliasm sees the revolution as a value in itself.'[178] It is often believed that millennarianism was a subversive doctrine of 'provincial radicals'[179] in the high Middle Ages. The true Medieval Chiliast was subversive in that he was:

> *... not humble or at all willing to suffer for Christ ... and that ... if Christians were always to have to suffer so, I would not want to be a servant of God.*[180]

Sometimes this even takes a distinctly anti-Christian or heretical emphasis. Kaminsky notes, for example, that the medieval Taborite militant radicals preached against the Roman Catholic system developing what he terms a 'schismatic religio-political program'.[181] Thomas Munzer showed his spiritual and religious radicalism in his distinction between the 'honey sweet and the bitter Christ' and there is a sense of this in Frank's own attitudes to religion.[182] Frank's subversion takes a most unusual form by perverting the Christian Father-Son relationship by stating that 'God the Father and God the Son create homo-erotic tension'. In this way, to Frank, 'God is the supreme paedophile'[183] as in his paintings *The Paedophile*, 1988, and *The Paedophile as if in Cushion — The Beach Scene*, 1988.

Frank's views on Jesus are equally idiosyncratic, remarking that he likes the 'idea of Jesus and his images of power and transcendence, of his walking on water'.[184] Frank specifies that his interest 'is in the images of Jesus, not Jesus himself'[185], which is in itself a subversive idea. Discussing the Medieval religious paintings he saw in Milan, Frank claims equally, irreverently, that he 'admired' 15th century portraits of 'a made-up' Jesus painted in hot pink with red lipstick', and suggests that 'effeminate portraits of Jesus ... were very radical interpretations'.[186]

Zamora notes how Jewish or Christian apocalyptic writers usually have a 'subversive vision' and exist 'outside the cultural and political mainstream'.[187] Frank's critiques of mainstream Modernist styles of art and his very up-bringing outside the rural New South Wales town of Singleton typify a similar sense of individuality, isolation and subversive detachment.

Similar subversive qualities can be found in his critiques of the Australian art scene and in his use of non-aesthetic materials such as sponge foam sofas, cake tins, coffee tables, serving trays, children's building blocks, car hubcaps and so on, which all create what Zamora refers to as an 'odd mixture of tones'.[188] A large portion of Frank's work, including for example his *Magritte's Poor Flowers*, 1988, is comprised of car hubcaps collected into a bouquet of flowers; an extraordinary conflation of traditional and avant-garde materials and motifs which subvert the art system, offering secular heresies of art, somewhat as Chiliast tendencies subverted orthodox religions.

As noted, Frank's childhood and teenage years were spent in a harsh rural environment (compared with urban lifestyles), the 'stratum living closest to the earth' which, in accordance with Mannheim's view, creates the 'robustly material and highly spiritual'.[189] The Chiliast's 'robust and corporeal drive'[190] is very much how one might describe the personality and behaviour of Dale Frank. However the Chiliast also has to express an inexpressible spiritual contact and can only find his symbols in the sensual analogies of everyday life. This can be seen in the title of five drawings, *Immortality, The Garden, Foulling the Bed*, 1981, where Frank's reference to tabooed topics like 'fouling the bed' — the robustly material — is contrasted with 'immortality' and the highly spiritual. A characteristic feature of Frank's work is that there is a robust materiality in his use of media: swirling paint, dribbling varnish, fabrics, towels, plastics and banal objects embedded into the paint surface in a bizarre fashion. Here the 'robustly material' is used in an exultant fashion combined with the spirituality of both his symbols and ideas.

Kaminsky additionally notes that the Chiliasts believe that 'God is in them', that 'God is everywhere, even in Hell' ... and 'therefore man has God perfectly even before he takes communion.'[191] The Taborites also apparently believed that 'the Chiliasts thought that Christ had already come secretly, like a thief in the night, and was working through them'.[192] In a similar fashion, Frank identifies with the idea of the power of having God within, as becomes clear in his series of seven drawings entitled *The Artist as God*, 1984, which suggest a Chiliastic state not megalomania. Another drawing with Chiliastic attitudes is *The Miracle and God the Father, Portrait*, 1982, which similarly depicts a self-portrait as God the Father.

Describing Chiliasm as an 'a-historical ecstasy which inspired both the mystic and the Chiliast'[193] and linking 'Chiliastic aloofness with ecstatic experience',[194] Mannheim explains that the mystic :

> *... lives either in recollection of ecstasy or in longing for it. His metaphors describe this ecstasy as a psychic situation ... It is perhaps this same ecstatic substance which turns with the Chiliast into the immediate here and now, but not in order simply to delight in it, but in order to whip it up and to make it part of himself.*[195]

As a Chiliast, Frank similarly 'whips up' the ecstatic and the 'now' in order to 'make it part of himself' through his use of divergent art styles and found objects. Such ecstatic images can be found in his spiral motifs, 'cosmic tours' and underground journeys, his seas and crystalline surfaces. In some of his paintings the shaman's vertigo forms concentric rings of brilliant colour which seem to move in a dizzying fashion, as in *The Masterpiece with a Diddle Worthy of a Fly*, 1987. According to Mannheim, the Chiliast 'is not actually concerned with the millennium that is to come'. What is important for him is that 'it happened here and now' and that it 'arose from mundane existence, as a sudden swing over into another kind of existence'.[196] Frank's mundane childhood might be said to have in part projected him into the state of the ecstatic and his concern with 'the end'. In this way, it is not just that the Chiliast is an apocalyptic thinker — rather it is that the apocalypse is immanent in the 'now'.

A Chiliast's sense of time and the now,[197] characterised by tense expectation[198] and the 'chance moment',[199] and anticipating 'a union with the immediate present', can also be seen in Frank's use of poured and flowing paint. It is Mannheim's view that 'Chiliastic time and the ecstatic are interrelated'. Immanent action can be seen in the following segment of a Medieval letter: 'Do not be tardy; He (Lord God Himself) is at the gates'[200] — meaning that God has come for Judgement Day because the end is 'now'. Kaminsky believes that the main purpose of these communities was 'self-preservation in an immanent period of catastrophe' and the end of 'the existing Age'.[201]

Clearly, the Chiliast has a fascination with endings. Schwartz also reports that the more exclusively one believes oneself to be concerned with The End, the more catastrophic the end appears[202], for apocalypse and millennarianism are eschatological in nature — concerned with final things. Title-references like 'Immortality', 'Salvation', 'Judgement' indicate that Frank's work is concerned with Judgement and the end of the present life. 'The End' is also evoked in Frank's subtitle *The Bus Stop at the End of the Universe.* While Apocalyptic 'endings and beginnings' are 'wilfully confused'[203] they are also about defining and exceeding such 'limitations'. It is interesting to consider the secular use of the word 'limit', which is derived from the religious term 'limbo' (Latin: *limbus*, a hem) — the supposed region on the border of Heaven and Hell. It is here in Frank's work that the two elements, religious (symbolism) and secular (art-making), converge back to their lexical origins.

Frank's references to endings and beginnings in his paintings are equally revealing, in the sense that art-making for Frank becomes a question, rather than an affirmation. For example, his inclusion of banal objects such as hubcaps, trays and cushions into his work seems to imply both the end of art and the beginning of anti-art, Chiliastic or iconoclastic art or some less definite alternative. More generally, Frank frequently refers to the limitations of other artistic approaches, in order to distinguish his art from theirs and thereby transcend their limitations.

Frank's preoccupation with the limitations of art might be characterised as an 'apocalyptic' battle between movements such as Formalism, Abstract Expressionism, Romanticism, Surrealism, Symbolism, Conceptualism and Dadaism. In his painting *The Masterpiece with the Diddle Worthy of a Fly*, 1987, the use of children's blocks may represent 'Formalism', while the dream images and conflicting ecstatic swirls might suggest Surrealism. The 'critical' element is involved because art styles are not quoted individually as a style in their own right but by levelling them in conjunction with others, albeit in a very chaotic scene. Frank's breaking of rules is yet another way of testing endings and beginnings and of undermining socially accepted art practice and artistic limits. Put another way, Frank's art functions at the metacritical level where materials and style are examined, subverted or exceeded in order to find another 'beyond', another limitation.

Flirting with disaster, Frank pushes himself, his spectators and his art to their absolute limits, fighting against the conventions of institutionalised beauty by creating a beauty of his own. In this way he again confuses endings and beginnings in order to identify the limits of an aesthetic and the creation of an Anti-Aesthetic. More often than not he uses tacky, tasteless materials, apocalyptic colours and the use of 'left-overs' of other people's 'good' and 'bad' taste as the raw materials for his creativity. Frequently Frank's paintings create an ugliness which seems unacceptable to a lay majority; this seems his way of redefining art's limits and asking the eternal question 'What is painting?' In this way Frank's fascination with limitations is related to his apocalyptic-Chiliastic thinking, of taking things to the very edge and over, in order to define the edge, the limit or the end. The End, decay, upheaval and unrest are as much features of existence as in the Middle Ages. In this respect, Mannheim interestingly posits that:

> *Chiliasm had its period of existence in the world of the decaying Middle Ages, a period of tremendous disintegration. Everything was in conflict with everything else ... It was a world in upheaval and unrest, in which the deepest impulses of the human spirit sought external expression.*[204]

Such characteristics of the Medieval era must surely have relevance for today's apocalyptic thinkers where 'end of world images linger in the dreams and speech of the people' and ultimately filter into scientific communities[205] and into the 'contemporary fascination with the End'.[206]

Writing in *The Pursuit of the Millennium*, Norman Cohn notes how social exhaustion, fatigue and collapse flourish in specific social situations and adds that 'Revolutionary millennialism drew its strength from a population living on the margin of society'. For Cohn millennialists 'were not simply poor' but could 'find no assured place in society at all' because they lacked the material and emotional support by traditional groups[207] so that the 'greatest wave of millennarian excitement ... was precipitated by the Black Death' and 'expressed ... in violence and massacre'.[208] A contemporary parallel to the Black Death could be found in the AIDS virus, diseases that Frank refers to in his work. Millennarianist revolutionaries may be from 'certain politically marginal elements in technologically advanced societies — chiefly young or unemployed workers and a small minority of intellectuals and students'.[209] Frank's profession as an artist, his country background, his nomadic travelling and childhood experience of dispossession places him well within this category.

For Cohn 'the old religious idiom has been replaced by a secular one' and that 'stripped of their original supernatural sanction, revolutionary millennarianism and mystical anarchism are with us still'.[210] As revolutionary anarchism it 'would not exist at all if it were not preceded by fatigue and followed by exhaustion'.[211] It is this sense of fatigue and exhaustion which is so frequently a feature of apocalyptic modes of the Post-modern movement and a powerful feature in the painting of Dale Frank.

According to Mannheim, Bakunin carried the Chiliastic attitude into the Modern world as 'radical anarchism'.[212] In turn, Frank elaborates a 20th century Chiliastic attitude in his art practice and transposes the religious images of apocalyptic Chiliasm (and, as I have suggested, the symbols of shamanism) within a relatively secular social system. Mannheim concludes that 'the relatively purest form of modern Chiliastic mentality, as embodied in radical anarchism, disappears almost entirely from the political scene'.[213]

While this may be the case in the strict political sense, it would seem that in the art of Dale Frank we have the continuation of the Chiliastic mode of thought, directed to the construction of millennial utopia (or shamanic paradise) in his art-making, and to the continuation of political anger, 'religious' images and his artistic rituals of reconstructing a shamanic Creation and a Chiliastic end. His anger and revenge seem to have evolved through his being robbed of his Paradise on Earth.

In Frank's work we see a religious development normally seen over a long period of time, one that has evolved from different types of societies and economies. Frank's shamanic 'initiations' appear to be more visible in his earlier works while Christian and priest-like concepts seem more obvious in his later works. Christian belief conveys an awareness of apocalypse that shamanism does not normally consider. In this respect, Frank's work continues a long history of Chiliastic rage, transforming his art-making and creating an art-form of great power, originality and anarchistic energy.

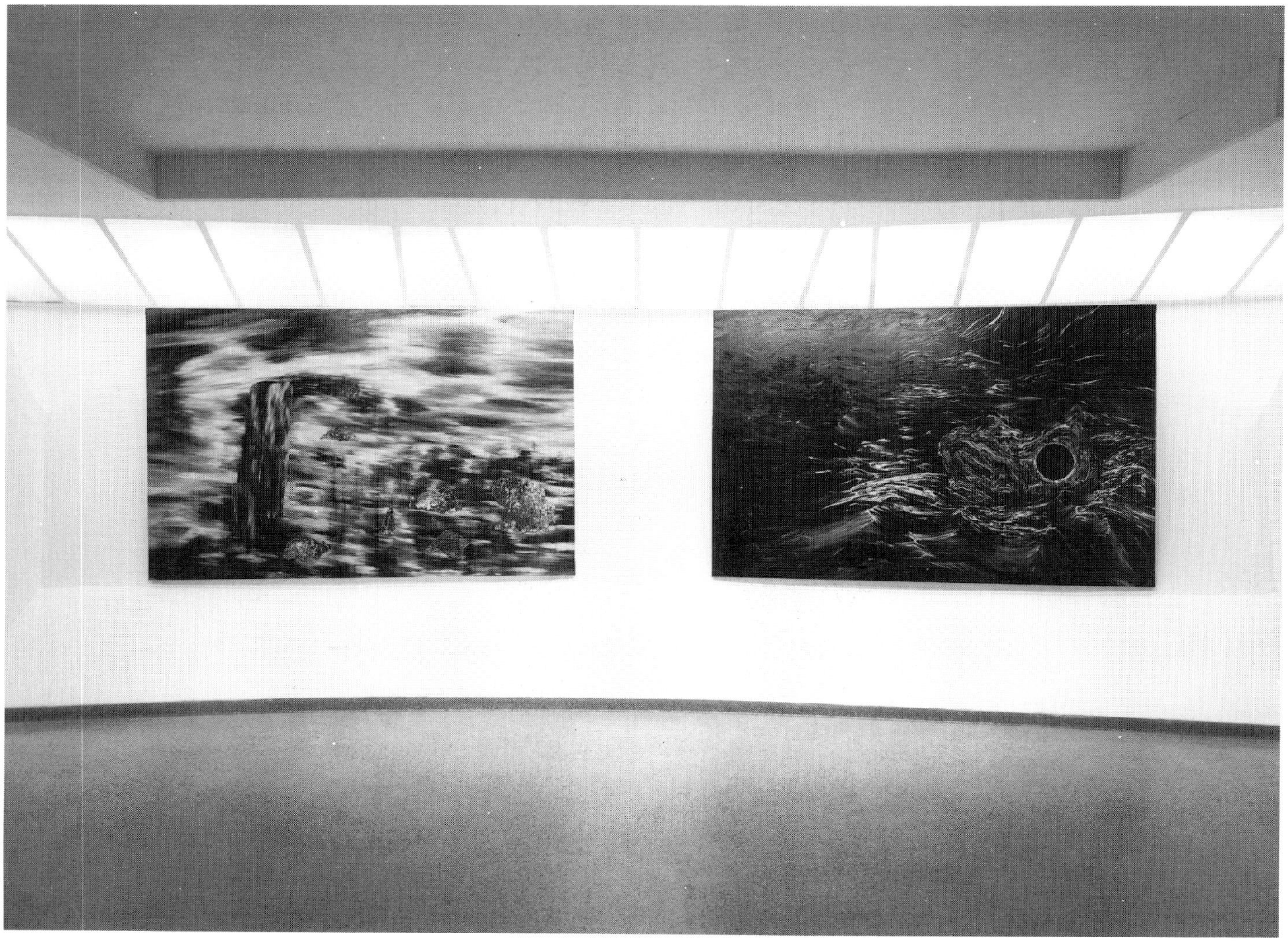

Installation view: Dale Frank, 'Australian Visions: 1984 Exxon International Exhibition', 25 September – 25 November, 1984, Solomon R. Guggenheim Museum, New York

THREE

Stylistic Analysis and Recent Works

Dale Frank's work is clearly difficult to categorise in terms of any one group, style, theme, myth or theory. Perhaps one of the most interesting aspects of his painting is its inclusion into international exhibitions with such variety of focuses as Romanticism, Surrealism, Neo-expressionism, Trans-Avantgarde, Bad Painting, Stylism and Post-Modernism.

Frank's ability to work through such a multiplicity of stylistic references, creating something entirely new, clearly corresponds to the shaman's need to improvise. It is very possibly this quality that contributes to Frank's bizarre incorporation of unexpected objects and styles in his work. This sort of innovation results in random or chance moves that align themselves equally with Dadaist thinking, Abstract Expressionist gestures and Surrealistic techniques and images. If Frank's work is difficult to deal with, it is because it involves a multiplicity of styles and materials. It is iconoclastic, anarchic, cannibalistic, chaotic, confusing, enigmatic — and often brilliant. One might see it in terms of David Carroll's book, *Paraesthetics*,[214] which discusses aesthetics 'turned against itself', while implying something improper or disordered, such as an aesthetic of chaos (a Post-Modern option of anarchy and chance). Frank takes a critical and philosophical approach to his art and art-making for him becomes a process of asking questions rather than affirming 'givens'. In this respect Frank refers to the limitations of other positions, in order to distinguish his art from theirs, in order to confront and go beyond his and their limitations.

Arguably, Frank's art is a battleground — a staged Dadaistic confrontation between Formalism, Abstract Expressionism, Romanticism, Surrealism, Symbolism and Conceptualism; each faction collapses exhausted upon the other. Put another way Frank may be seen as a Dadaist, setting up a situation, igniting and collapsing it, breaking rules by playing games, and exiting from the scene intact in order to repeat the process. His work thus provokes a stage for a continual dialogue between the problems of painting and its destruction, and the art world — perhaps hinting at a subversion of the history of 20th century art and his own work.

Frank's complex work is often stylistically promiscuous or eclectic and is deliberately so, for specific intellectual reasons. He is in part commenting on the art of others, and in part *resurrecting* an 'essence' of modernist styles from the past which many might now consider 'dead', a religious concept affecting his art practice.

While not obvious to the casual observer, this 'stylistic promiscuity' and chaotic appearance is nearly always ordered by a strong, consistent philosophical and critical position. Frank's revival of modernist art styles often shares the sense of parody exhibited by shamans,[215] indeed this parodic approach is one of the most consistent characteristics of his work. Consistent too, but often unnoticed by others, is the relationship of shamanic symbols and motifs (eyes, flowers, voids, seas, cosmos) and the artist's work practices (poured and heated paints, layered resins, cut shapes, plastic sheeting and metals). In other words, such practices are often the product of such shamanic concepts as the *poisoning* of the canvas' surface (1985–1986). Shamans will often poison other shamans or they may 'heal' by absorbing poison from others.[216] In Frank's later paintings he quite openly discusses his sense of poisoning the painting's surface, creating his 'miasmic' paintings, by employing complex chemical reactions and combustions.

Interestingly, the use of poisons often results in the growth of crystals on the painting's surface. To the shaman, crystals are helping spirits and are magical substances that facilitate flight into the sky.[217] As Dale Frank indicates in his conversation, their presence in his work causes considerable pleasure. Two of his crystal paintings are *The Line and Round of the Green Fly*, 1986, and *The Levitation of the Polynesian — the Hidden Knife and Erection*, 1985.[218]

Another bizarre shamanic aspect of Frank's work practice is his use of metals. Increasingly, throughout Frank's work, we find metallic materials, such as gold and silver paints and nails in *The Cosmology of the Nocturne Whilst the Poker-Faced Bandit*, 1987, and the metal car hubcaps which create extraordinary visual, semantic and temporal conjunctions when found on the surface, in such as works *Art Nazis Must Die*, 1989, and *Magritte's Poor Flowers*, 1988. In *The Good Grandmother Painting: Painting Pictures with Doodles and Diddles (The Triumph)*, 1987, a metal tray closely resembles the shaman's oval mirror, used as an aid in ecstatic ascent. For the shaman metallic objects, nails, shields and magical sticks represent the sun[219] and offer protection from evil spirits playing a part in the ecstatic journey and mystical experiences.[220] Pierced discs can be called the 'orifice of the sun' through which the shaman might enter the underworld[221] and provide interpretation for Frank's use of car hubcaps. Unlike the stylistic variables, Frank's motifs retain intense personal, symbolic and mystical meanings.

By combining references to modernist styles and such shamanic activities, Frank juxtaposes art making and parody. A long-term central theme in Frank's work is 'the act of painting', which relates in part to Ralph Balson's 'Matter Painting', so that 'the matter, the paint, was allowed to flow together to produce its own rhythm, its own structure — a natural paint structure'.[222] Frank tries to find out what the substance of paint will give, to make his painting a 'Matter Painting'.[223] Brooms, mops, heated and cracked paint create a methodology with bizarre conjunctions, technique and scale jostling and confusing the eye of the viewer. In conversation, Frank relates his work to an exploration of materials in the manner of the Romantic movement of the 19th century.

The dynamic and enigmatic nature of Frank's work pivots around a vital and central concept of anarchic Chiliastic conflict — whether conceptual, visual, practical or theoretical — and provides an opposition to mainstream art. The disjunction between 'styles' creates what he calls a 'trap', a demilitarised zone where the beautiful and ugly battle for precedence. Another way of describing his art might be as a state of existing in Limbo, between Heaven and Hell, between one style and another. An essential ingredient in all Frank's work is that of tension between different elements. By flirting with disaster, Frank pushes himself, his art and his spectators to their absolute limits — a process which he associates in conversation with 'fighting against institutionalised beauty by creating a beauty of his own'.

Mario Praz writes that 'true mysticism tends to the negation both of expression and of art'.[224] Evelyn Underhill also writes that mystics take up the 'imagery of negation'. It seems Frank is involved with the *via negativa* — a journey into the mystery of Divinity which is a way of experiencing the divine darkness and a way of 'letting go into God'. Peter Moore suggests that the blankness at the heart of mysticism helps us to understand the void. It also enables us to have a better understanding of Frank's voids. A letting-go of words and images is essential to postmodern spiritual practice. Undergoing 'the *via negativa* is by way of suffering and pain'. In religious literature this is called the 'dark night of the soul' that reminds us of our nothingness. Fox writes that this can be an 'experience of immense spiritual depth and a source for a new birth'. This aspect can be seen in Frank's *The Painting (The Vicious Conspiracy)*, 1984, where Frank becomes a light shining out of the darkest void, that is suggestive of a spiritual rebirth. In this way Divinity is not only God of Light but also of a 'superessential darkness'. The mystic's process of rejection of 'language' (art) becomes a political-theological starting point. In this way Frank is involved with the *via negativa*, which, although it is an approach to God, is also a way of wiping one's mind clean of an 'entire culture'. In this way what we might term Frank's 'anti-aesthetic' appears to derive from a mystical point of view. This mystical anti-aesthetic seems to account for the chaotic jumble of styles, the repulsive surfaces and materials and apocalyptic-kitsch colours in his work. Hal Forster associates the notion of the anti-aesthetic with one 'aspect of the utopian dream of a time of pure presence, a space beyond representation'.[225] It is very possible that Frank's anti-aesthetic is involved with a utopian paradise, a space and a time that *are* beyond representation, a utopian dream that is merely hinted at and disguised from the prying eyes of the viewer. In Forster's opinion the 'anti-aesthetic' is a 'critique which destructures the order of representation in order to reinscribe them'.[226] It seems Frank does this, constructing a critique which destructures art styles and subsequently combines them together in the symbolic expression of a radical, politico-religious aesthetic.[227]

Through his use of discarded and tacky materials, colours and arbitrary painting, Frank's work often appears to be crude. He likes to use the 'left-overs' of other people's 'good' and 'bad' taste as his raw materials have been included in exhibitions of Bad Painting or Kitsch. One might also consider that his 'bad taste' is not 'kitsch' so much as another aspect of the decadence which is sometimes associated with the shaman.[228] Frank will agree that he does not use kitsch as an end in itself. It could be thought of as a by-product of the shamanic association with decadence and decay which generally prefigures chaos and collapse, qualities defined by some critics as reflecting a Post-Modern crisis. Frank's choice of reject materials and revolting surfaces is also a deliberate application of the Romantic anti-aesthetic of the Sublime: an ugliness unacceptable to a lay majority. This is Frank's way of defining limits and asking the eternal avant-garde question: 'What is painting?'

These concerns become particularly apparent in Frank's new works, his enigmatic 'blanket' and 'rug' paintings — for example, *Classicism* and *Flowers*, both of 1990. These works should initially be seen as appropriations from mass production, not art. At their most basic level they function as a found image or Duchampian Readymade, where an everyday object is placed within an art context. *Classicism* and *Flowers* reflect a vacancy or absence of the artist's hand from the work and speak of the cheap and tasteless, flaunting their hideous, shiny pile surface.

Frank's rug paintings, with their soft nastiness, echo a Derridean paradox, that of 'the pleasure of displeasure' and 'the presentation of the unpresentable'[229] — a political act in itself, possibly related to the Chiliast's liking for transgression. Here the viewer is placed in the dilemma of an attraction for the 'softness' and a repulsion for the 'cheapness' in an impasse where High Art and Kitsch are inextricably mixed. As Habermas suggests, aesthetic consciousness is 'addicted to a fascination which accompanies the act of profaning'.[230]

Frank certainly appears to 'profane' both his surfaces and our vision. Nevertheless, the labelling of Frank's work as 'kitsch' is misguided, since the objects and colouring of Frank's paintings are rather more to do with his working in an apocalyptic and visionary genre than the banal. The 'displeasing' qualities of his work also have correspondences with shamanic decadence, referred to by Eliade.[231] Rug works such as *Classicism* and *Flowers* are untouched by paint and reflect a desire to keep art unfinished — an 'unwork' rather than a work. In this way Frank's creations serve to confront both theory and art with their limitations and to transform and displace each in terms of the other.[232] With such blankets and rugs, Frank confronts the limitations of his own strategies.

At this point we might recall that Frank embeds cloth, towels, sheets, blankets and fringed cushions into his painted surfaces. Works such as *The Art of the Artful Hook, Line and Sinker of the Pocket Fisherman Willow Pillow and Sincere*, 1988, and *The Paedophile*, 1988, and *Sex and the Sweet Trap Spot the Faithful Shadow*, 1988, where the fringed cushions might recall in a humorous way, the Formalist squares of Malevich and Hans Hoffmann. While these objects confront us with an element of surprise, they also relate to shamanic interests. Some shamans believe they may capture souls and make them enter cushions in order to help the dead person sleep, acting as the soul's 'material receptacle'.[233] As Eliade notes, spirits can also reside in costumes, wraps and blankets.[234] Towels or blankets are seen in works such as *The Deep Sleeper*, 1990, and *Pop Goes the Weasel*, 1989, which is composed of printed red and black towels with coloured squares and yellow paint dragged across the surface.

Frank's soft pile surface might also secretly reflect the shaman's love of animal fur and skins for his clothing and the drum[235] and perhaps represent substitute skins ? It is possible to surmise that the incorporation of cloth and pile rugs into Frank's paintings has some kind of spiritual significance as animal skins, fur and feathers are believed to be ascensional symbols.[236]

Another long-term theme in Frank's art is that of 'mirror images' or the shamanic or schizoid double reflected in works like *The Two Moons*, 1984, and the multiple 'I/eyes' or psychological 'other' of schizophrenia. A recent work, *Classicism*, 1990, portrays twin tigers, mirrored on the surface. The use of tigers has special significance to some shamans as metamorphosis into an animal ancestor. A tiger may also symbolise magical flight and be a sign of sacred knowledge.[237] Some shamans believe that they 'can turn into a tiger' and that 'on the fourteenth day after his death the shaman becomes a tiger'. The tiger might take the shaman on his back to a 'mythical place where tiger-men live'.[238]

Classicism, a very balanced 'rug painting', presents a picturesque, academic, idealised landscape with an implied perspective. The furriness of the tigers and the furriness of the rug incorporate a sense of irony and, Frank suggests, tease the viewer with the suspicion that they aren't to be taken seriously. Also built into the image, and remarked upon by Frank, is their sense of aggression and submissiveness. A sense of Symbolist ambivalence, located between desire and death, and a struggle between the desire for earthly domination and voluptuous abandon is also embedded into these works.

Frank's appetite for disparate practice, his deliberate use of social detritus and his fetishistic fascination for the tacky and cheap also typify the iconoclasm of the Chiliastic anarchist and shaman. While shamans support the community they are generally perceived as being 'separated from the rest of the community by the intensity of their own religious experience'[239] and through the fear they engender with their ability to make spells. It is possibly this shamanic aspect that engenders Frank's quality as an 'outsider' from specific art styles and movements.

Another recurring image in Frank's work is that of 'flowers' — a symbol that emerges more in his later work, perhaps owing more to the early modernist theory of Symbolism and Surrealism than to the Pop art flowers of Warhol. This image seems once again exemplified in Frank's fascination with defining limits, in/out/across boundaries of art and non-art. Frank's floral 'rug paintings' began with a manufacturer's catalogue, where the rug was photographed in a fine art frame. As Frank observes, as a mass-produced object it isn't art, but he gives it back to art by placing the piece in a gallery — which changes the context yet again. Accordingly, Frank's *Flowers* is a 'presentation with a sense of reverence' rather than irony. In such a sense, one could suggest that 'flowers' has significance as an icon for art. Such recurrent images in Frank's work convey strong Symbolist overtones in the tradition of Moreau and Redon, whose flowers also suggest death. Here there is a strong rapport between the decadence of the shaman and the decadence of the Symbolist. Other works that reflect this floral theme include Frank's bizarre work *Magritte's Poor Flowers*, 1988, where car hubcaps form a metallic bouquet, or *Art with Flowers*, 1989 (flower printed contact), *Bouquet for Gustave and Rene,* (Moreau and Magritte) 1989, or the flowers of *Art* (blue mink acrylic),1989. However, the shaman may use flowers to make a diagnosis about his ill patient. If, in his shaman's ecstasy he sees the patient walking among fresh flowers, 'a cure is certain'; but 'if the flowers are faded, death is inevitable'.[240] It is reasonable to consider that the predominance of the flower motif in Frank's later work plays a similar diagnostic role, or that they are, as Frank says, 'symbols of death' and the source of some poisons.[241] The appearance of flowers in his more mature work suggests shamanic concepts of healing and the making of death spells — as a role of the experienced shaman — and may explain why flowers are missing from his early 'initiatory' works. The motif of flowers emphasises the consistency of the motif, yet they are made and presented very differently — in the form of paint and hubcaps, floral plastic sheeting or rugs united by a flower motif.

Frank's works operate in a manner that David Carroll has termed a 'Paraesthetic' — art turned against itself: improper, 'disordered'. In the rug painting *The Apparition of the Head of John the Baptist in Formal Florid Goa*, 1990, flowers appear yet again. This work, a readymade, fearlessly presents the cheap and nasty surface of Arabic-influenced Italian Kitsch, a 'low art' form which epitomises one more removal of an image from its source. The rug paintings are also transgressive for we know that they were made in a factory as rugs. By presenting what many critics would call the 'unpresentable' in a gallery setting, Frank presents the Sublime. The flower motif continues Frank's association of flowers with death, reflecting both historical ornamentation, symbolism and the unreality of the image. It is possible that this work might also be perceived as a decorative ceiling, to be viewed in the manner of a Tiepolo, in which the heavenly blue between the flowers represents an absence or silent void into which the central flowers have been tossed. There might also be a reference here to Dali's bleeding roses or to the flowers in Moreau's *The Apparition (Salome the Head of St John the Baptist).* Like Moreau, Frank's art and titles are composed of riddles and archaic forms creating a matted web of shamanic thinking, Chiliastic anarchy and apocalyptic 'coded' language.[242] As Frank has noted in conversation, the rug's flowers could also be seen as an appropriation of the floral motif in Tantric art, reflecting another aspect of Frank's appropriation of isolated motifs without their philosophical belief systems.

In *The Apparition of the Head of John the Baptist in Formal Florid Goa*, 1990, the central floral motif forms a mandala where the surrounding heavenly blue creates a physical and meditative experience. Frank suggests that this blankness might also reflect the experience of art or artists without meaning and thereby situates itself in a half-way place between life and death, without a knowledge of either. Another example, *A Painting of a Painting's Nightmare of an Unsuccessful Artist,* 1984, also reflects the double-bind of the artist being caught between trying to find non-existence from existence and seeking life in the void. These works also seem to question the reason for painting, by appropriating the meaning of art and the essence of painting through symbolism. In this respect Frank very interestingly quotes the following lines in which Zola suggests that Moreau:

> *... led painting into the realms of mystery, doubt and fascination. The paintings are at the same time exasperating, full of elements which are added on like collage ... Everyday objects become totally unrecognisable, luxury becomes lewdness in his pictures; the static is shown in contrast to the active; inertia is set against dynamism ... the real and the imaginary become inextricably entangled with one another ... Death is triumphant is a festive background.*[243]

This quotation is deeply evocative of the spirit of Frank's art. Like Huysman's decadent novel, *A Rebours*, Frank's art is enveloped in the odour of social depravity, exhaustion and the overheated atmosphere of society. The rug painting, *The Apparition of the Head of John the Baptist in Formal Florid Goa* also echoes the way in which *fin de siecle* art utilises the St John the Baptist motif.

The baffling nature of Frank's art seems typified by the way his recent work simultaneously compares Symbolist elements reminiscent of Dadaist and Surrealist painting. For example his collage painting *Did the Parrot have Something to do with it ?*, 1990, offers a social and political critique of the Australian art world by combining squares and rectangles of coloured, transparent plastic overlapping layered pages of formal layout material from *Tension* magazine. This work might also be about the process of editing, and in Frank's view, the *Tension* editor's 'neglect' of certain artists. There is also a violence or explosiveness inherent in the layout's titles; 'Minefield', 'Backlash', 'Fire Sale'. The emphasis on text appears to make reference to Cubism, Dadaism and Schwitter's *Merz* collages. Typography and areas of plastic 'woodgrain' also emphasise both the Cubist connection and the plastic woodgrain veneer, and seems to play with the Bauhaus philosophy of 'truth to materials' by negating the principles of good design. Overall the visual repulsiveness of such smooth surfaces typifies Derrida's notion of the 'pleasure of displeasure'.

Frank's games with squares, rectangles, tartans, checks, blocks and cylinders are essentially a resurrection of Formalist art. Frank's layering of geometric shapes also refers to Hans Hoffmann's 'push-pull' oppositions, of Cubist form and Fauvist colour. On occasion, references to Albers might also be found in Frank's areas of paint and overlapping transparent plastic.

While some viewers may be fascinated by such coloured, transparent overlaps, its appeal to Frank lies in the black emptiness between the coloured planes. This planar emptiness has direct references to cut-out holes, suggestive of the void, in previous works like *The Apparition of the Head of John the Baptist in Formal Florid Goa* and once again reasserts thematic, symbolic consistency. Frank finds the voids in his paintings to be reminiscent of earlier images of death such as the Romantic paintings of Caspar David Friedrich. *Dorian's Eye to the Painter's Yellow Sea and Winter Willow (Therese's Pretty View in View of the Rocky Palette)*, 1984, is as previously suggested, a view from within a grave. In other paintings his practise of stitching the holes alludes to the void and his notion of the 'transparent' canvas which is both 'there' and 'not there'. Indeed, his woollen threads, might be compared to the way in which shamanic bridges 'positivise' a negative space and restrain the viewer from 'falling' into the void. Despite the symbolism, these webs evoke a zealous formalism, functioning in a way that seems variously charming, symbolic and unsettling.

Bachelard's concept of the 'sweet magnetism of the viscous' seems to define a central quality both of Frank's painting and that of Balson, who similarly explored the ways in which paint might be allowed to 'flow together to produce its own rhythm, its own structure'.[244]

For Daniel Thomas, Balson was 'a poet of a universal, shifting flux'.[245] Frank, like Balson, is such a poet, working as Jean Clay puts it, 'between plastic and formal components' characterising the formalist approach of many Romantic painters,[246] while also making specific references to the Cobra group's and Art Povera's more recent concern with art materials. Combining the immaculately constructed surface with flamboyant spatters of paint, Frank explores the surface as a plastic element and Abstract Expressionist gesture, subverting and sustaining a gestural violation of the surface in a simultaneous process of creation and destruction. In other words, Frank's painting both flattens the pictorial space and builds on or cuts into it, as paint layers chaotically rise to the surface in slabs, planes or marbling.

Flowing paint or colour also suggests *stains*, either underneath the paint layers or blood red pourings onto the surface. During their initiations, some shamans cut their bodies, creating blood flows, for offerings of blood can be seen as expiatory.[247] As a young man Frank cut a cross into the skin over his heart. Such paint-flows might also be interpreted as 'Christian symbols of life, of man's redemption through the shedding of Christ's blood'. Red is the symbolic colour of Christian martyrdom[248] for 'the symbolism of blood constitutes the rite of expiation and the faith in pardon — a faith which is itself connected with the confession of sins and repentance. The symbolism of blood might well suggest an offering'.[249] *I Love You*, 1990, for example, depicts Frank's ritualistic offering of his blood and himself to us — possibly after his death. From another perspective, these same red 'stains' of paint also be seen as 'symbols of defilement, taboo or a sublimation of dread',[250] for stains and flows engender the viewer's ancient 'dread of the impure'. Pettazone defines defilement as 'an act that involves an evil, an impurity, a fluid, a mysterious and harmful something that acts dynamically — that is to say, magically'.[251] From a political perspective the flowing stain 'designates precisely the situation of having gone astray' which is 'more radical' and forecasts the more modern symbols of 'alienation and dereliction'.[252] In addition to its redemptive and threatening overtones, Frank's painting also operates in what I have termed an anti-aesthetic manner, drawing into itself both parodic references to Abstract Expressionism and serious references to experimentation with the surface, as in Romantic art, Surrealism and Abstraction.

Works that display expressionistic dribbles and stains, brilliant, kitsch colours, metal or objects embedded into the support emphasise the materiality of the painting's surface. While the quality of iron is a response to materiality and the 'ironness of iron, the sackiness of sacking',[253] it also reflects the shaman's attraction to the ecstatic and magical nature of metals found in works like *Art Nazis Must Die (Self-Portrait)*, 1989. Frank thus associates the materiality of paint and the rhythm of painting with the rhythm of the universe — this is particularly evident in the powerful acid-green painting *Knowing Known the Poison*, 1988. In paintings such as *The Cosmos with Ornamentation (The Spotted Sailor)*, 1987 and *I Knew the Mandlebrot Before it was a Superstar*, 1990, surging flows create taches (colour blotches), cosmic 'sunspots' with filaments that suggest the Mandlebrot icon of Chaos Theory. The latter pertains to order in chaos and chaos in order — the accidental according to certain laws. Frank's working process also parallels this theory, beginning with an arbitrary starting point, and utilising unpredictable results from insignificant actions.

Part of the fascination of Frank's work clearly lies in his ability to resurrect and quote previous styles of high modern art while bringing them to both cosmic and everyday levels — an attitude which is often very sceptical of High Art ideals. The interaction of the 'High Art' within the realm of the theoretical, cosmic and the mundane creates strange explosive/implosive disjunctions. Frank brings together many distant 'realities' — the seemingly banal, the physical and the metaphysical paradoxically creating and negating values at the same time, in a manner reminiscent of the destructive, apocalyptic, iconoclastic or negative aspects of both the Chiliastic and Romantic traditions.

Romantic art has often been linked with rebels and dissent.[254] Hayden White also makes links between Romanticism, Formalism and Anarchism and considers that in the 19th century 'Anarchism is the ideological implication of Romanticism' and a 'secularised form that Orgiastic Chiliasm took', which 'fed into Fascism in the 20th century in the same way that Romanticism has'.[255] What one might think of as a fusion of Anarchistic, Chiliastic, Romantic and at times Formalist tendencies occurs repeatedly in Frank's later oeuvre.[256] Frank's 'wanderings of the imagination',[257] his visionary journeys and redemptive offerings of blood, and his painting technique could be perceived as being Romantic. Frank's early initiatory 'nightmare' paintings and his Romantic ennui[258] might also find a parallel in the Post-Modern sense of 'exhaustion'.[259] The Romantic artist's characteristic 'tension', 'paroxysm', 'jarring and clamorous discords' and 'forcing of tones' all have their equivalents in

Frank's fluorescent, high-keyed colour and chaotic jumble of styles and just as some Romantics take pleasure in 'destruction and transgression',[260] Frank uses destructive techniques of burning and cutting and 'transgressing' combinations of disparate modern art styles. Transgressions such as 'uncompromising rituals of breaking' are also aspects of millennarianist rebellion.[261]

Suggesting other terms which apply equally well to Frank, Mario Praz links the Romantic, transgressive joy of sadism to the joy of remorse and expiation,[262] and a consequent inversion of values. Such 'inversions' can be found both in Frank's reversal of moral and religious themes, and such formal devices as his overloaded surface in *The Good Grandmother Painting: Painting Pictures with Doodles and Diddles (The Triumph)* 1987, where a wooden coffee table and metal tray project almost a metre out from the painting's surface. His early work's dismemberment themes and his later work's confused styles and colours suggest the 'beauty of the horrid'[263] and the decadent Romantic fascination with the 'uncontrolled, the macabre, the terrible, the strange' and with a 'beauty tainted with pain, corruption and death'.[264] These tendencies are all reflected in Frank's portrayal of his own 'tortured and dismembered body, his expiatory flows of blood, and his fascination for suffering, death and decay'.[265] As Praz notes, the Romantics also often develop a cult for 'tainted' or 'cadaverous beauty',[266] delighting in representing the dramatic, extreme point of human agony. In a similar manner Frank depicts his body being dismembered before his own eyes, or as St Bartholomew 'flayed', or Christ wrongly judged and crucified. The image of the artist 'mocked and rejected like Christ'[267] exemplifies a Romantic suffering very like Frank's. Suffering and cadaverous beauty is also reflected in Frank's appreciation and collection of Crucifixions and Depositions of the dead Christ.[268] As in Romantic painting, Frank brings ecstasy and horror together,[269] provoking 'the pleasure of displeasure'.

This strange air of ecstasy and horror also tempts critics such as Angela Vettese and Camille Sbrissa[270] to place Frank within the contexts of Neo-Surrealism and show a tendency toward the 'graphic automatism'[271] evident in works like *Cosmos with Ornamentation … Knowing Known the Poison Gundy*, 1989, and *Poking up Daisies*, 1990. Another feature, Frank's vertiginous concentric circles, suggests the ecstatic religious visual experience that becomes more explicit in *The Masterpiece with the Diddle Worthy of a Fly*, 1987. It is interesting to note here that Eliade associates the shaman's unmastered spirits with 'mediumistic automatism'.[272] Frank also uses other Surrealist techniques such as pouring, dribbling and Rorschach images.

This kind of surrealism conforms with a 'renouncement of the world of logic and the play of fantasy' coinciding with the conviction that 'there are treasures hidden in the recesses of the human mind'. Vettese also associates this particular form of Surrealism with those who 'aim at laying bare the layers, symbols and images of the mind'.[273] Viewed in such terms, Frank's visionary dreams of eyes, flowers and seas are patently Surreal. Angela Vettese also links Frank's images as his 'unconscious in turmoil'[274] with the Neo-Gothic taste for 'fantastic quasi-medieval atmospheres'[275] — a trait which is suggested by Frank's allusions to Medieval life, his symbols, images and titles such as *Portrait, A Track to Medieval Artist and Fountains*, 1982. Other references to St John the Baptist, 1990, *The Immaculate Crucifixion to Forgive all Art Sinners*, 1990, *The Two Saints*, 1985, and his images of St Bartholomew and St Sebastian, devils, saints, God and Christ, similarly conform at times to the medieval religious atmosphere in Frank's work.

All these characteristics prompt the more general hypothesis that Frank explores what Eco terms the 'hyperreal,' or the 'postmodern', 'neo-medieval' wave,[276] looking at mass culture, for symptoms of a 'quest for our roots'.[277] In Frank's case this medievalism reflects a multi-temporal and spiritual sense of belonging to another age, or, as Matthew Fox suggests, a 'rediscovery of the creation mystics of the Middle Ages'.[278] Eco considers the question of 'dreaming of the Middle Ages' as a 'Post-modern temptation' of 'intemporal ecstasies'.[279] Eco's concepts are equally applicable to Frank and best described in terms of what Eco calls the Middle Ages of 'tradition', of occult philosophy and the 'mystical weddings of the micro with the macrocosm'.[280] Frank's multi-temporal references once again reflect what one might think of as his shamanic ability to cross ontological boundaries, a trait which makes him as much a part of the Primordial Tradition as the Post-modern. Eco's Middle Ages of 'Tradition', like Frank's, fuse a historical and psychological insecurity of the Middle Ages with his similar responses in the 20th century.[281]

In summary, Frank's sense of Post-modern spirituality reflects a world-wide, reawakened interest in mysticism and spirituality.[282] This in turn reconciles culture with Nature and its interconnection with the Cosmos as a whole.[283] In this respect Frank's work possibly embodies two impulses of Post-modernism. On the one hand he offers visions of a Deconstructive, Anarchistic Chiliastic catastrophe. On the other hand he provides us with images of what Fox terms a Reconstructive, Shamanic, 're-enchantment' and re-creation of the world.[284] He also perceives the Post-modern spiritual practice as 'Creation spirituality' that attempts to open 'the mystic inside',[285] exemplified by Frank's visionary life. Fox also writes that 'Spirituality is about doing, becoming and Power,' unleashing the 'divine powers in us all'. He believes that the mystic has somehow managed to imbibe the powers of the universe,[286] engendering a cosmic force in Frank's spiritual and artistic practice. Frank, like the artist Gablik discusses, turns to a 'shamanic consciousness' and a 're-enchanted shamanic art' that will awaken a sense of responsibility for the earth[287] and its interrelation to the world.

Stylistically Frank simultaneously exudes a Post-modern sense of collapse, a *fin de siecle* atmosphere of overheated decadence and a melting and merging of many styles of art which is Post-modern in its sense of eclecticism and catastrophe. An aspect of Frank's Post-modernism is his parodic quotation of previous modern art styles, a parody which parallels the shaman's trickster behaviour.[288] Frank's style clearly shares the Post-modern fashion of 'critiquing' many styles rather than working in one rigid manner, and often playfully combines Formalist geometric abstract shapes combined with expressionistic ecstatic swirls — a tendency particularly evident in recent works like *The Masterpiece with the Diddle Worthy of a Fly*, 1987. Producing a sense of shock or surprise in the viewer, Frank's quotation might also be seen as an aspect of the shaman's role as a provocative 'magician' and 'trickster'[289] who confuses 'codes'.[290] In this way Frank perhaps 'seeks to question rather than exploit cultural codes, to explore rather than conceal social and political affiliations'.[291] Frank's creativity consistently reflects a spiritualised Post-modern, Chiliastic anarchy in its refusal of stylistic orthodoxies.

At the same time, Frank also explores a crucial sense of multi-temporalism, evincing ecstatic experience, exploring the motifs of primordial Creation, Apocalypse, Revelation, Medieval life and the 21st century, and even suggesting the experience of becoming one with Christ. At their extremes Frank's thematics extend both to primordial Creation (the creative aspect) and the apocalyptic End of the World (the destructive aspect).

Perhaps the most useful general theory encompassing these traits is Achille Bonito Oliva's notion of Trans-avantgarde[292] in the Post-modern. Bonito Oliva considers the Trans-avantgarde as a language, a tool of change, a passage from one work to another, from one style to another. This sense of transition clearly corresponds to Frank's eclectic juxtaposition of Formalism, Expressionism, Surrealism, Symbolism and Abstraction within one work. According to Bonito Oliva, 'the new image has found a natural habitat in the history of art and of styles'[293] — a phrase which nicely describes Frank's cultural world-view.

While Frank considers his quotations to offer a process of 'resurrection', Bonito Oliva suggests that this approach denotes a timelessness that consists in the recovery of languages, positions, and methodologies pertaining to the past'.[294] Trans-avantgarde painting slows down this speed in the viscosity of painted matter, and thereby introduces a protracted time — a duration which echoes art's eternal desire for immortality.[295] This too, could well describe Frank's painting.

Frank is eclectic in his methods and styles despite his consistent philosophy and ideology, producing in his work what Bonito Oliva terms 'continuous shiftings of meanings'[296], often taken to puzzling extremes. The viewer is never *quite* sure how to confront or analyse Frank's work.

Bonito Oliva suggests that Trans-avantgarde images explore 'figuration, of abstract marks, of opulence of material and colour, without ever submitting to standardisation'[297] and neatly describes the qualities of Frank's fluoro colours, eclectic styles, metallic paints and inclusion of bizarre objects.[298] For Frank, past and present styles are recovered as a sort of *objet trouve*, detached from their semantic references. Quotation thus becomes a process whereby cultural models are recovered for open-ended creativity.[299]

In essence, Frank sets aesthetics against itself and places style in opposition to style, performing a critical function by asking 'What is painting?' Frank's dialogue with, and quotation of, Abstract Expressionism, Formalism, Dadaism, Romanticism, Symbolism and Surrealism, anarchically breaks with pictorial conventions by pushing each to its limits and beyond, setting one in confrontation with another with typical iconoclastic, Chiliastic energy and anger.

As I have suggested, Frank's experiment with styles, materials and approaches defies conventional categories. Frank creates an aesthetic situated on both sides of Aesthetics — invoking the beautiful and the ugly, attraction, repulsion. In David Carroll's terms this 'Paraesthetic' approach points to a complex of questions, which lead in turn to other questions. In this situation art must be constantly reworked and — from the critic's point of view — must be constantly redefined.

Throughout this book I have tried to demonstrate correspondences between Frank's motifs and mysticism, between Shamanism and Chiliasm. Frank fascinatingly defies conventional categories and demands consideration in a broad range of contexts including Shamanism, Chiliasm, Romanticism, Modernism, the Post-modern and Trans-avantgarde. That his work falls into so many contexts is very impressive in such a young artist. It is perhaps inadvisable at this point to try to characterise Frank's achievement in terms of any over-specific category or concept, or even, indeed, in terms of this book's focus upon Shamanism, Chiliasm and contemporary artistic innovation. Rather than wishing to typecast Frank too specifically, I have attempted here to demonstrate the rich pluralism of his art by reference to the fascinating interplay between his painting and the assumptions of these three traditions.

To conclude: Frank's work may or may not correspond entirely to definitions of the orthodox Shaman, Chiliast or Post-modernist. Nevertheless his art frequently seems to partake in various ways of all these traditions, interweaving and reassessing their assumptions in many extremely provocative and innovative ways. His subsequent work will almost certainly explore, elaborate and re-permutate aspects of these and other traditions. Few other contemporary Australian artists have engaged in such a rich amalgam of spiritual, social and aesthetic traditions. Few other artists offer such perplexing and also such exhilarating work.

It is precisely because Frank's work appeals to this challenging and pluralistic array of references that his work merits considerable attention, and in all probability will continue to surprise those following developments in contemporary Australian and International art.

FOOTNOTES

1 Eliade, M., *Shamanism: Archaic Techniques of Ecstasy*, Princeton N.J.: Princeton University Press, 1972, pp. 4, 375.
2 Eliade, M., p. 33.
3 Harner, M., *The Way of The Shaman*, New York: Bantam Books, 1986, p. xiii.
4 Lewis, I.M., *Ecstatic Religion*, Harmondsworth: Penguin Books, 1978, p. 50.
5 Ricoeur, P., *The Symbolism of Evil*, Boston: Beacon Press, p. 353.
6 Murray, H., *Myth and Mythmaking*, Boston: Beacon Press, 1968, p. 334.
7 Eliade, M., p. 509.
8 Eliade, M., p. 322.
9 Eliade, M., p. 313.
10 Eliade, M., pp. 313, 375.
11 Guthrie, W., *Orpheus and Greek Religion*, London: Methuen & Co. Ltd., 2nd revised edition, 1952, pp. 264–265.
12 Guthrie, W., p. 266.
13 Guthrie, W., pp. 264, 271.
14 Harner, M., pp. 161–164.
15 Warden, J. (ed), *Orpheus, The Metamorphoses Of A Myth*, Toronto: University of Toronto Press, 1982, p. xiii.
16 Eliade, M., pp. 3, 140.
17 Campbell, J., *The Masks of God: Primitive Mythology*, London: Secker and Warburg, 1960, p. 231.
18 Campbell, J., pp. 230, 231, 240.
19 Campbell, J., p. 241.
20 Campbell, J., p. 248.
21 Eliade, M. (ed in chief), 'Shamanism: An Overview', *The Encyclopaedia of Religion*, Vol. 13, New York: Macmillan Publishing Company, pp. 202, 213, 217 and Campbell, J., pp. 229.
22 Eliade, M., 'Shamanism: An Overview', pp. 202, 211.
23 Eliade, M., pp. 13, 33.
24 Eliade, M., pp. 13, 14, 33 and Campbell, J., p. 251.
25 Eliade, M., pp. 5, 67, 80, 99, 143.
26 Campbell, J., p. 265.
27 Eliade, M., pp. 126, 128, 130, 132, 134, 135.
28 Eliade, M., pp. 90, 91.
29 Eliade, M., pp. 13, 14, 15, 99.
30 Eliade, M., p. 33.
31 Murray, H., *Myth and Mythmaking*, p. 311.
32 Murray, H., *Myth and Mythmaking*, p. 317.
33 Eliade, M., p. 509 and Campbell, J., p. 239.
34 Eliade, M., p. 24.
35 Eliade, M., pp. xi, 13, 14, 15, 20, 21, 25, 26.
36 Eliade, M., p. 107 and Dodds, pp. 140–143.
37 Eliade, M., p. 37, note 6.
38 Eliade, M., p. 67.
39 Eliade, M., pp. 34, 36.
40 Eliade, M., pp. 36, 86.
41 Interview, Dale Frank and Jane Magon, 18th August, 1991.
42 Eliade, M., p. 38.
43 This kind of resurrection is reflected in Christian hagiography, where one might think of St Anthony, St Sebastian, St Bartholomew and so on.
44 Guthrie, W., pp. 19, 21.
45 Harner, M., p. 30.
46 Harner, M., p. 64.
47 Foss, P., 'Eyes Fetishism and the Gaze', *Art and Text*, No. 20, February–April, 1986, p. 29.
48 Eliade, M., pp. 36, 37.
49 Foss, P., p. 29.
50 Drury, N., *Don Juan, Mescalito And Modern Magic*, London: Routledge & Kegan Paul, 1978, pp. 17,18, and Harner, M., p. 159.
51 Interview, Dale Frank and Jane Magon.
52 Interestingly Julia Kristeva also writes that melancholic persons settle the lost thing or object within themselves ... This presents us with the first state of the self's doubling, which initiates a series of contradictory identifications. With doubling, 'my other is hostile to me' and that persecution entails a double meaning. In hypnotic passion one sees doubles, in Kristeva, J. *Black Sun*, Columbia University Press, New York, 1989, pp. 166, 167, 168, 246.

53 Eliade, M., p. 328.
54 Harner, M., p. 76.
55 Eliade, M., note 37, p. 153, p. 352.
56 Eliade, M., p. 153.
57 Eliade, M., pp. 36, 37, 153, 352.
58 Dodds, E., *The Greeks and the Irrational*, Berkeley: University of California Press, 1951, pp. 140, 160.
59 Interview, Dale Frank with Jane Magon.
60 Harner, M., pp. 21–23.
61 Harner, M., pp. 21–23.
62 Eliade, M., pp. 256, 330.
63 Eliade, M., p. 57.
64 Bettelheim, B., *Symbolic Wounds*, London: Thames and Hudson, 1955, p. 218.
65 Eliade, M., p. 53.
66 Eliade, M., pp. 142, 146.
67 Eliade, M., in Murray, H., *Myth and Mythmaking*, p. 71.
68 Harner, M., pp. 13, 54, 81, 82 and Eliade, M., pp. 138, 384.
69 Dale Frank in conversation with Jane Magon, 1991.
70 Eliade, M., pp. 51, 52.
71 Harner, M., pp. 37, 159, 160.
72 Eliade, M., p. 389 and Harner, pp. 159, 160.
73 Eliade, M., p. 94.
74 Eliade, M., pp. 167, 168.
75 Eliade, M., pp. 96, 97,99.
76 Eliade, M., pp. 34, 171, 174.
77 In Greek mythology, where Zeus swallows Phanes — the origin of all — he mingled with his own limbs 'the power and strength of the god' (Guthrie, p. 81). In this way the god engulfs creator and creation in his own body ... and brings them forth again as they were before (Guthrie, pp. 81, 104).
78 Fry, N., in Murray, H., *Myth and Mythmaking*, pp. 123, 127, writes that: During the descent the hero may be swallowed by the dragon into the monster's belly reflecting the 'night journey' of an introverted soul. Jesus, too, was portrayed as descending into hell through the mouth of a huge dragon or shark. (p. 128.)
79 Holloway, M., 'Bleak Romantics', *Australian Visions: 1984 Exxon International Exhibition*, Exhibition Catalogue, New York: Solomon Guggenheim Museum, 1984, p. 19.
80 Harner, M., pp. 31, 46, 83–91. It is interesting that a mythical bird is seen only twice in the life of a shaman, once in his life at his spiritual birth and once at his death. The mythical bird is also believed to carry the shaman's soul into the underworld. Sometimes the shaman's soul is described as a bird (Eliade, pp. 36, 38). Frank's *Dead Bird in the Studio*, 1985, was described by Frank as marking a special time in his life, like a spiritual awakening.
81 Vastokas, J., 1970, quoted in Harner, M., *The Way of The Shaman*, New York: Bantam Books, 1986, p. 37.
82 Frank's drawings are similar to Alaskan Eskimo masks; see photograph and text of Vastokas, J., 1970, quoted in Harner, M., *The Way of The Shaman*, New York: Bantam Books, 1986, p. 37.
83 Harner, M., p. 38.
84 Eliade, M., p. 82, 58.
85 Eliade, M., p. 84
86 Interview, Dale Frank with Jane Magon, 1991.
87 Dodds, E., p. 37.
88 Macchioro, V., *From Orpheus To Paul*, New York: Henry Holt And Company, 1930, p. 39.
89 Macchioro, V., p. 43. These flows recall the place where Orpheus descended into Hades to recover his wife.
90 Eliade, M., pp. 33, 54, 80.
91 Eliade, M., pp. 134, 173.
92 Eliade, M., p. 204 and Stone, M., 'Lists of Revealed Things in the Apocalyptic Literature' in *Magnalia Dei The Mighty Acts of God*, New York: Doubleday and Company, 197 , p. 433. Stone discusses geographical or cosmic voids that feature in the apocalypse where God 'scrutinises the depths of the abyss'.
93 Kontova, H., 'Dale Frank', *Flash Art*, No. 122, 1985, p. 70.
94 Eliade, M., pp. 203, 204.
95 Eliade, M., pp. 397, 398, 484, 486, Note 110, p. 489.
96 Eliade, M., p. 419.
97 Eliade, M., in *Myth and Mythmaking*, p. 68 and Eliade, M., pp. 250, 262, 265.
98 Eliade, M., pp. 171, 173, 174, 175.
99 Eliade, M., notes the use of the metaphor relating the shaman's drum to an expanse of water; 'through the drum as through a lake'. Notes 90, p. 247.
100 Dale Frank in conversation with the author.
101 Eliade, M., in Murray, H. (ed), *Myth and Mythmaking*, pp. 61, 62, 67.
102 Eliade, M., p. 125, 126.
103 Eliade, M., pp. 169, 194, 270, 284.
104 Eliade, M., p. 126

105 Eliade, M., pp. 154, 464, 465, 498.
106 Harner, M., p. 149.
107 Forestier, L., in Balakian, A. (ed), *The Symbolist Movement In The Literature of European Languages,* Budapest: Akademiai Kiado, 1982, pp. 108, 118. Forestier indicates that mirrors intercede between man and the cosmos: 'the play of mirrors reveals the existence of primal images' and are 'secret, sacred signs of the Cosmos'.
108 Interview Dale Frank and Jane Magon, 14 February, 1991.
109 Eliade, M., p. 143 and Hall, J., *Halls Dictionary of Subjects and Symbols in Art,* London: John Murray, 1986, p. 509. Hall writes that the 'Fallen World' is interpreted as a symbol of the void which is also a wound or Christ's wound, inherent in mortality and one that cannot be healed.
110 Eliade, M., p. 104 and Frank in conversation with Jane Magon, 1990, 1991.
111 Howitt in Eliade, M., *Shamanism: Archaic Techniques of Ecstasy,* pp. 52, 88, 91, 320, 322. Harner writes that many shamans would regard a shattered crystal as equivalent to or indicative of the 'ending the world'. p. 143.
112 Frank in conversation with the author, 1991.
113 Lewis, I.M., p. 49.
114 Eliade, M., pp. 90, 91.
115 Howitt in Eliade, p. 143. Harner writes that 'every shaman tells a different story of the creation.' Shamans refer to the same event but the way of telling it differs. p. 57, 58. As in *Genesis* they portray 'a single act of creation in time as a creation myth', see Flew, A. (ed), *A Dictionary of Philosophy,* London: Pan Books in association with the Macmillan Press, 1983, p. 77. Another literary reference might be: 'In the beginning God created the heavens and the earth. Now the earth was a formless void, there was darkness over the deep, and God's spirit hovered over the water'. See in Jones, A., (ed), 'Genesis', *The Jerusalem Bible,* London: Darton, Longman & Todd, 1966, p. 15.
116 Burkert, W., *Orphism and Bacchic Mysteries: New Evidence And Old Problems of Interpretation,* Berkeley: The Center for Hermeneutical Studies, 1977, p. 12.
117 In *Genesis* and many other religious myths, a relationship can be found between Creation and the primordial waters. Many of Frank's early works reflect the ominous and primordial 'darkness over the deep'.
118 Lunar myths are important in the organisation of the first coherent theories concerning death, resurrection, fertility regeneration and initiation. Eliade, M., *The Myth of the Eternal Return, or, Cosmos and History,* Princeton: Princeton University Press, 1974, p. 86.

In Frank's paintings he battles evil for 'the evil of history is linked with cosmic evil, the primordial peril where the cosmic drama becomes a Messianic drama'. Cosmic evil includes 'murders, slaughters — quarrels, lying words, disputes, anarchy and disaster' — all the elements of Frank's visionary world of the 21st century and the world of illusion. See also Ricoeur, P., pp. 200, 205, 208.
119 Lewis, I.M., p. 50.
120 Gill, S.D., (ed, Eliade, M.), 'North American Shamanism', *The Encyclopaedia of Religion,* Vol. 13, New York: Macmillan Publishing Company, p. 217.
121 Schwartz, H., (ed, Eliade, M.), *The Encyclopaedia Of Religion,* Vol. 9, New York: Macmillan Publishing Company, 1986, pp. 527, 528.
122 Eliade, M., *The Myth of the Eternal Return, or, Cosmos And History,* Princeton: Princeton University Press, 1974, pp. 57, 60.
123 Thomas, D., 'Ralph Balson', *Art and Australia,* Vol. 2, No. 4, March, 1965, p. 291.
124 Kontova, H., 'Dale Frank', *Flash Art,* No. 120, 1985, p. 70.
125 Hall, J., *Dictionary of Subjects and Symbols in Art,* Norwich: Fletcher & Son Ltd., 1986, p. 86.
126 Stone, M., 'Lists of Revealed Things in the Apocalyptic Literature' in *Magnalia Dei: The Mighty Acts of God,* New York: Doubleday and Company Inc., 1976, p. 414.
127 Jones, A. (ed), 'The Book of Revelation', *The Jerusalem Bible,* London: Darton, Longman & Todd, 1966, p. 436.
128 Laing, R.D., *The Divided Self,* Harmondsworth: Penguin Books, 1969, pp. 200–205.
129 Kristeva, J., *Black Sun,* Trans. L. Roudiez, New York: Columbia University Press, 1989, pp. 3, 151, 119.
130 Stone, M., p. 433.
131 Dale Frank in conversation with the author. This example of cosmic travel has been interpreted by Kristeva who writes that 'the depressed person is ... a dweller in the imaginary realm'. p. 61.
132 Himmelfarb, M., *Tours of Hell,* Philadelphia: University of Pennsylvania Press, 1983, p. 3.
133 Himmelfarb, M., p. 2, p. 51.
134 Himmelfarb, M., p. 3.
135 Kristeva, J., pp. 223, 224.
136 Schwartz, H., p. 522.
137 Jones, A. (ed), 'The Book of Revelation', *The Jerusalem Bible,* London: Darton,Longman & Todd, 1966, pp. 448, 449.
138 Jones, A., p. 438.
139 Jones, A., p. 62.
140 Zamora, L., *Writing the Apocalypse,* Cambridge:Cambridge University Press, 1989, p. 14.

141 Zamora, L., p. 14.
142 Interview Dale Frank with Jane Magon, 14 February, 1991.
143 Zamora, L., p. 15.
144 Interview, Dale Frank with Jane Magon, 31 January, 1991.
145 Interview, Dale Frank with Jane Magon, 31 January, 1991.
146 Zamora, L., p. 1.
147 Zamora, L., p. 11 and Schwartz, p. 527.
148 Zamora, L., p. 11.
149 Zamora, L., p. 7.
150 Zamora, L., p. 9.
151 Dale Frank in conversation with Jane Magon, 1990.
152 Zamora, L., p. 3
153 Dale Frank in conversation with Jane Magon, 1990.
154 Lincoln, B., 'The Earth Becomes Flat' A Study of Apocalyptic Imagery', *Comparative Studies in Society and History*, Vol. 25, Cambridge: Cambridge University Press, 1983, p. 152.
155 Schwartz, H., p. 530.
156 Lerner, R., 'Millennialism, Christian' in *Dictionary of the Middle Ages*, Vol. 8, New York: Charles Scribner's Sons, 1982, p. 384.
157 Schwartz, H., p. 522.
158 Schwartz, H., p. 530.
159 Schwartz, H., p. 522.
160 Kaminsky, H., 'Chiliasm and the Hussite Revolution', *Church History*, Vol. 26, 1957, p. 50.
161 Interview, Dale Frank with Jane Magon, 31 January, 1991.
162 Mannheim, K., p. 190.
163 Schwartz, H. p. 524, 525.
164 Schwartz, H., p. 529.
165 Kaminsky, H., 'Chiliasm and The Hussite Revolution', *Church History*, Vol. 26, 1957, p. 62.
166 Schwartz, H., p. 527.
167 Kaminsky, H., p. 49.
168 Schwartz, H., p. 524, and Eliade — M. Eliade writes that 'nomadism' is a feature of shamanism. p. 9
169 Schwartz, H., p. 526.
170 Frank discussed his childhood memories of constant anger with the author, early in 1991.
171 Schwartz, H., p. 525.
172 Kaminsky, H., p. 50.
173 Kaminsky, H., pp. 55–56.
174 Kaminsky, H., p. 57.
175 Kaminsky, H., p. 59.
176 Kaminsky, H., p. 64.
177 Mannheim, K., p. 198.
178 Mannheim, K., p. 196.
179 Kaminsky, H., p. 48.
180 Kaminsky, H., p. 59.
181 Kaminsky, H., p. 45
182 Mannheim, K., p. 194.
183 Interview, Dale Frank and Jane Magon, 14 February, 1991.
184 Interview, Dale Frank and Jane Magon, 14 February, 1991.
185 Interview, Dale Frank and Jane Magon, 14 February, 1991.
186 Interview, Dale Frank and Jane Magon, 14 February, 1991.
187 Zamora, L., p. 2.
188 Zamora, L., p. 12.
189 Mannheim, K., p. 192.
190 Mannheim, K., p. 213.
191 Kaminsky, H., p. 61.
192 Kaminsky, H., p. 57.
193 Mannheim, K., p. 233.
194 Mannheim, K., p. 203.
195 Mannheim, K., p. 193–4
196 Mannheim, K., p. 195.
197 Schwartz, H., p. 522.
198 Mannheim, K., p. 195.
199 Mannheim, K., p. 212.
200 Kaminsky, H., p. 48.

201 Kaminsky, H., p. 50.
202 Schwartz, H., p. 521.
203 Schwartz, H., p. 529.
204 Mannheim, K., p. 204.
205 Schwartz, H., pp. 528, 529.
206 Schwartz, H., p. 530.
207 Cohn, N., *The Pursuit of the Millennium*, London: Temple Smith, 1970, p. 282.
208 Cohn, N., p. 282.
209 Cohn, N., pp. 282, 286.
210 Cohn, N., p. 286.
211 Cohn, N., p. 202–203.
212 Mannheim, K., p. 196 and note 1, p. 196 and p. 218.
213 Mannheim, K., p. 223.
214 Carroll, D., *Paraesthetics*, New York: Methuen 1987, p. xiv.
215 Eliade, M., *Shamanism: Archaic Techniques of Ecstasy*, Princeton N.J.: Princeton University Press, 1972, pp. 154, 24 and Campbell, J., *The Masks of God: Primitive Mythology*, London: Secker and Warburg, 1960, pp. 55, 265.
216 Eliade, M., pp. 305, 307, 308.
217 Eliade, M., p. 52, 88, 91.
218 Unfortunately the crystals do not seem to photograph very clearly.
219 Eliade, M., p. 172, 148, 433. These car hubcaps might be 'orifices of the sun' through which the shaman might enter the underworld or they might also function as the shaman's wheel on which he occupies a 'central position' for his flight into the air.
220 Eliade, M., p. 29, 148, 172, 177.
221 Eliade, M., pp. 148, 433.
222 Thomas, D., 'Ralph Balson', *Art and Australia*, Vol. 2, No. 4, March, 1965. p. 290.
223 Thomas, D., p. 290.
224 Praz, M., *The Romantic Agony*, London: Oxford University Press, 2nd edition, 1951, p. 200.
225 Forster, H., 'Postmodernism: A Preface' in *The Anti-Aesthetic*, Seattle: Bay Press, 1991, p. xv.
226 Forster, H., p. xv.
227 Forster, H., p. xi.
228 Eliade, M., pp. 67, 68, 83, 256, 258, 376, 500.
229 Carroll, D., p. 143.
230 Habermas, J., 'Modernity — An Incomplete Project' in *The Anti-Aesthetic*, Seattle: Bay Press, 1991, p. 5
231 Eliade, M., pp. 67, 68, 83, 256, 258, 376, 500.
232 Carroll, D., p. 187.
233 Eliade, M., pp. 210, note 79, 211.
234 Eliade, M., pp. 147, 178, 179, 350.
235 Eliade, M., pp. 150–154, 170, 177, 179, 339.
236 Eliade, M., p. 177.
237 Eliade, M., pp. 171, 177, 178
238 Eliade, M., p. 339, notes 15 and 16.
239 Eliade, M., p. 8 and Campbell, J., p. 254.
240 Eliade, M., p. 304.
241 Dale Frank in conversation with Jane Magon, 1991.
242 Zamora, L., *Writing The Apocalypse*, Cambridge: Cambridge University Press, 1989, p. 15.
243 Delevoy, R., *Symbolists and Symbolism*, New York: Rizzoli International Publications Inc., 1982, p. 42.
244 Thomas, D., p. 290.
245 Thomas, D., p. 291.
246 Clay, J., *Romanticism*, New York: Phaidon, 1981, p. 100.
247 Eliade, M., pp. 124, 256, 257, 263, 275, 277, 308, 337. A scar is still evident where Frank at the ages of 12 and 14 cut into his palm, more for philosophical reasons, asking himself 'How could I die just from the disruption of flesh, or was death instead caused from loss of spirit?' It seems that now these activities were brought about more as questions about immortality.
248 Hall, J., *Hall's Dictionary of Subjects and Symbols in Art*, London: John Murray, reprint 1986, p. 49.
249 Ricoeur, P., *The Symbolism of Evil*, Boston: Beacon Press,p. 97.
250 Ricoeur, P., pp. 8, 12, 40.
251 Ricoeur, P., p. 25.
252 Ricoeur, P., p. 73.
253 Thomas, D. p. 290.
254 Bonito Oliva, A., *Trans-avant Garde International*, Milan: Giancarlo Politi Editore, 1982, pp. 28, 252, and Praz, M., p. 61, and J.L. Talmon, *Romanticism and Revolt*, New York: W.W. Norton and Company, pp. 136, 162.

255 White, H., 'The Poetics of History' in *Metahistory The Historical Imagination in 19th Century Europe, Baltimore:* The John Hopkins University Press, 1973, pp. 22, 29.

256 Like other Romantic heroes Frank is the rebel type (the Chiliastic anarchist) the fallen angel, Medievalist, the millennarianist or shaman who lives 'in voluntary exile', see Praz, M., pp. 61, 66, 67, 68, and Schwartz, H., p. 524, 525, 526, and Eliade, M., p. 9.

257 Praz, M., p. 38.

258 Praz, M., p. 68

259 Huyssen, A., 'Mapping The Postmodern' in *New German Critique,* No. 33, Fall, 1984, p. 48.

260 Praz, M., p. 104.

261 Schwartz, H., (ed, Eliade, M.) 'Millennarianism', *The Encylopaedia of Religion,* Vol. 9, New York: Macmillan Publishing Company, 1986, p. 524.

262 Praz, M., p. 105, 106.

263 Praz, M., pp. xiv, xv.

264 Praz, M., p. 38, 45.

265 Interestingly Hayden White describes 'redemption' as a 'Romantic drama' and one that we could easily apply to Frank's concepts. White, H., p. 9.

266 Praz, M., pp. 38, 45, 120

267 Honour, H., *Romanticism,* New York : Harper and Row, p. 266.

268 Mannheim has suggested that Grunewald's crucifixions might have had connections with the Chiliastic Anabaptists. See Mannheim, K., *Ideology and Utopia,* London: Routledge and Kegan Paul Ltd., 1936, pp. 194–95, note 3. There is an interesting correlation in interpretation between Grunewald's and Frank's empathy for decaying, crucified Christs.

269 Praz, M., p. 109, 120, 126, 145.

270 Vettese, A., 'Europe and America: two aspects of the new surreal', *Flash Art,* No. 122, April/May 1985, pp. 20–25. and Sbrissa, C., 'Milan', *Art Line,* Vol. 2, No. 10, Winter, 1985, pp. 18,19.

271 Vettese, A., p. 22.

272 Eliade, M., p. 450.

273 Vettese, A., p. 22

274 Vettese, A., p. 24.

275 Vettese, A., p. 21.

276 Eco, U., *Travels In Hyperreality,* New York: Harcourt Brace Jovanovich, 1986, p. 61.

277 Eco, U., pp. 61, 62, 65.

278 Fox, M., 'A Mystical Cosmology: Toward A Postmodern Spirituality' in Griffin, David Ray (ed), *Sacred Interconnections,* Albany, New York: State University of New York Press, p. 20.

279 Eco, U., pp. 65, 72.

280 Eco, U., p. 71.

281 Eco, U., p. 79.

282 Fox, M., pp. 15–33 and Griffin, David Ray (ed), *Sacred Interconnections,* Albany, New York: State University of New York Press, p. ix–13.

283 Griffin, David Ray (ed), *Sacred Interconnections,* Albany, New York: State University of New York Press, pp. xii, 3 and Fox, pp. 9, 28, 29, 30.

284 Gablik, S., in Griffin, David Ray (ed), *Sacred Interconnections,* Albany, New York: State University of New York Press, p. 184. and Fox, M., in Griffin, David Ray (ed), *Sacred Interconnections,* p. 12.

285 Fox, M., p. 16.

286 Swimme, B., quoted in Fox, M., p. 17.

287 Gablik, S., quoted in Griffin, D. R., p. 9, 192.

288 Eliade, M., pp. 4, 5, 24, 315 and Campbell, J., pp. 55, 248, 249.

289 Campbell, J., p. 247 – 249.

290 Hassan, I., 'The Question of Postmodernism' in H.R. Garvin, *Romanticism, Modernism, Postmodernism,* Lewisberg, 1980, pp. 123,125, and Huyssen, A., p. 7.

291 Forster, H., p. xii

292 Bonito Oliva, A., *Trans-avantgarde International,* Milan: Giancarlo Politi Editore, 1982.

293 Bonito Oliva, A., pp. 8, 10.

294 Bonito Oliva, A., p. 12.

295 Bonito Oliva, A., p. 68.

296 Bonito Oliva, A., p. 18, 24.

297 Bonito Oliva, A., p. 16.

298 Bonito Oliva, A., p. 8, 16, 34, 56, 72, 119, 121, 122.

299 Bonito Oliva, A., p. 62.

The
Colour Plates

Plate 1
The Key to Ships at the Gate (Self-Portrait)
Acrylic paint on wood
136 x 99 cm
1982

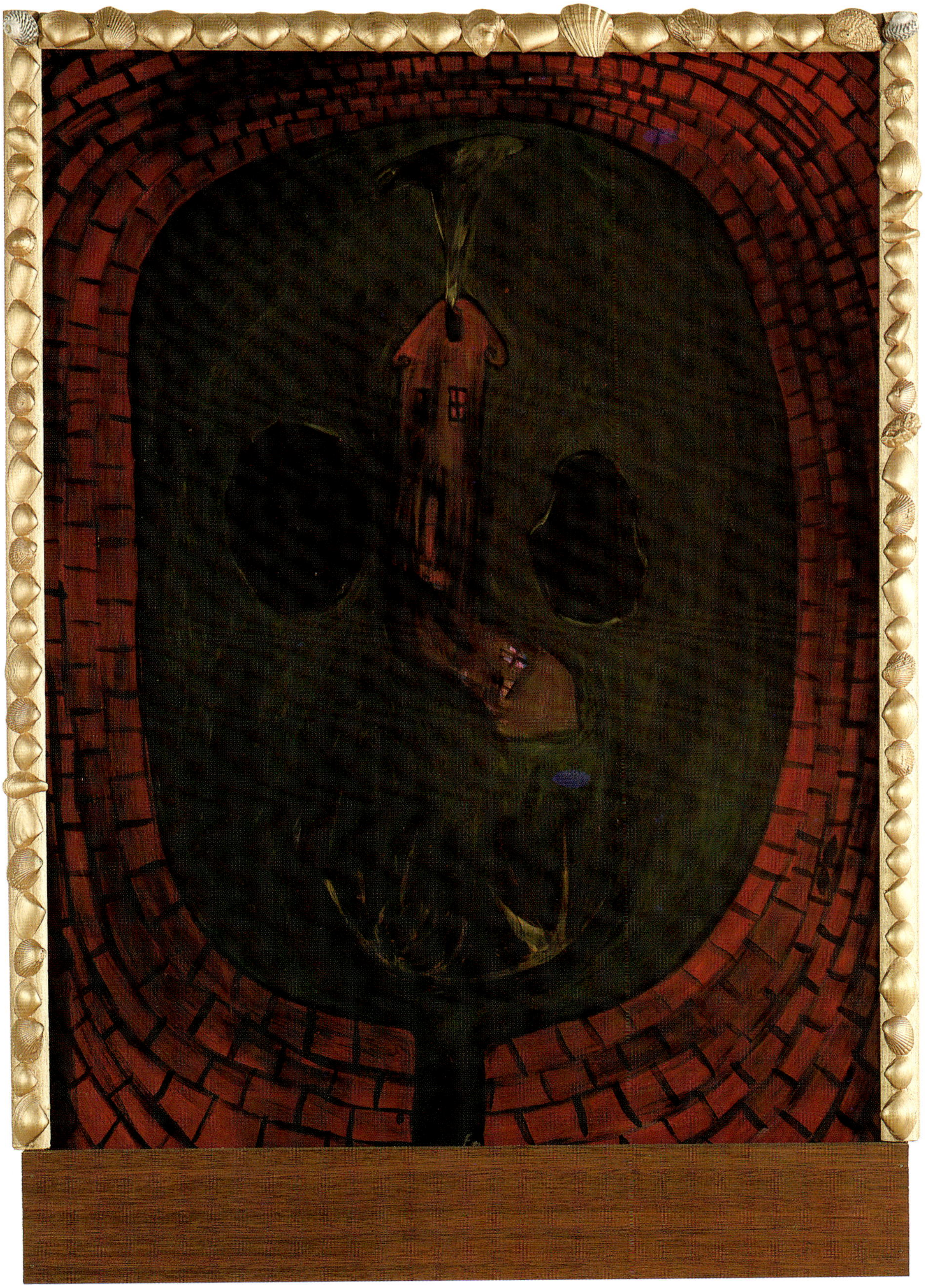

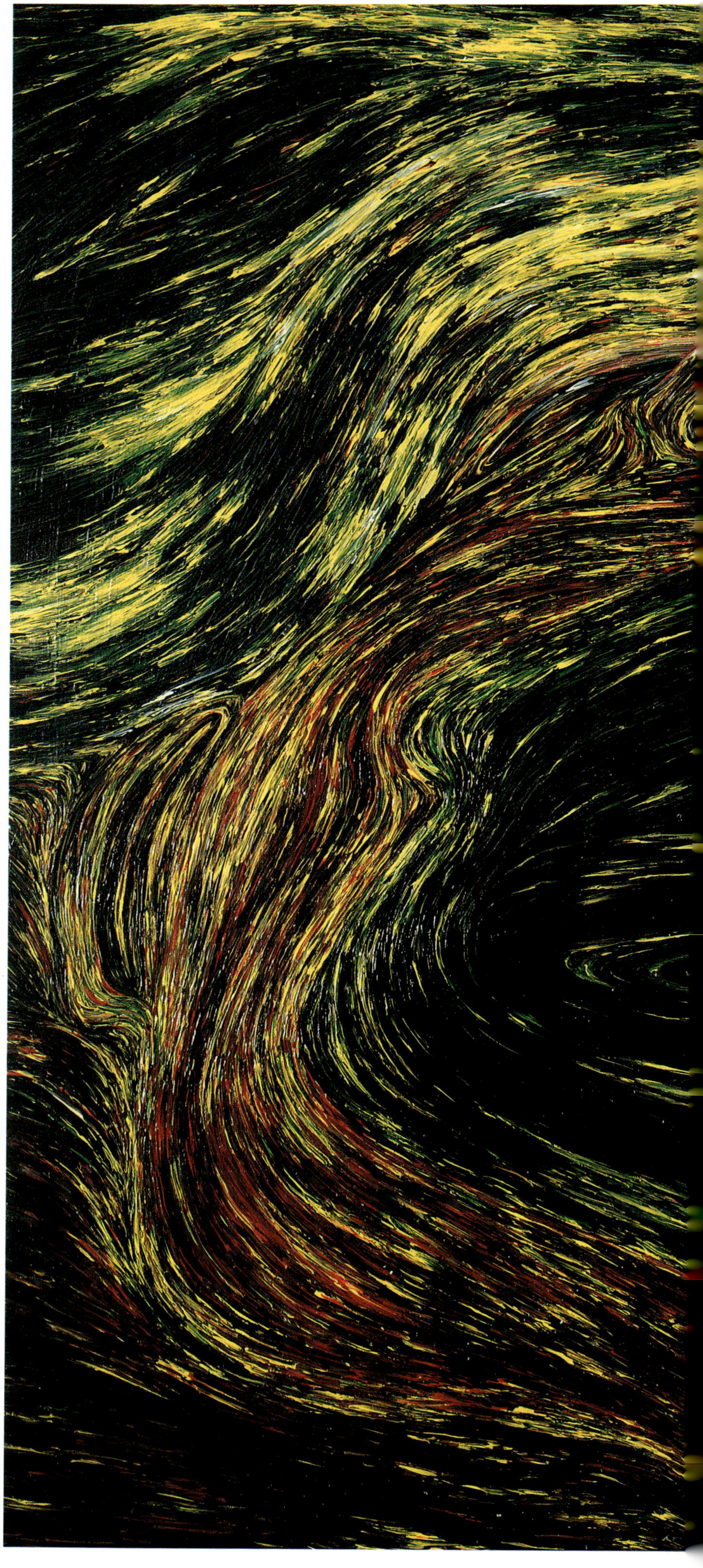

Plate 2
The Miners Rich Vein and a Double Portrait of the Possible Miner from the Front — Triple Portrait
Acrylic paint on canvas
175 x 254 cm
1983
Collection of National Gallery of Victoria, Melbourne

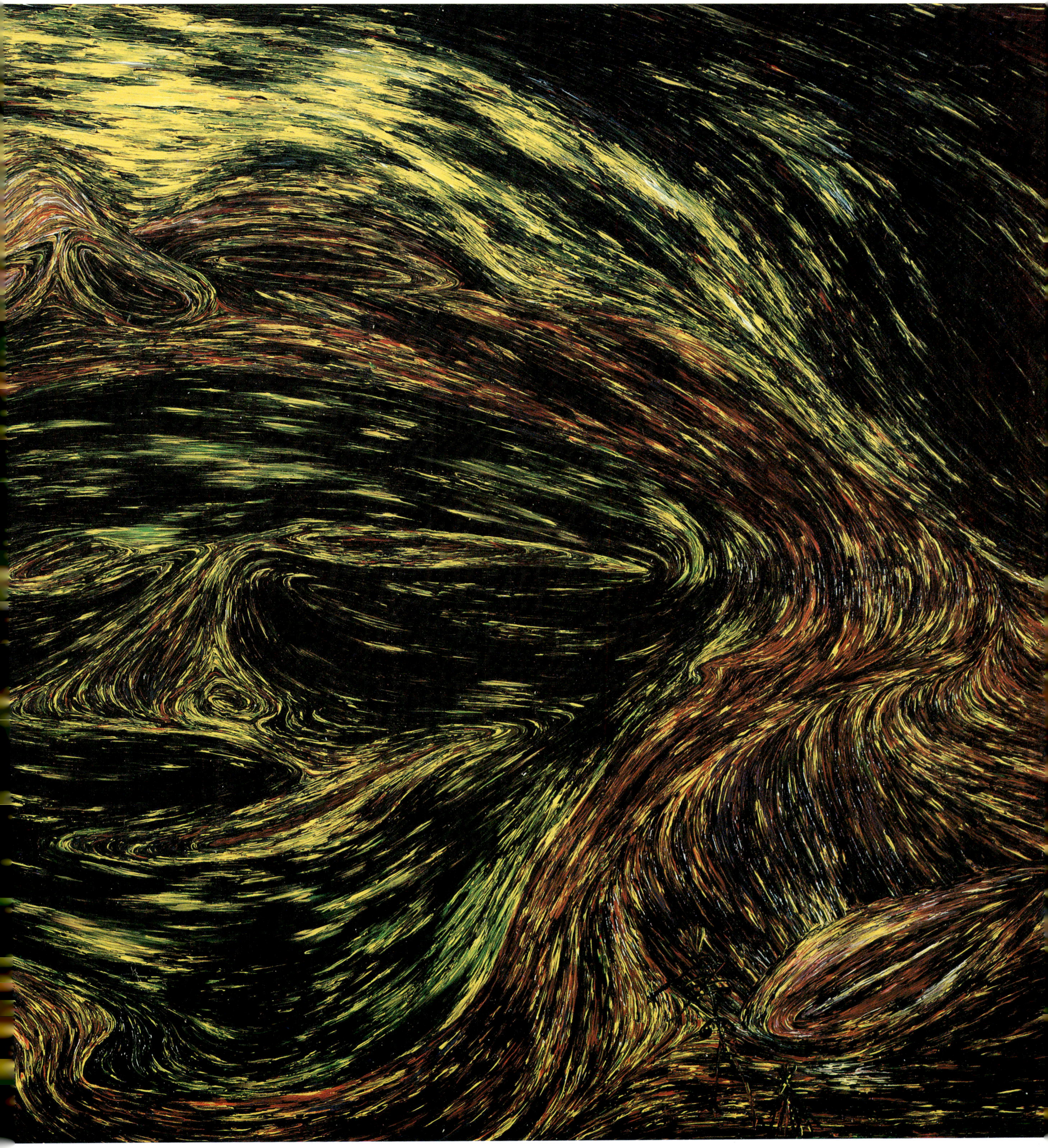

Plate 3
The Snail Fleeing — Portrait of Paul Groot with a Small Self-Portrait
Acrylic paint on canvas
175 x 251 cm
1983
Collection of the Art Gallery of South Australia, Adelaide

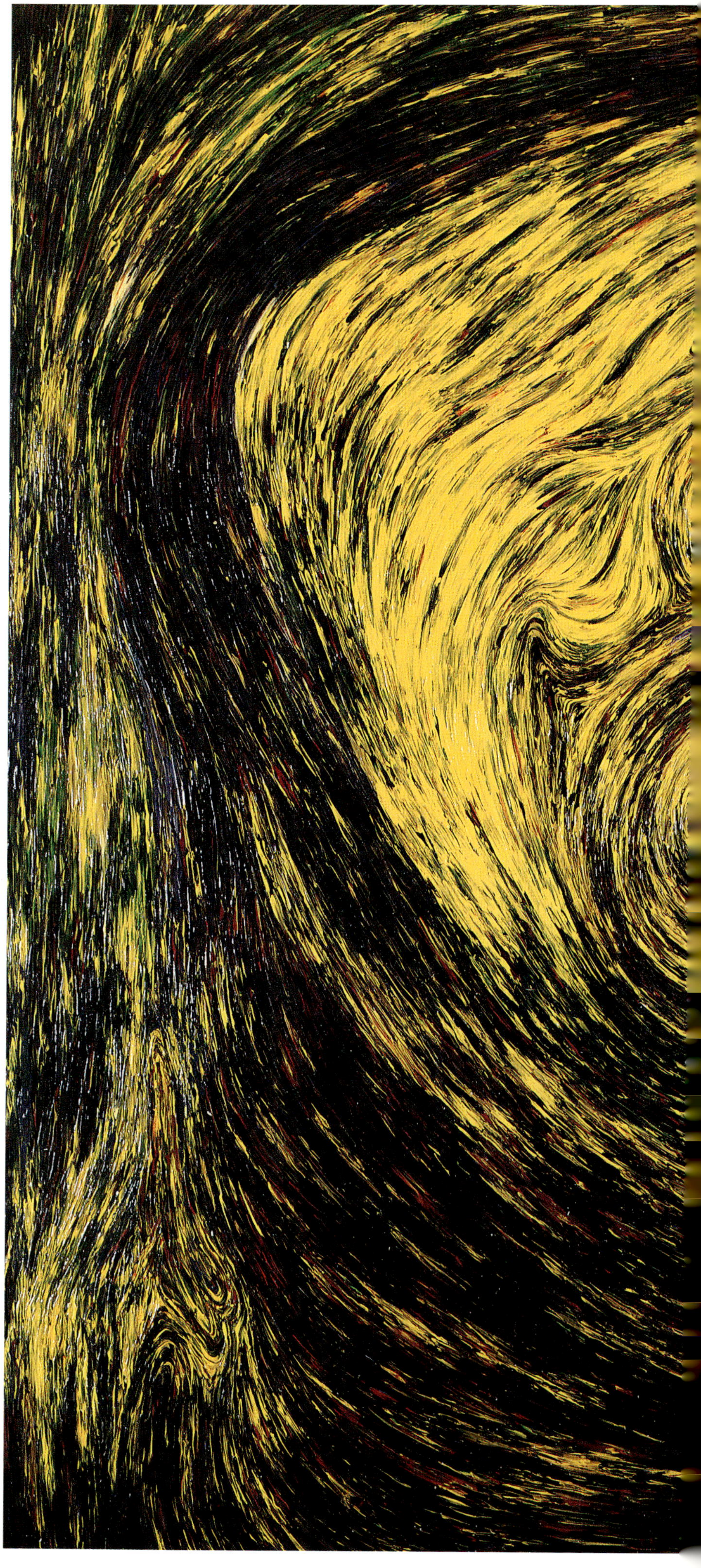

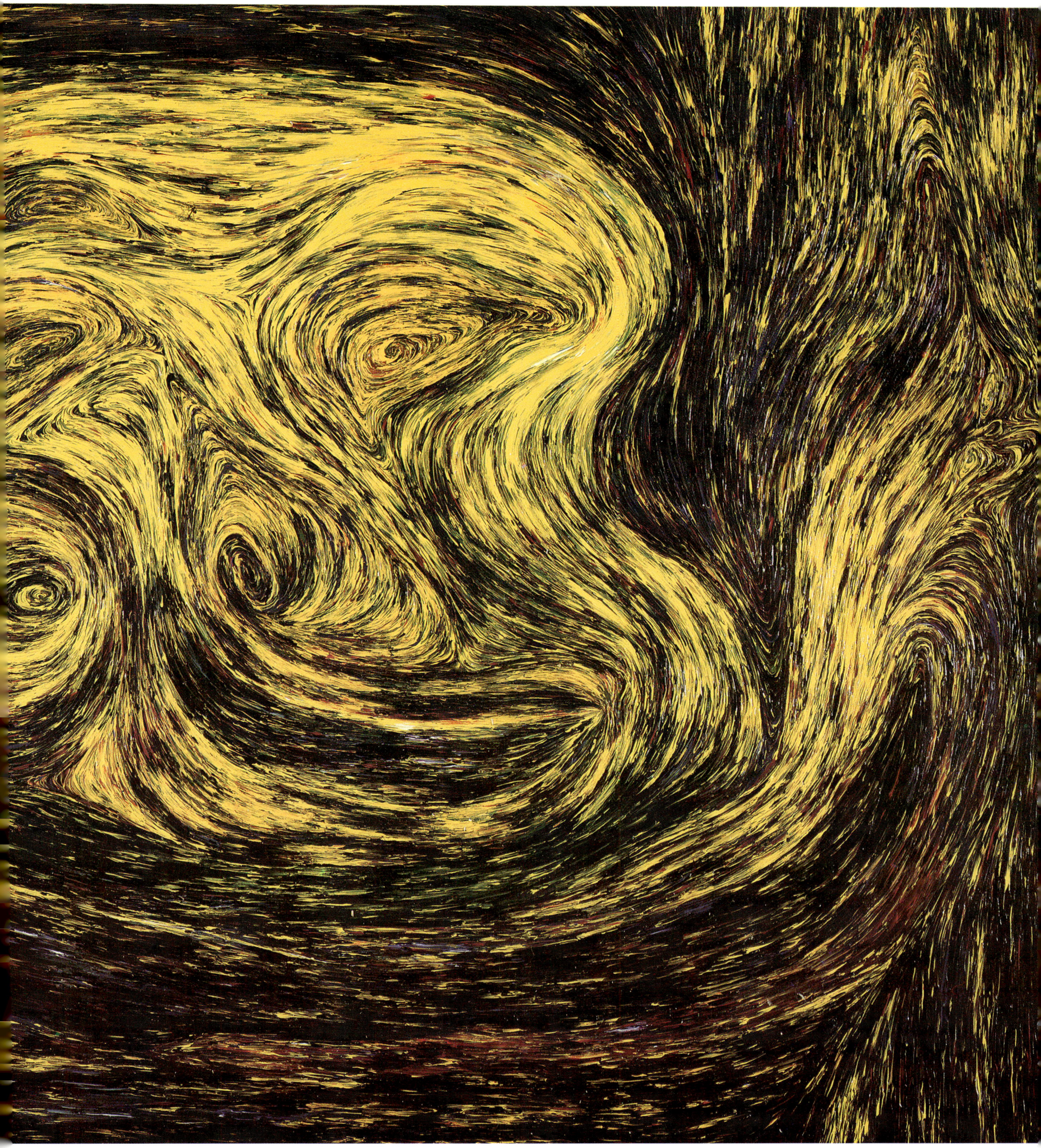

Plate 4
Self-Portrait: The Full of Fear Soldier in View of the Trench and Gases
Acrylic paint on canvas
200 x 180 cm
1983
Collection of Australian National Gallery, Canberra

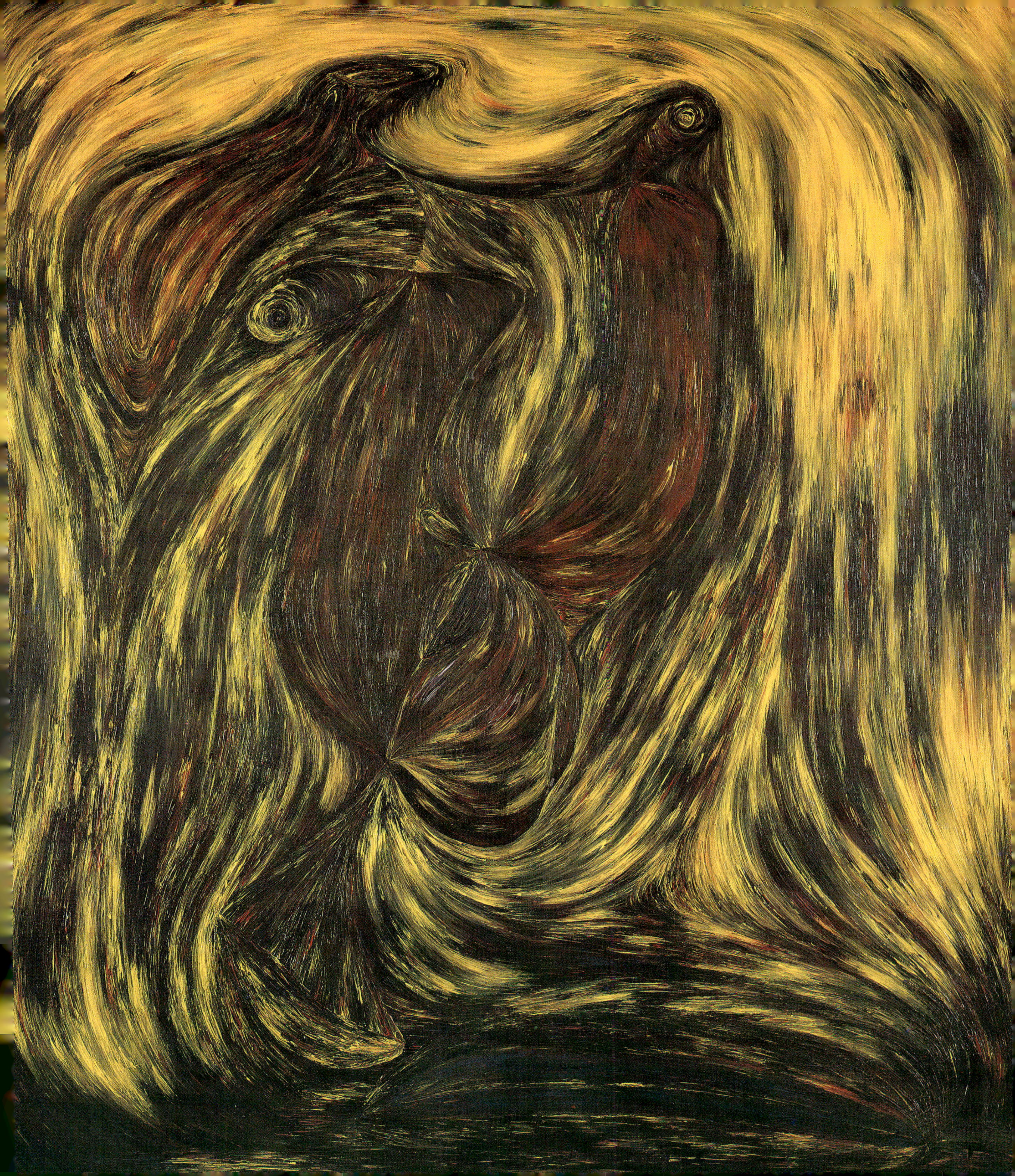

Plate 5
The Vicious Conspiracy
Acrylic paint on canvas
160 x 200 cm
1984

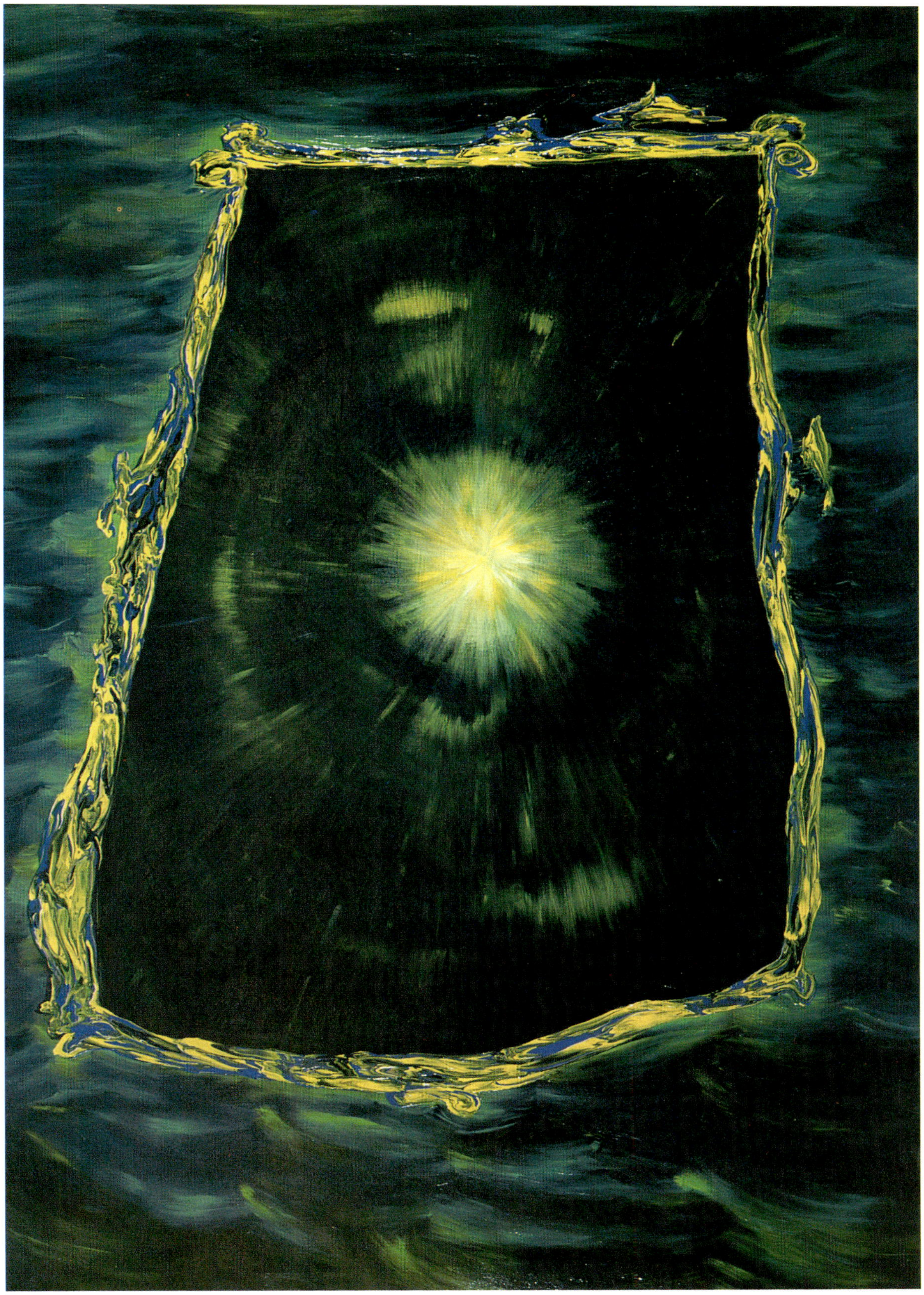

Plate 6
The Sea and the Sore Eye
Acrylic paint on canvas
180 x 240 cm
1984
Private collection, Milan, Italy

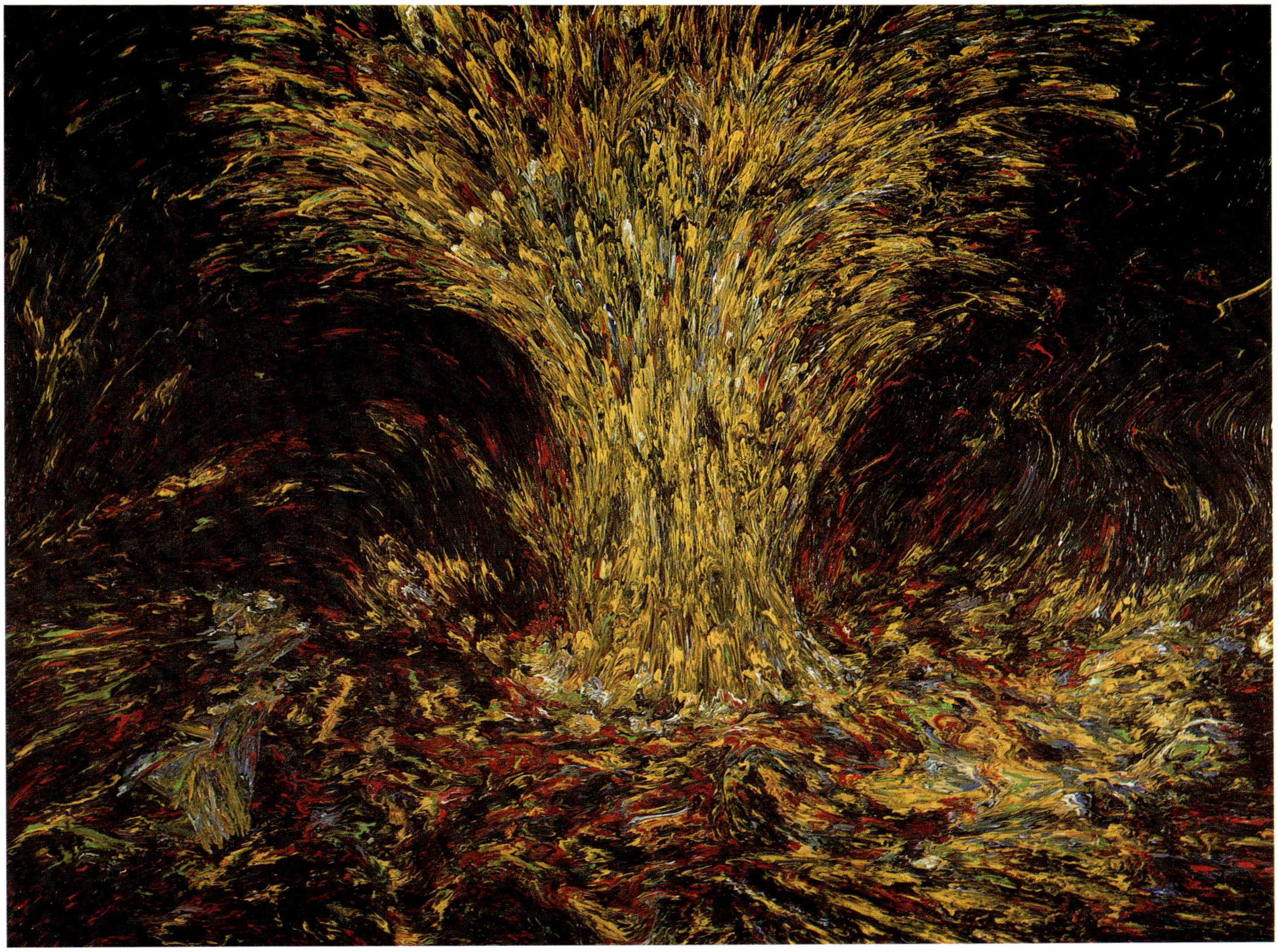

Plate 7
The Two Moons
Acrylic paint on canvas
200 x 300 cm
1984

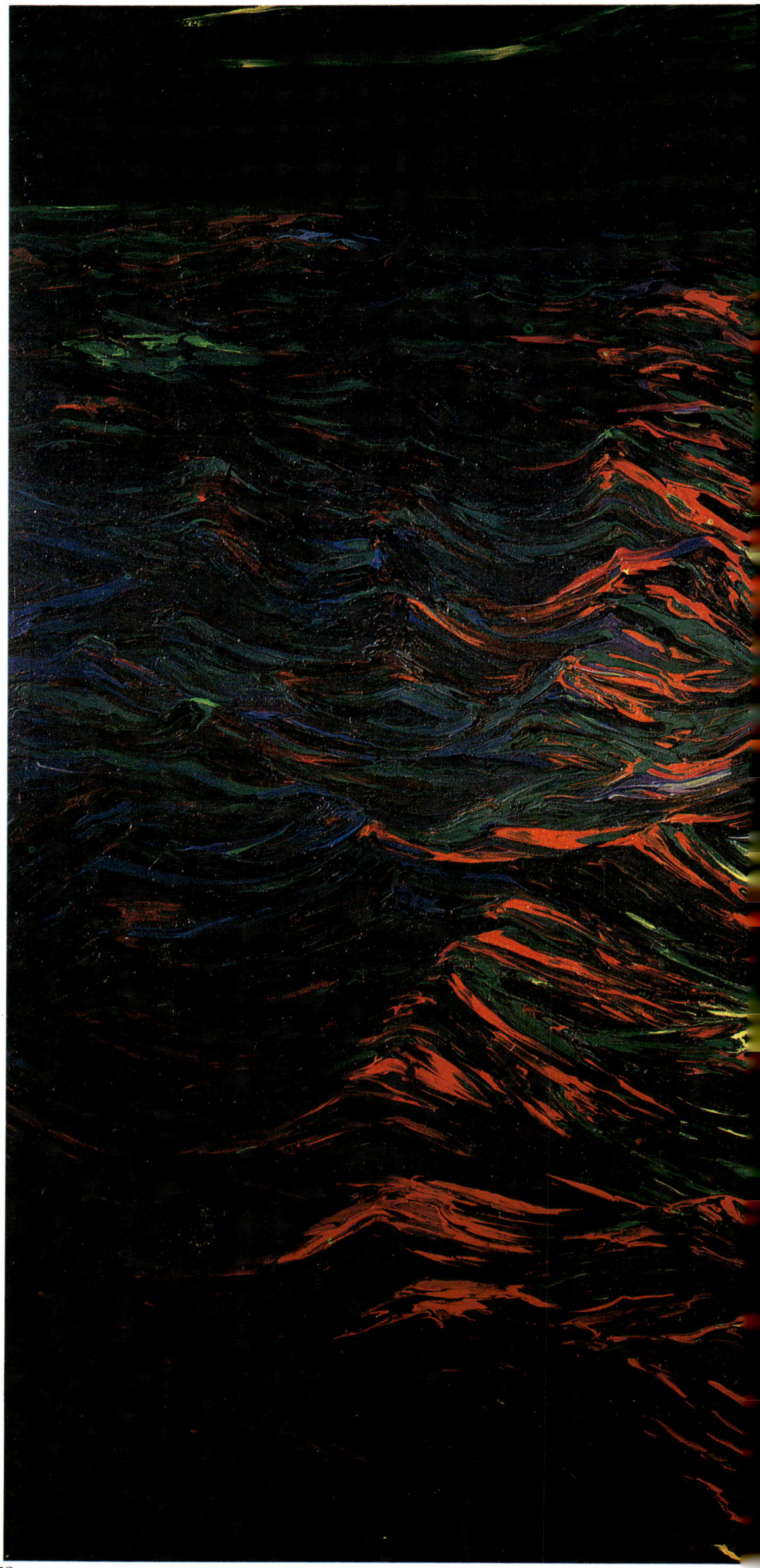

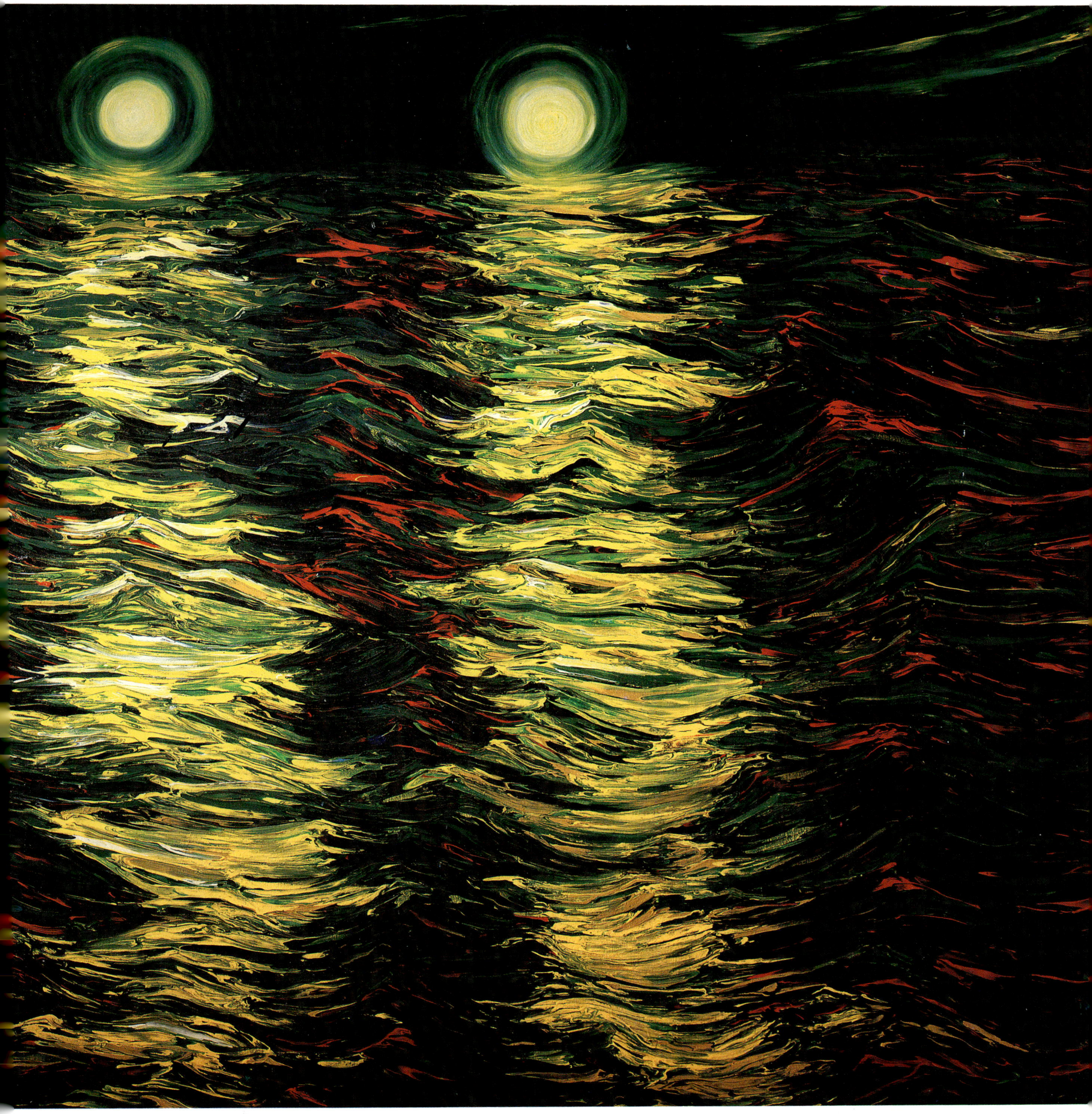

Plate 8
The Wake
Acrylic paint on canvas
200 x 260 cm
1984
Private collection, Milan, Italy

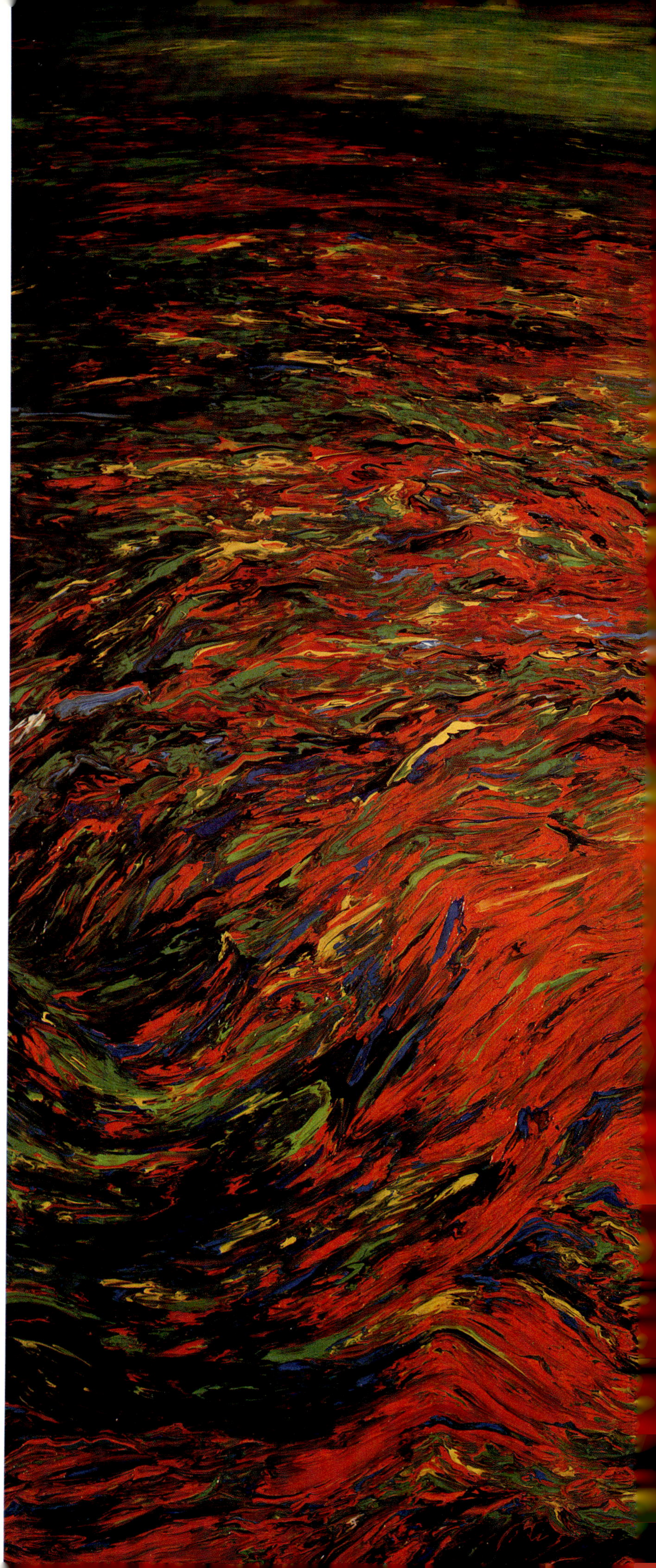

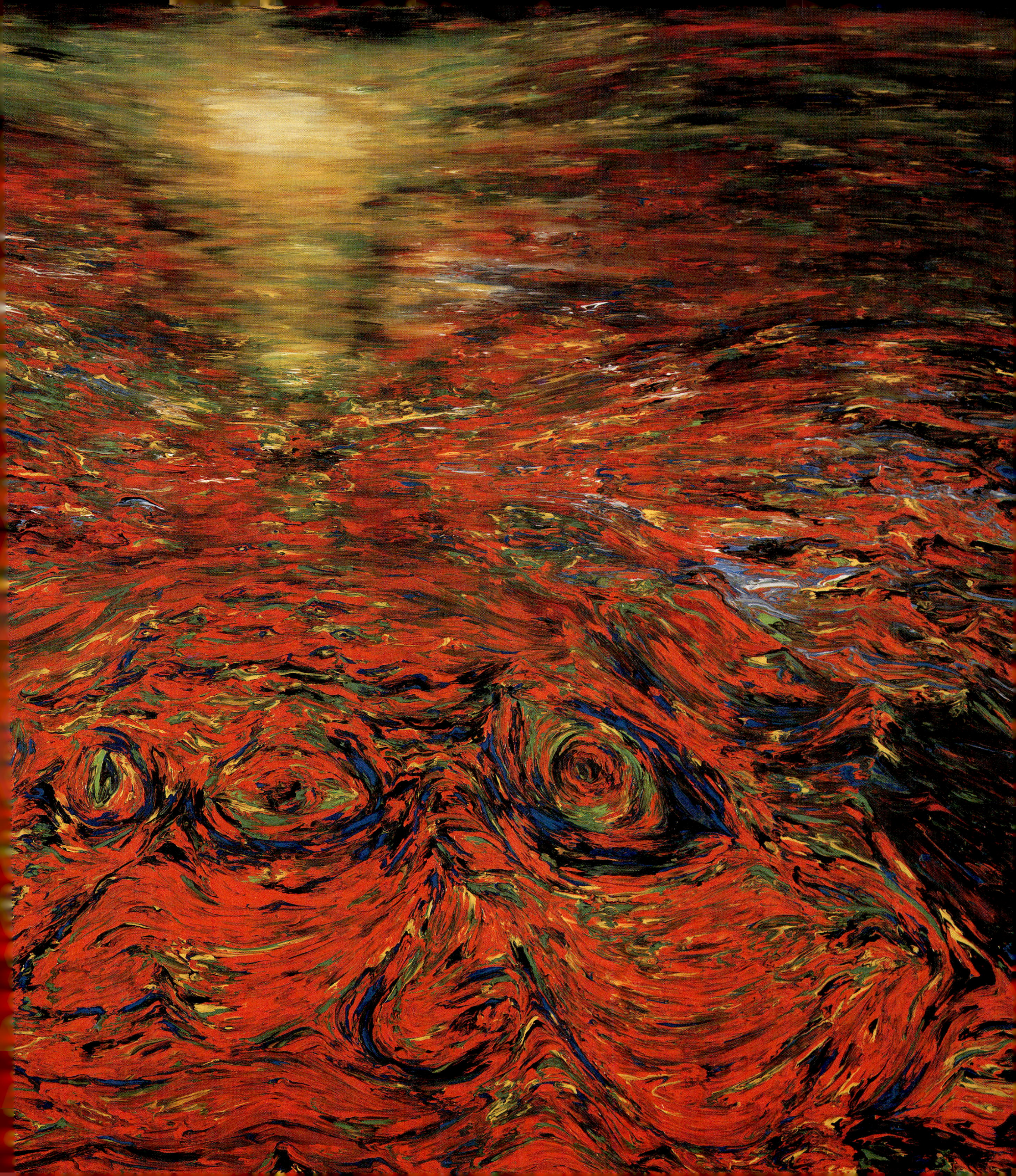

Plate 9
The Oily Sea and the Painter
Acrylic paint on canvas
200 x 300 cm
1984
Private collection, Sydney

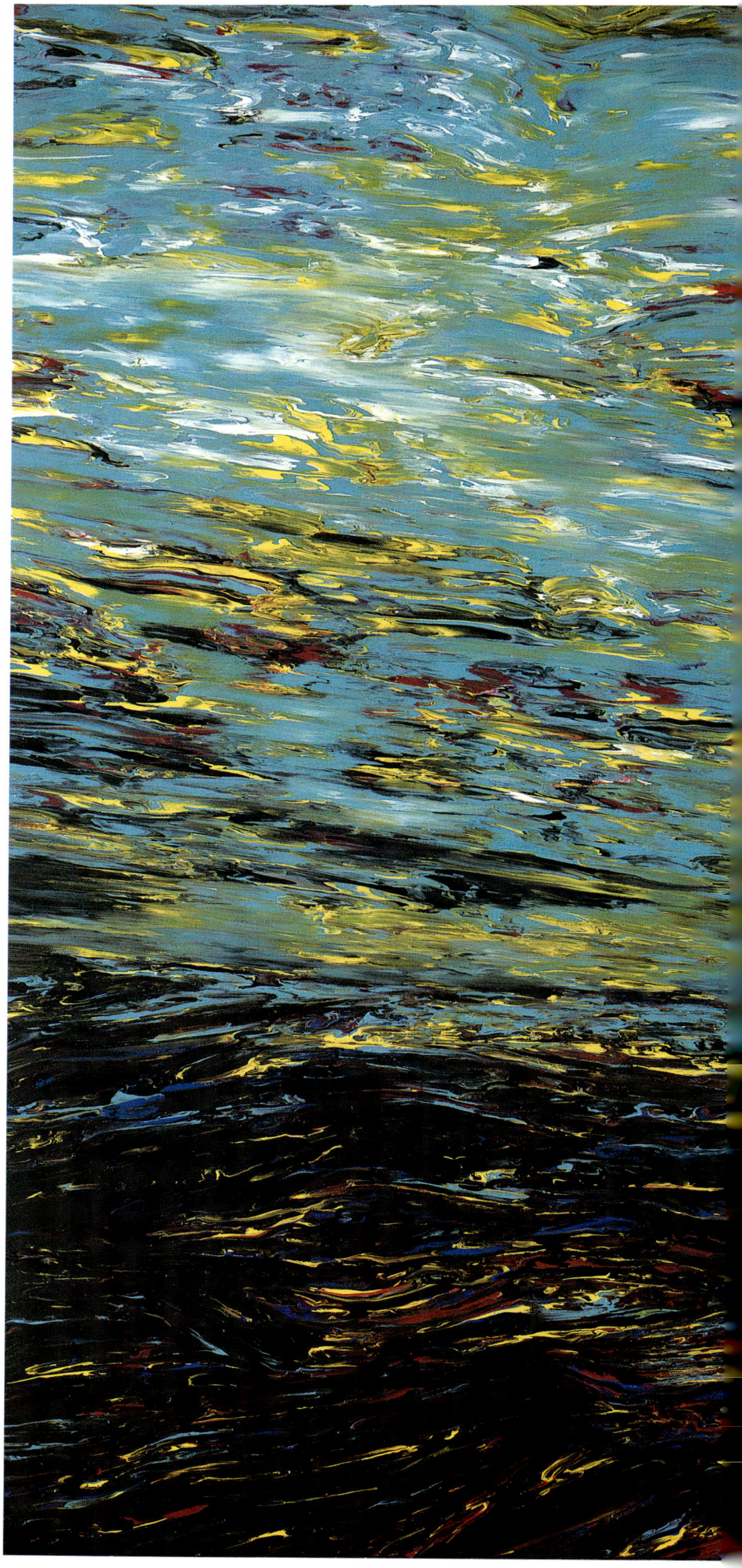

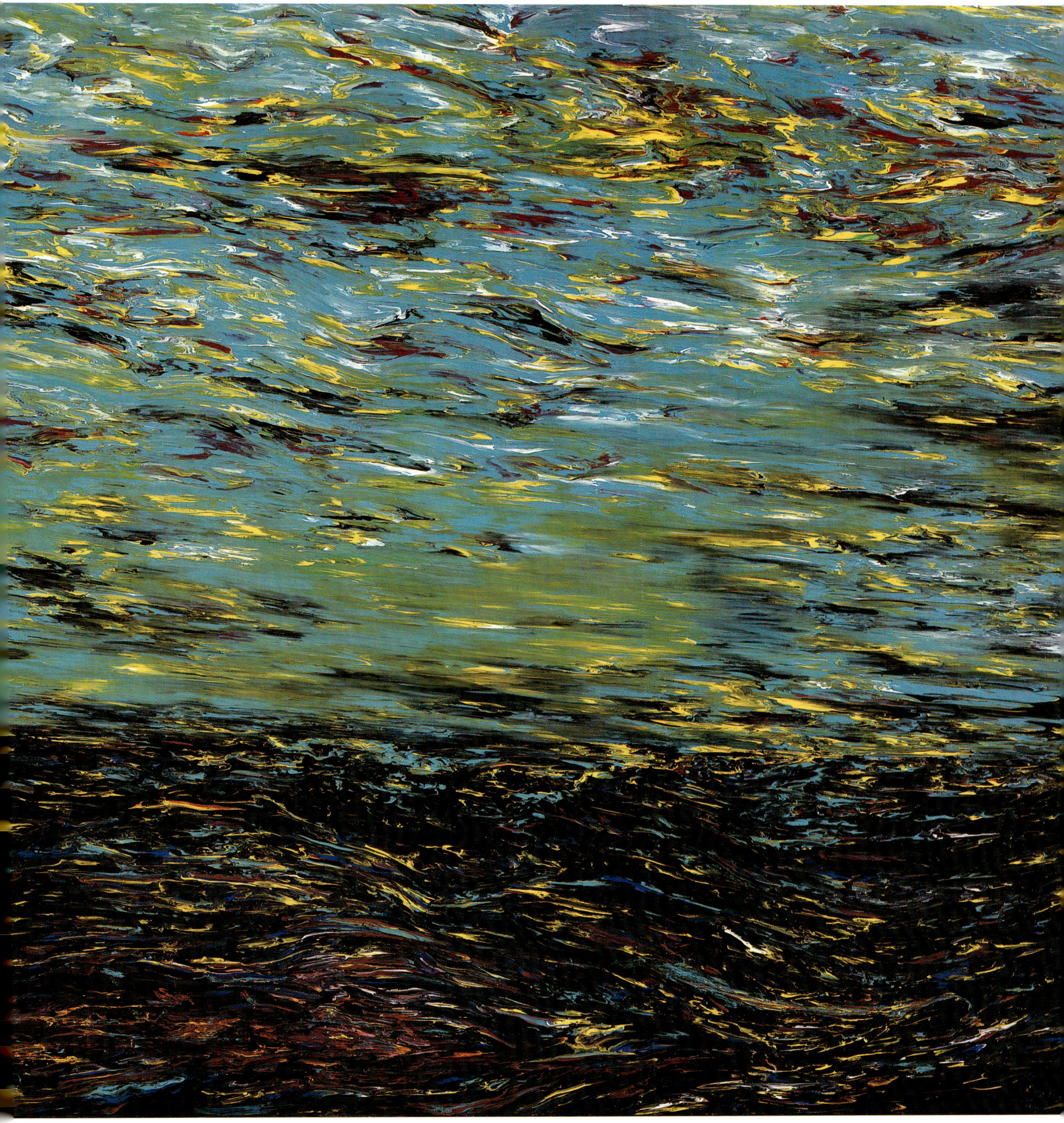

Plate 10
The Stagnant Sea
Acrylic paint on canvas
200 x 300 cm
1984
Private collection, Terni, Italy

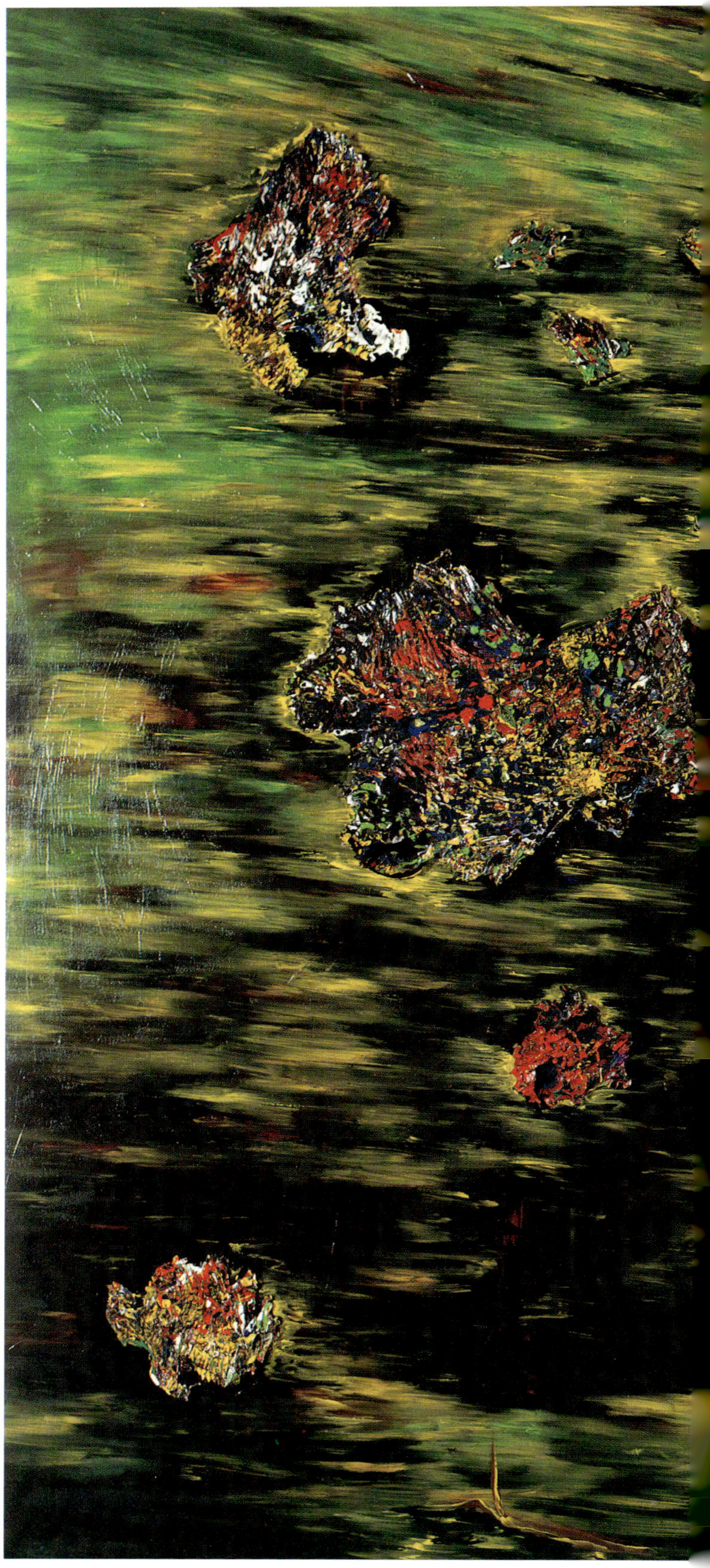

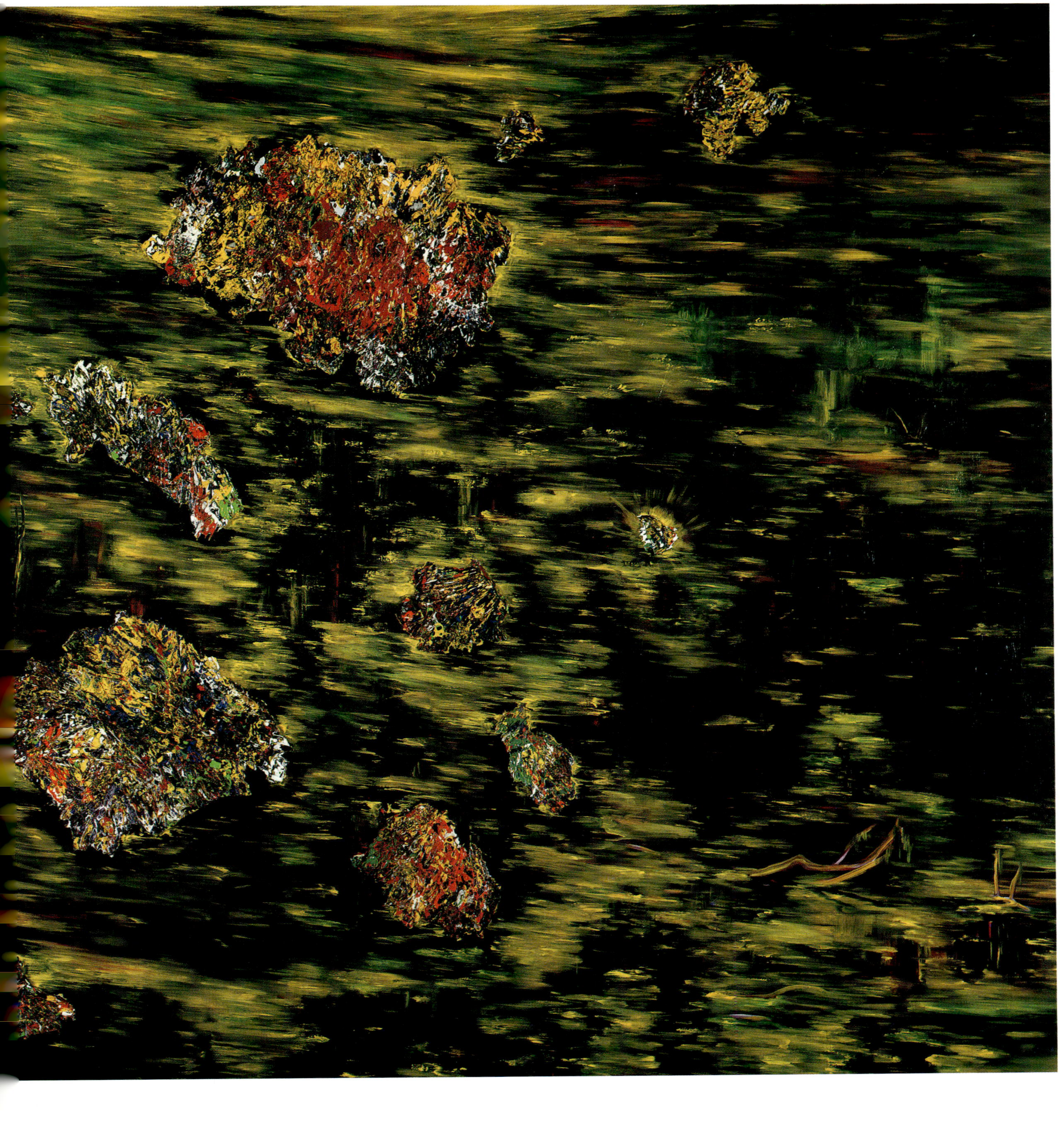

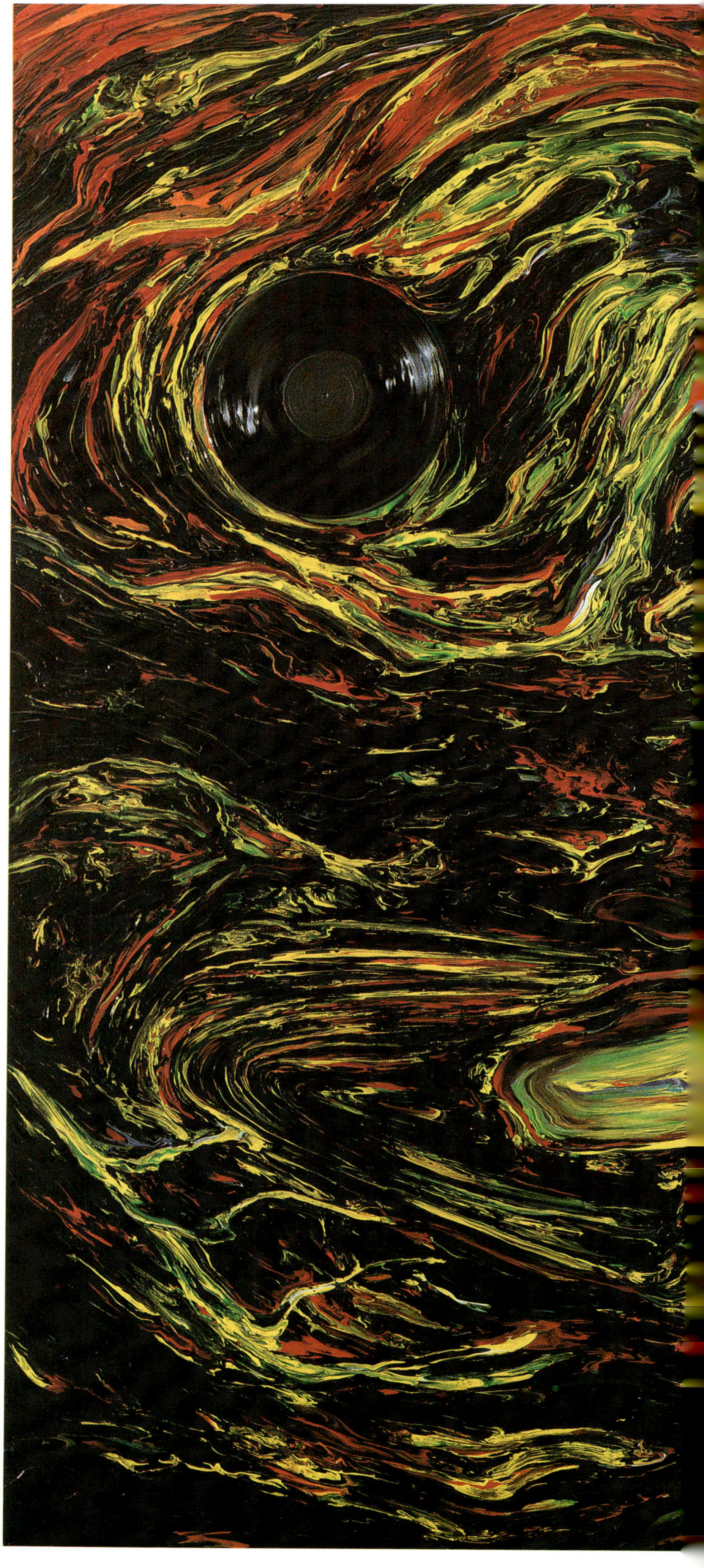

Plate 11
The Inland Sea (New Moon to the Warren)
Acrylic paint on canvas
180 x 270 cm
1984

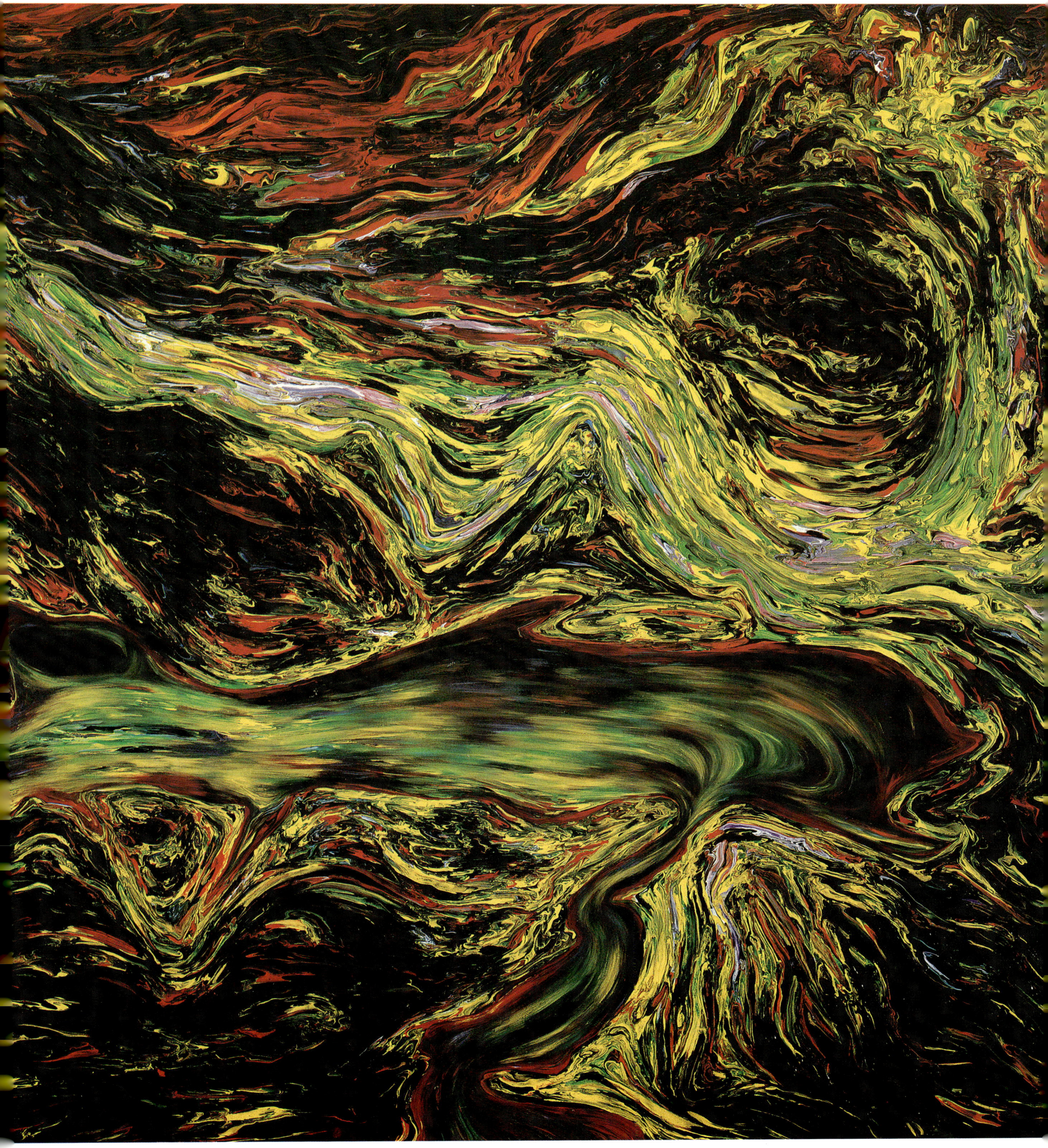

Plate 12
Dorian's Eye to the Painter's Yellow Sea and Winter Willow (Therese's Pretty View in View of the Rocky Palette)
Acrylic paint on canvas
190 x 300 cm
1984
Private collection, Sydney

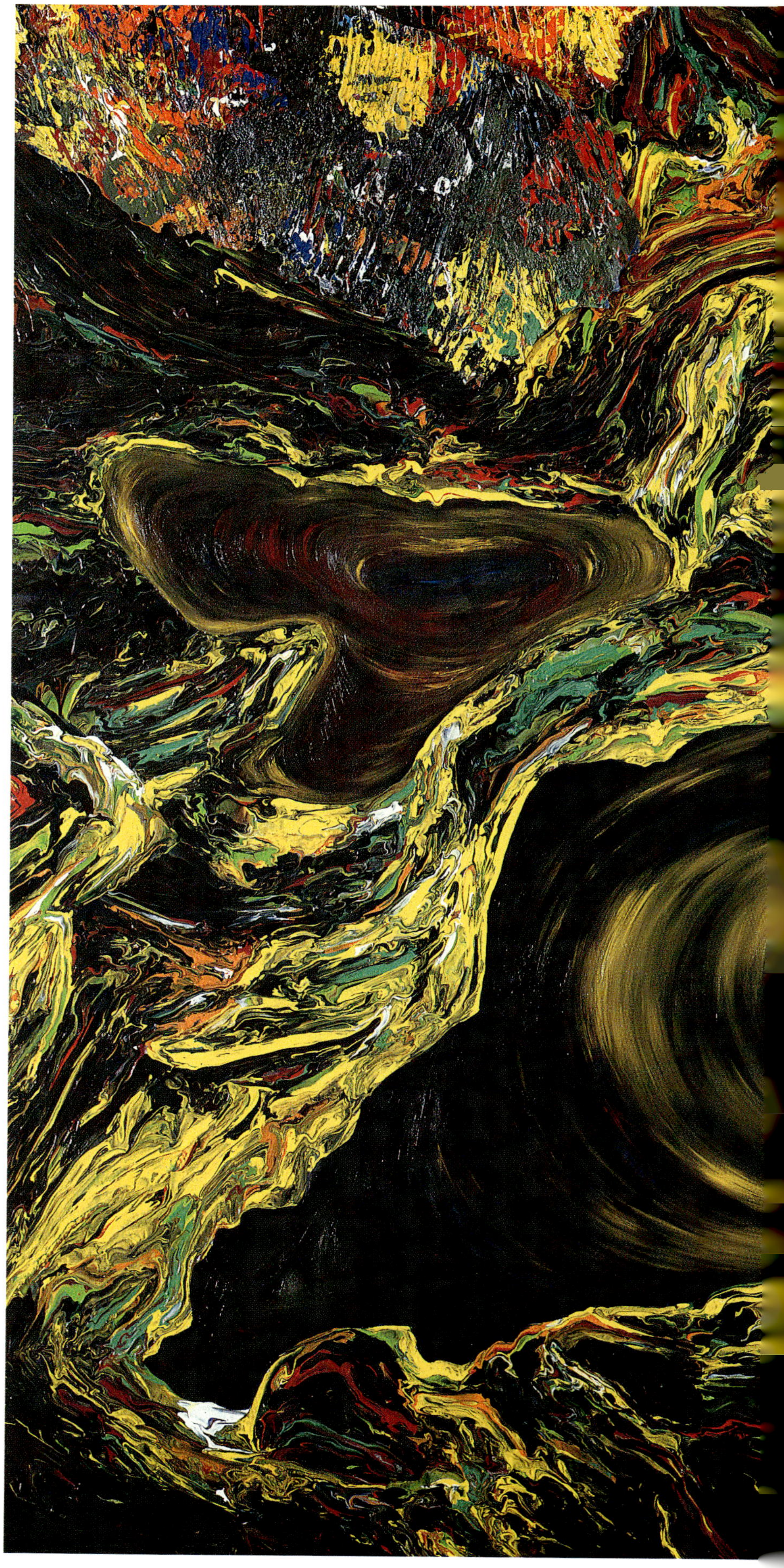

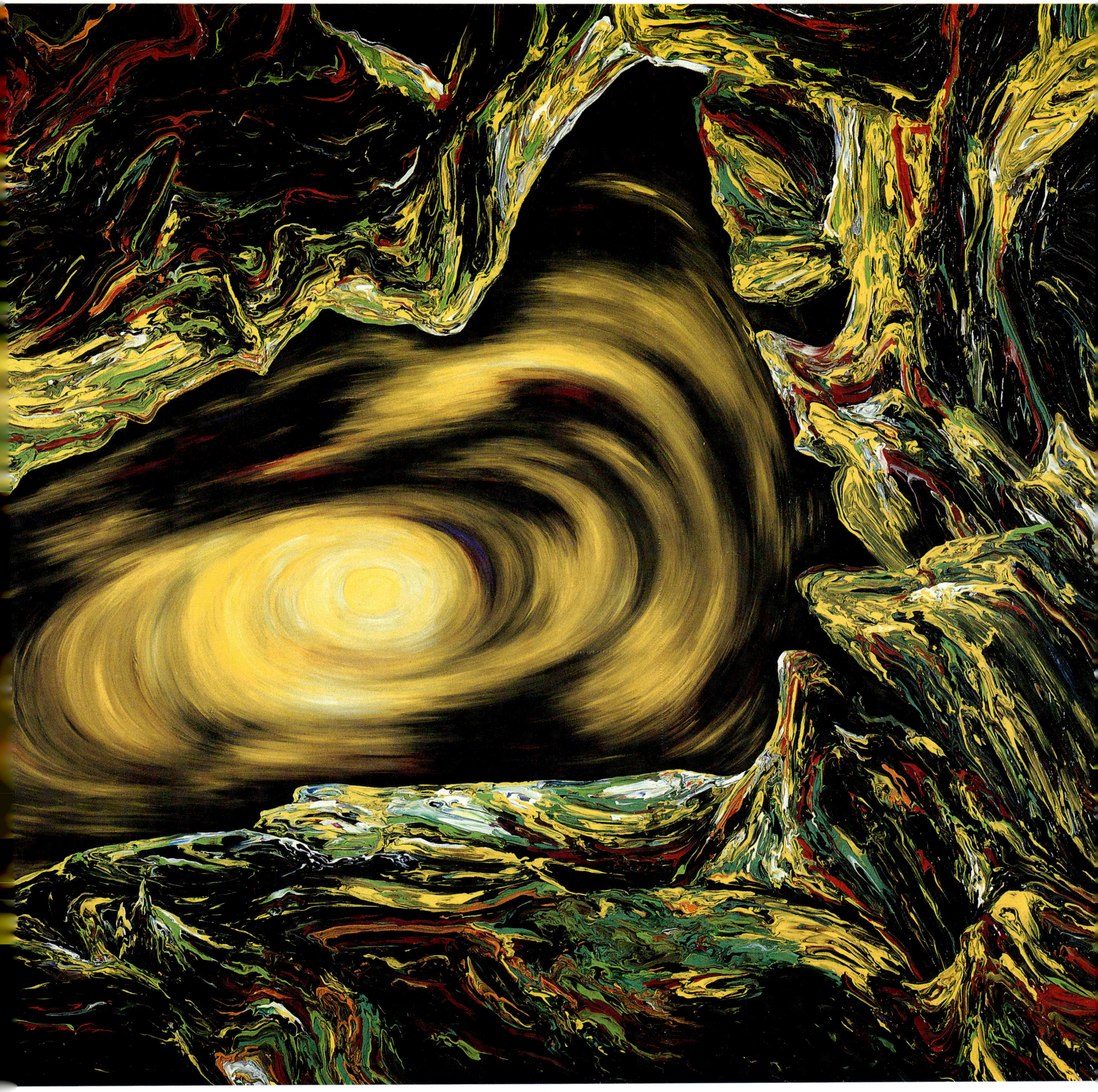

Plate 13
The Studio — The Two Lover Paintings while the Artist Slept
Acrylic paint on canvas
210 x 320 cm
1985

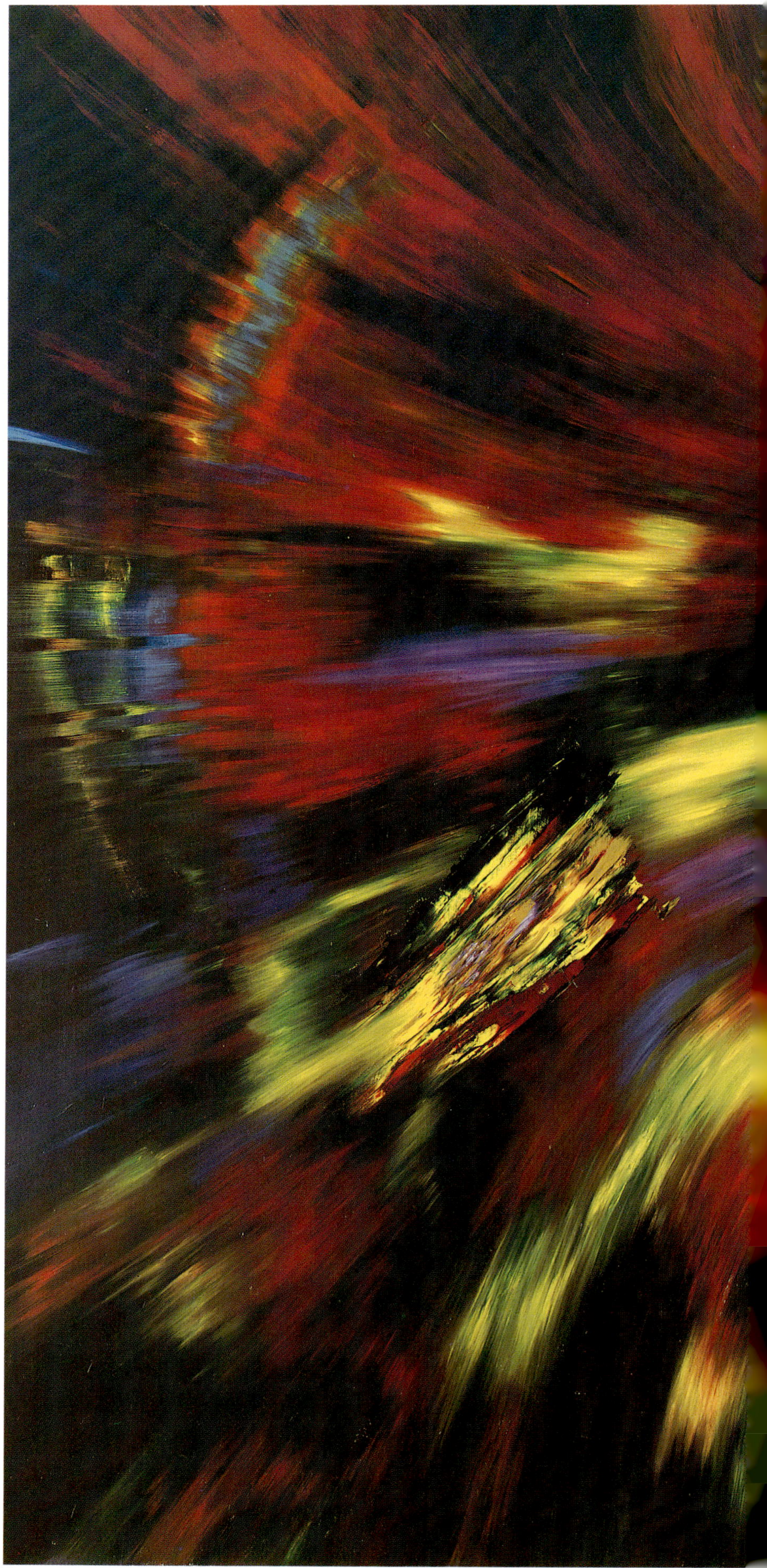

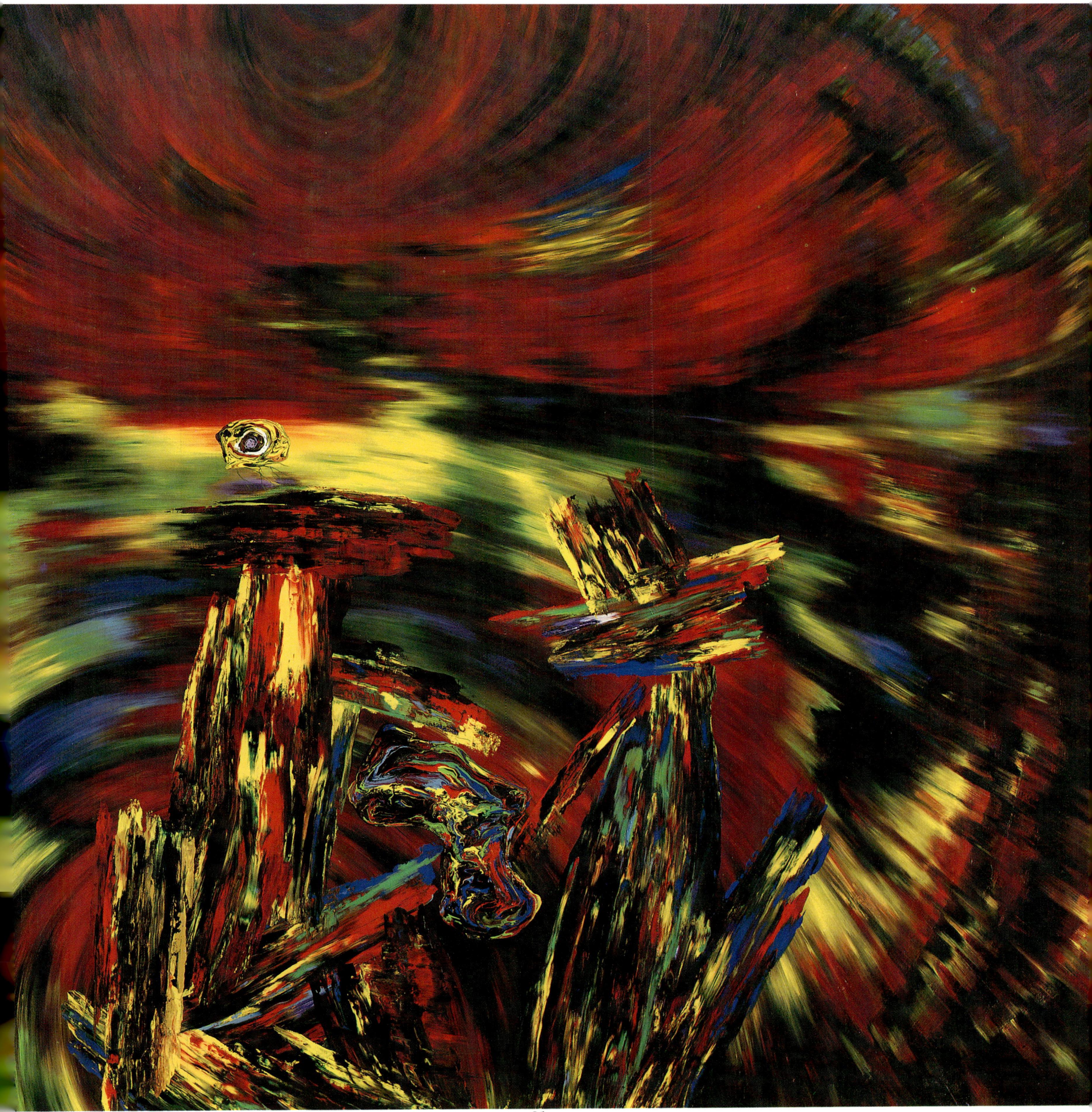

Plate 14
The Studio — The Shallows and the Sticky Eye that seems to have no Finish to Spite Itself
Acrylic paint on canvas
210 x 300 cm
1985

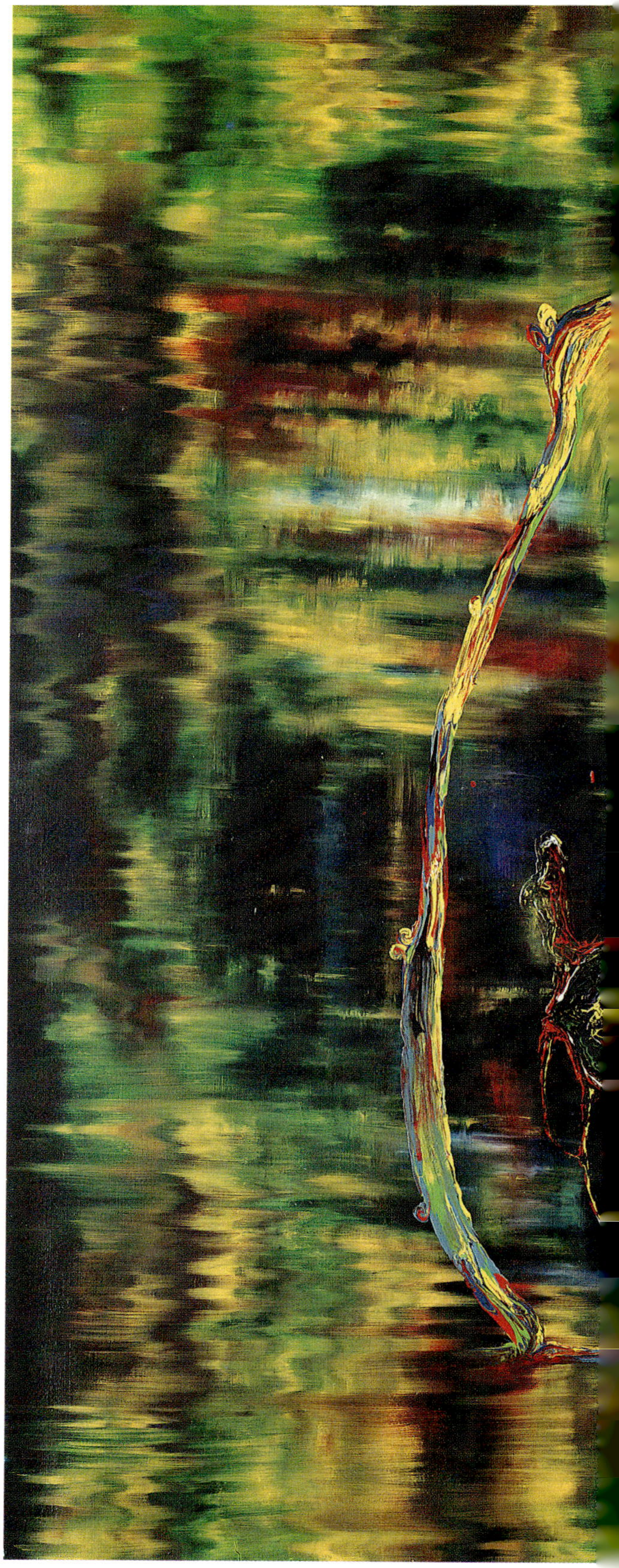

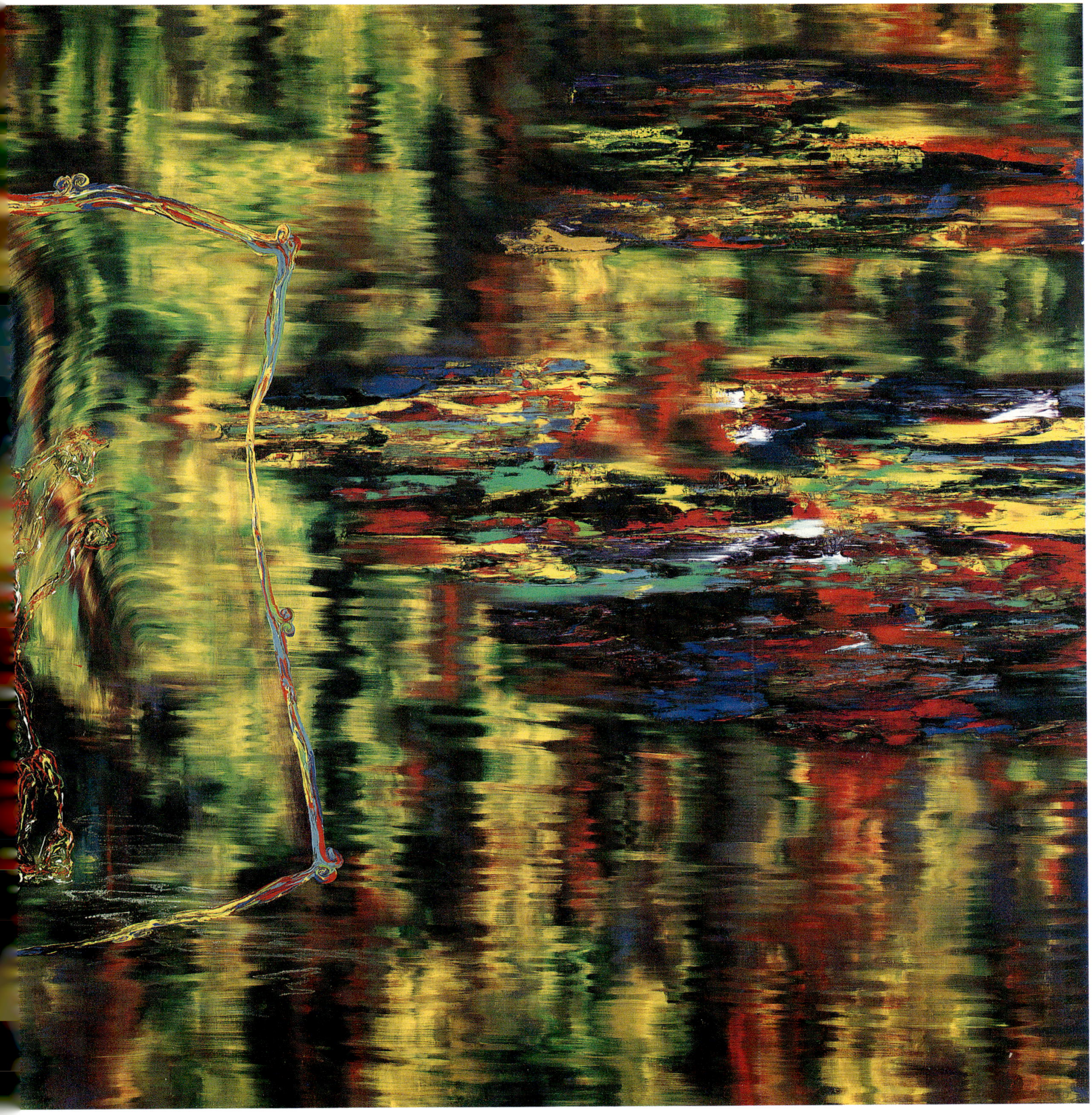

Plate 15
Two Paintings out for a Midnight Swim
Acrylic paint on canvas
200 x 179 cm
1985

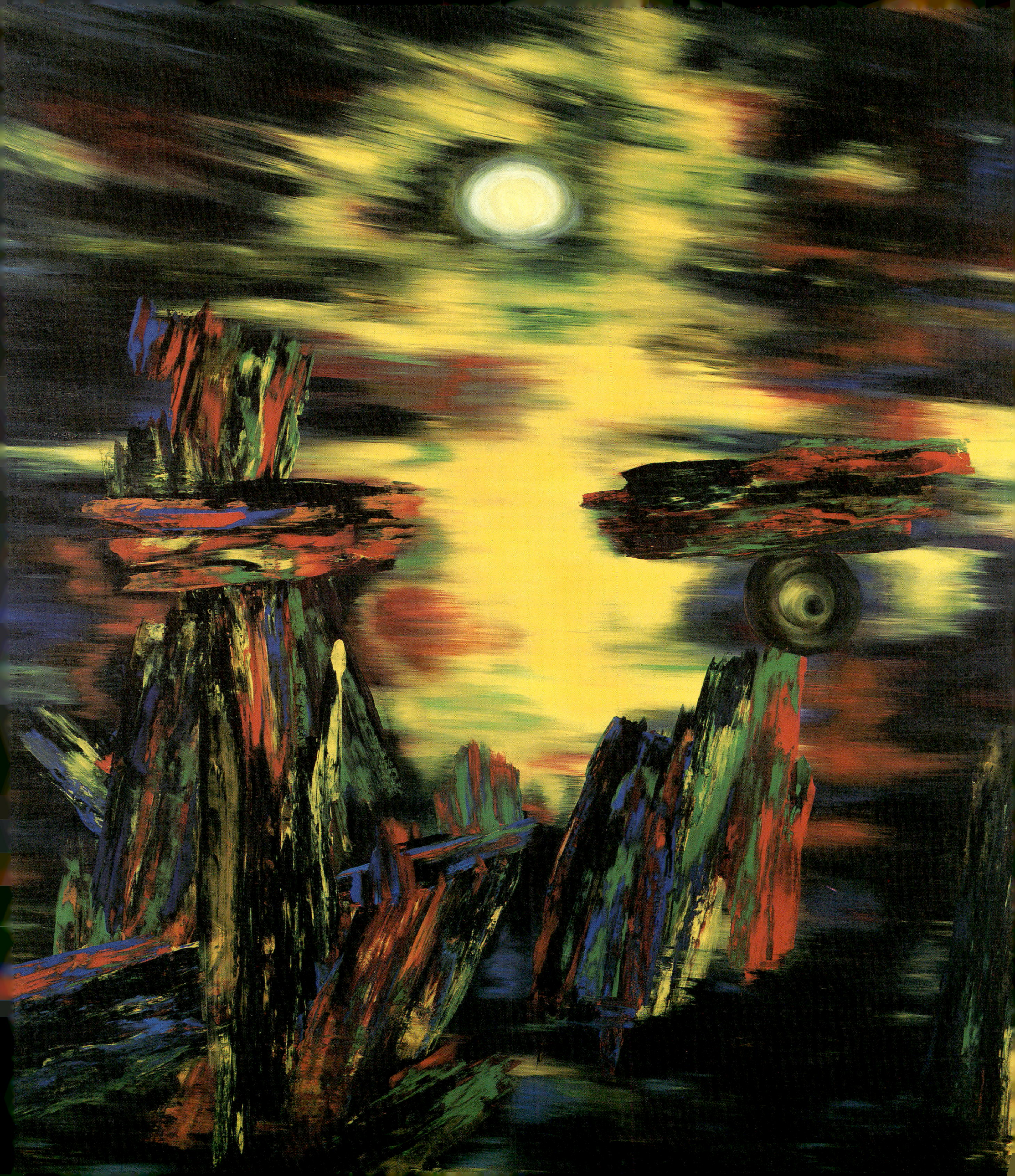

Plate 16

The Very Bad Painting of a Bad Mother Painting with Floatation Aids

Acrylic paint on canvas

200 x 150 cm

1986

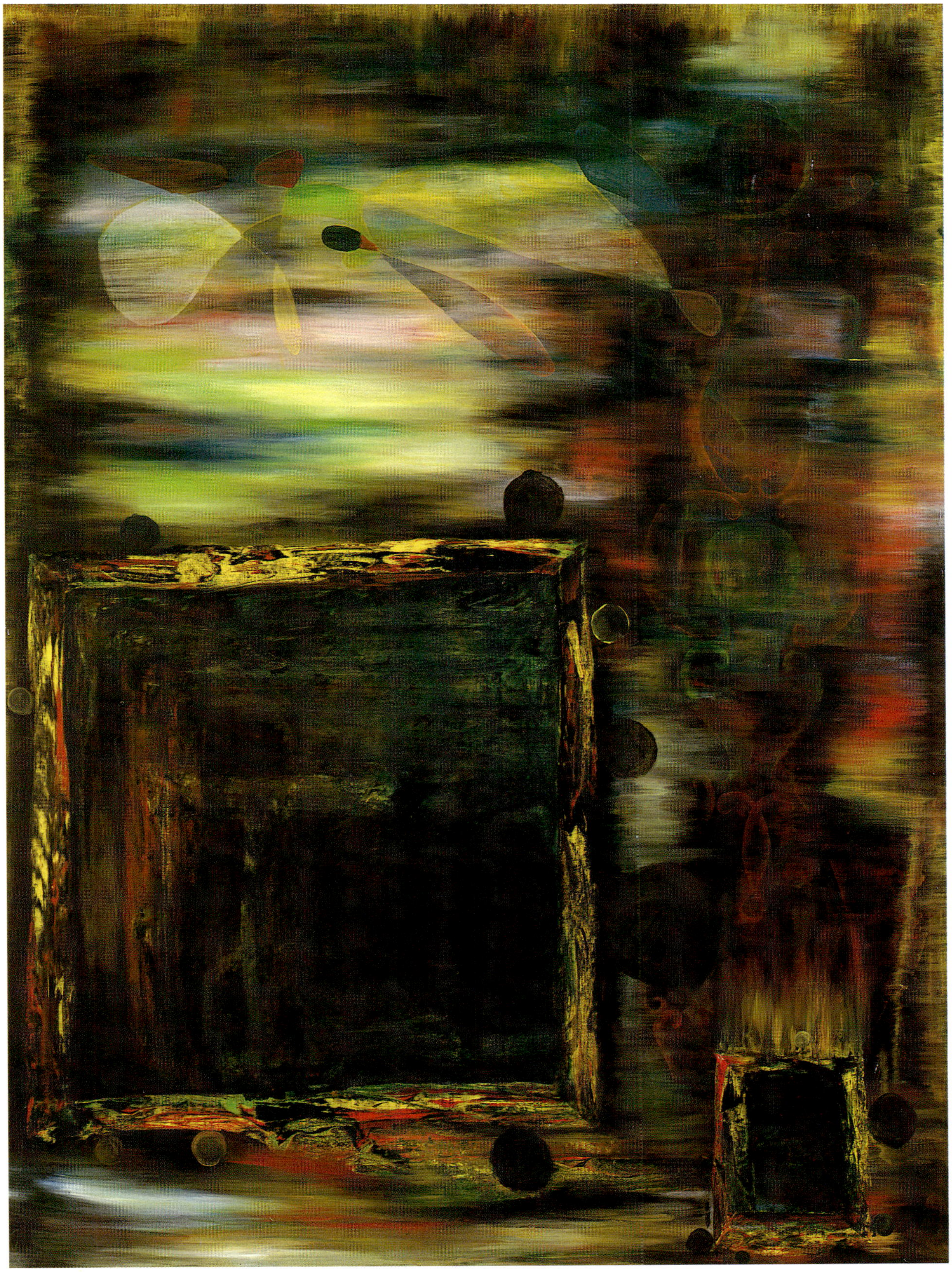

Plate 17
The Cosmology of the Nocturne Whilst the Poker-Faced Bandit
Acrylic paint, green oxides, varnishes, steel nails, on reinforced fibreglass plastic sheet
150 x 120 cm
1987

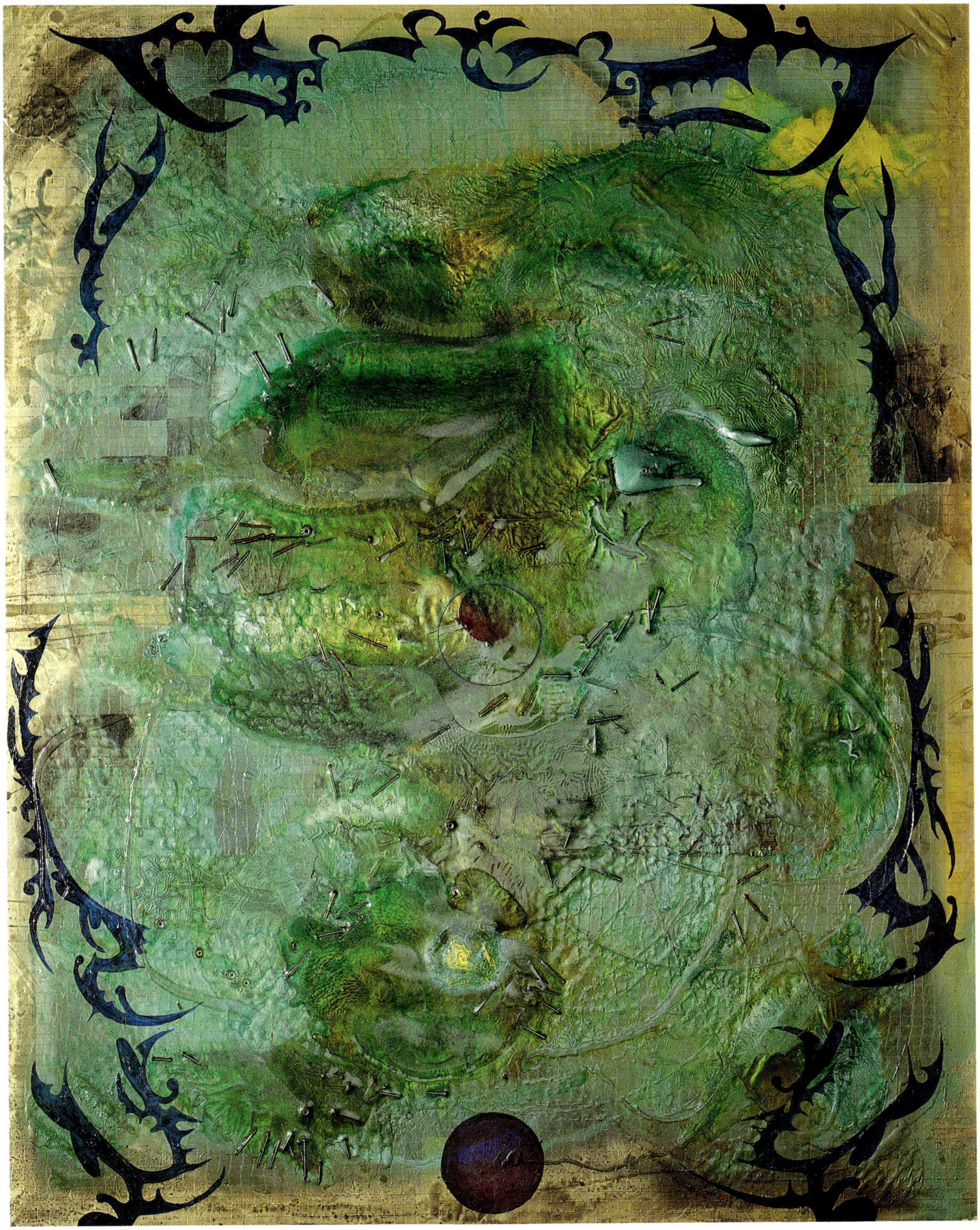

Plate 18
The Masterpiece with a Diddle Worthy of a Fly
Acrylic paint, wood blocks, on sponge rubber on canvas
150 x 120 x 12 cm
1987
Collection of ICI Corporation, Australia

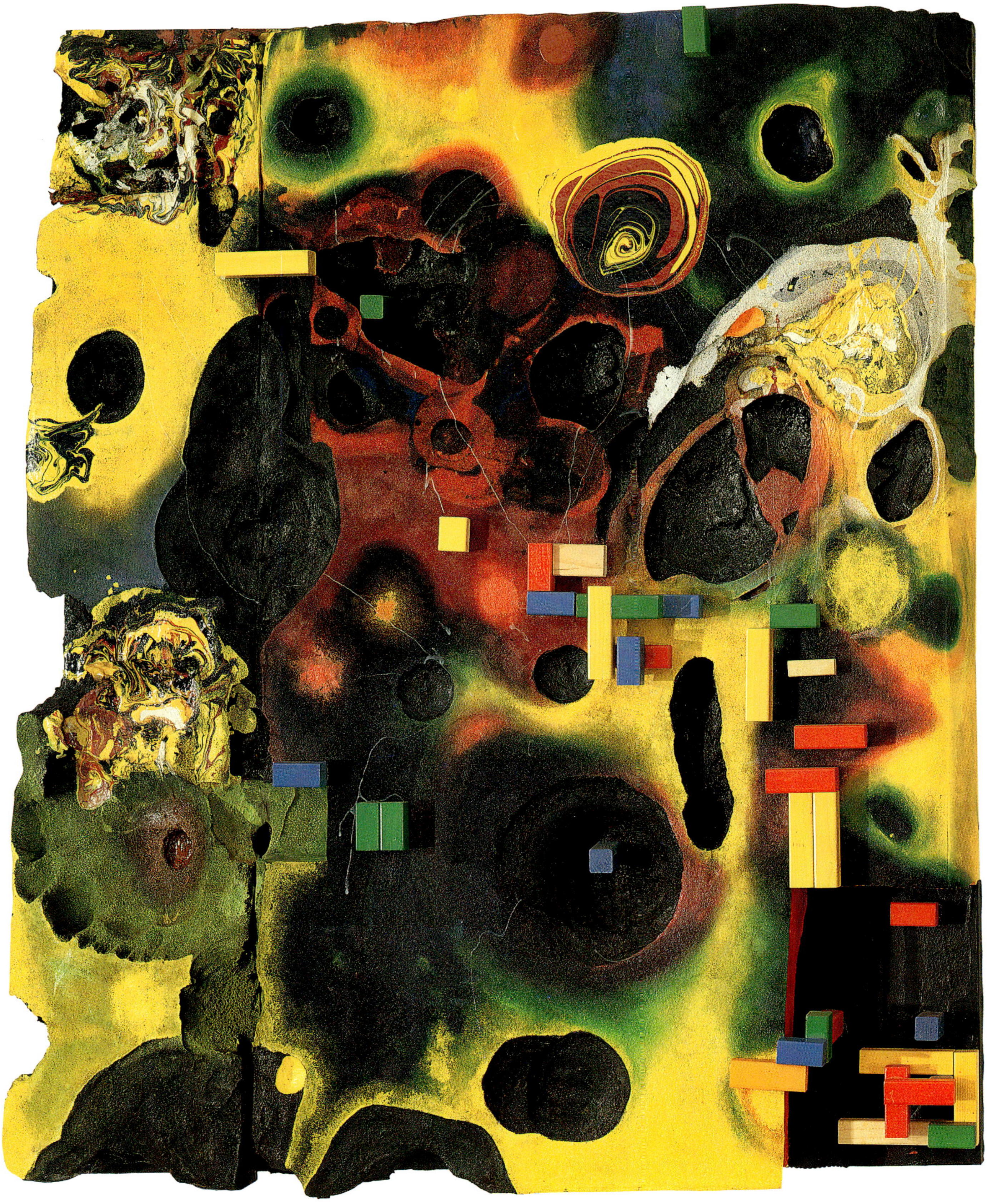

Plate 19

Symphony in Yellow and Lime when the Great Australian Artist met the God of Thyme

Acrylic paint on canvas

(previously, a studio seascape, 1985; a self-portrait, 1983)

200 x 180 cm

1987

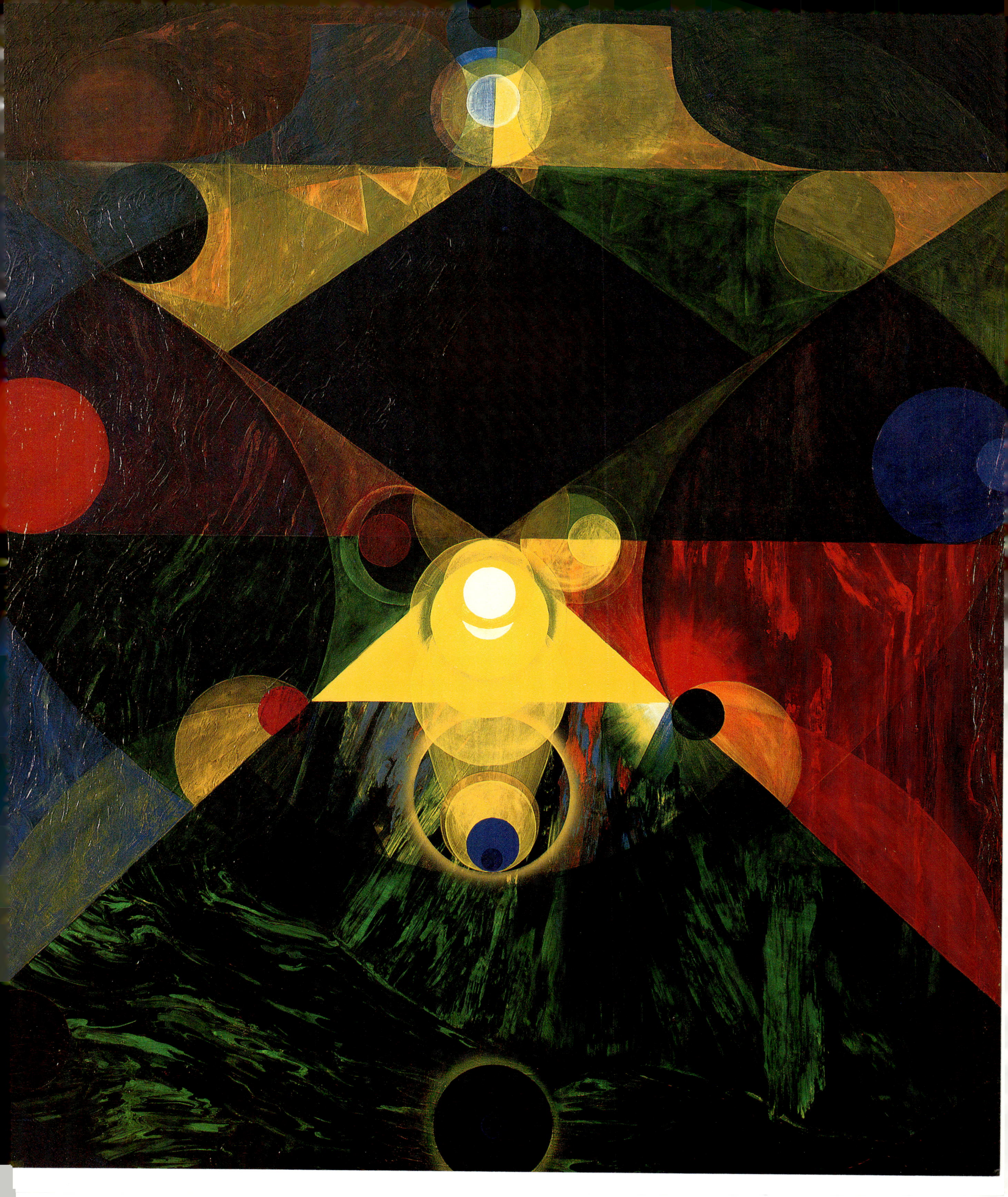

Plate 22
The Goulley Wog (Art 2)
Acrylic paint, bakelite plate on wood
184 x 122 cm
1988
Private collection, Brisbane

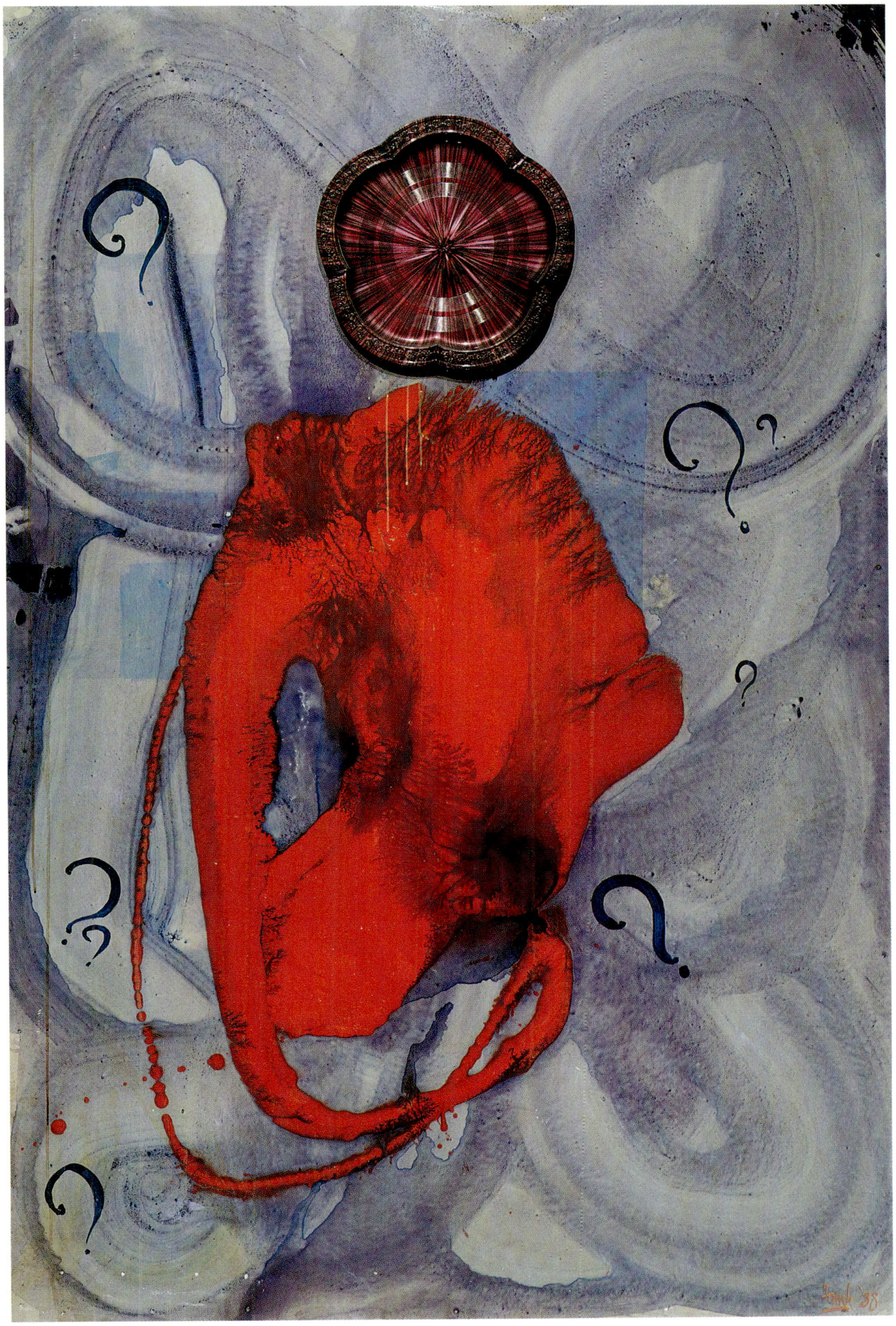

Plate 23
Okay Get Down and Shout — Under the Tank Stand
Acrylic paint, varnishes, printed acrylic paper, on canvas
240 x 400 cm
1989
Collection of Hugh Jamieson, Sydney

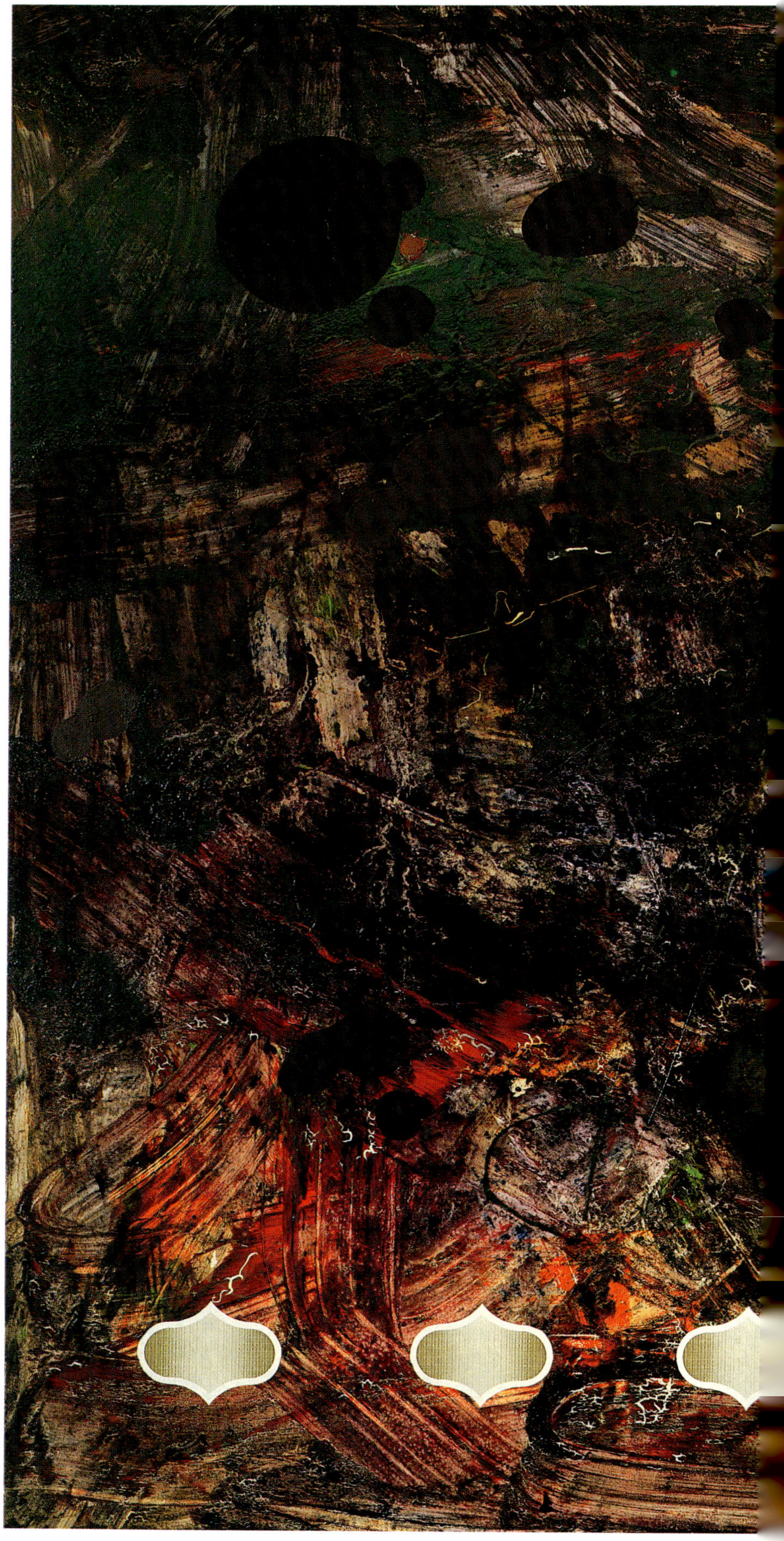

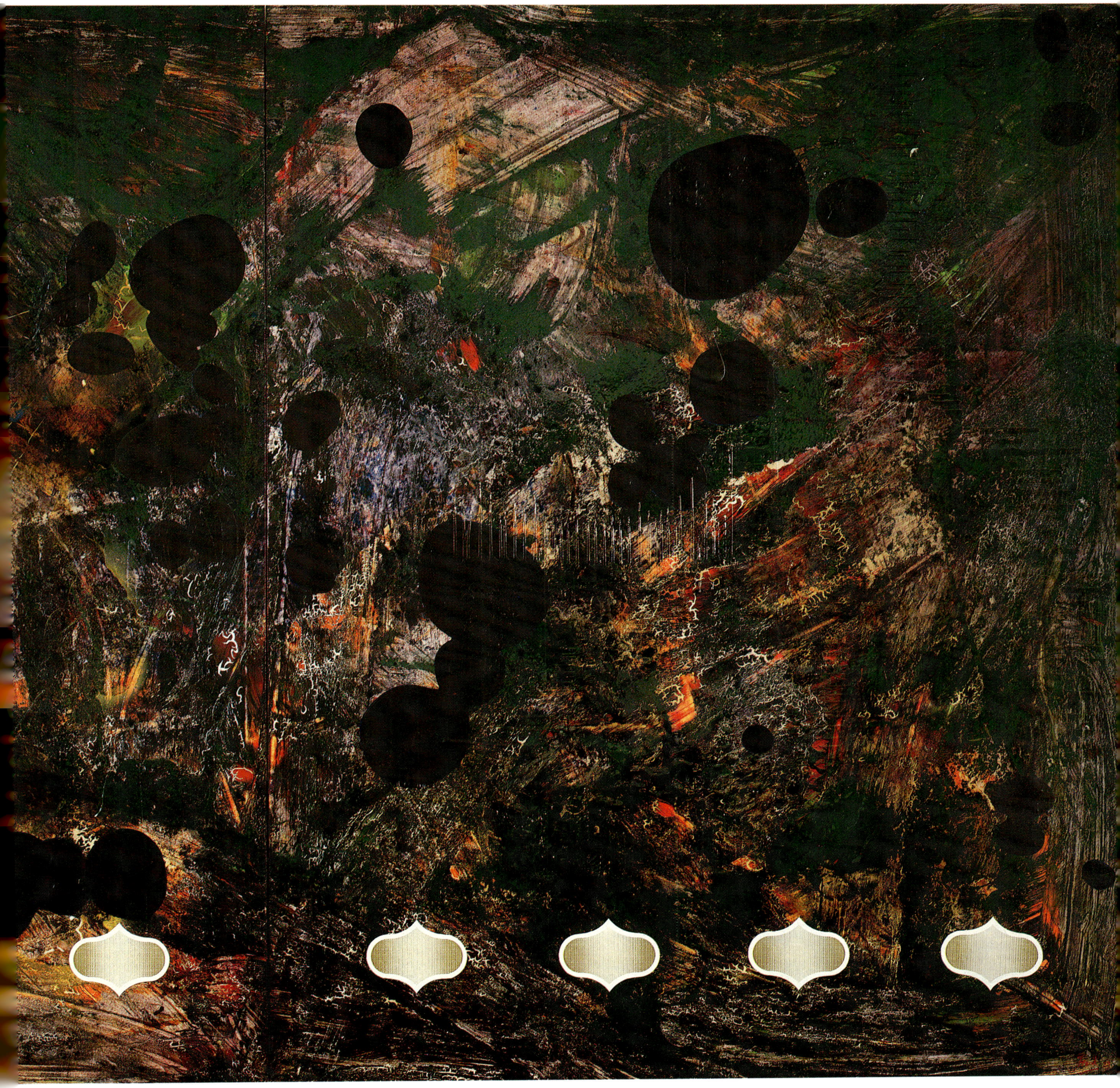

Plate 24
Art Nazis Must Die
Acrylic paint, oil paint, varnishes, chrome hub-caps on canvas
200 x 300 x 5 cm
1989

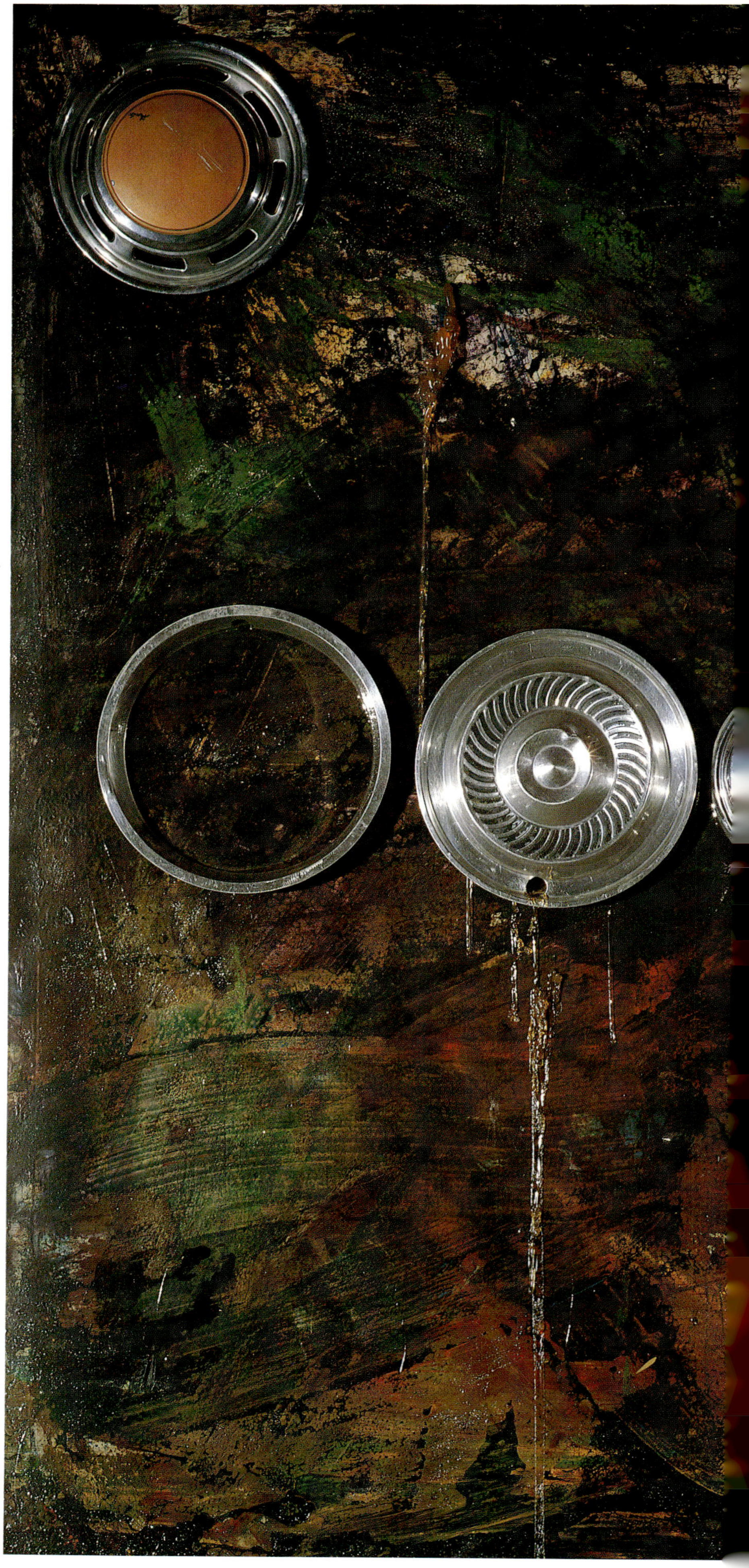

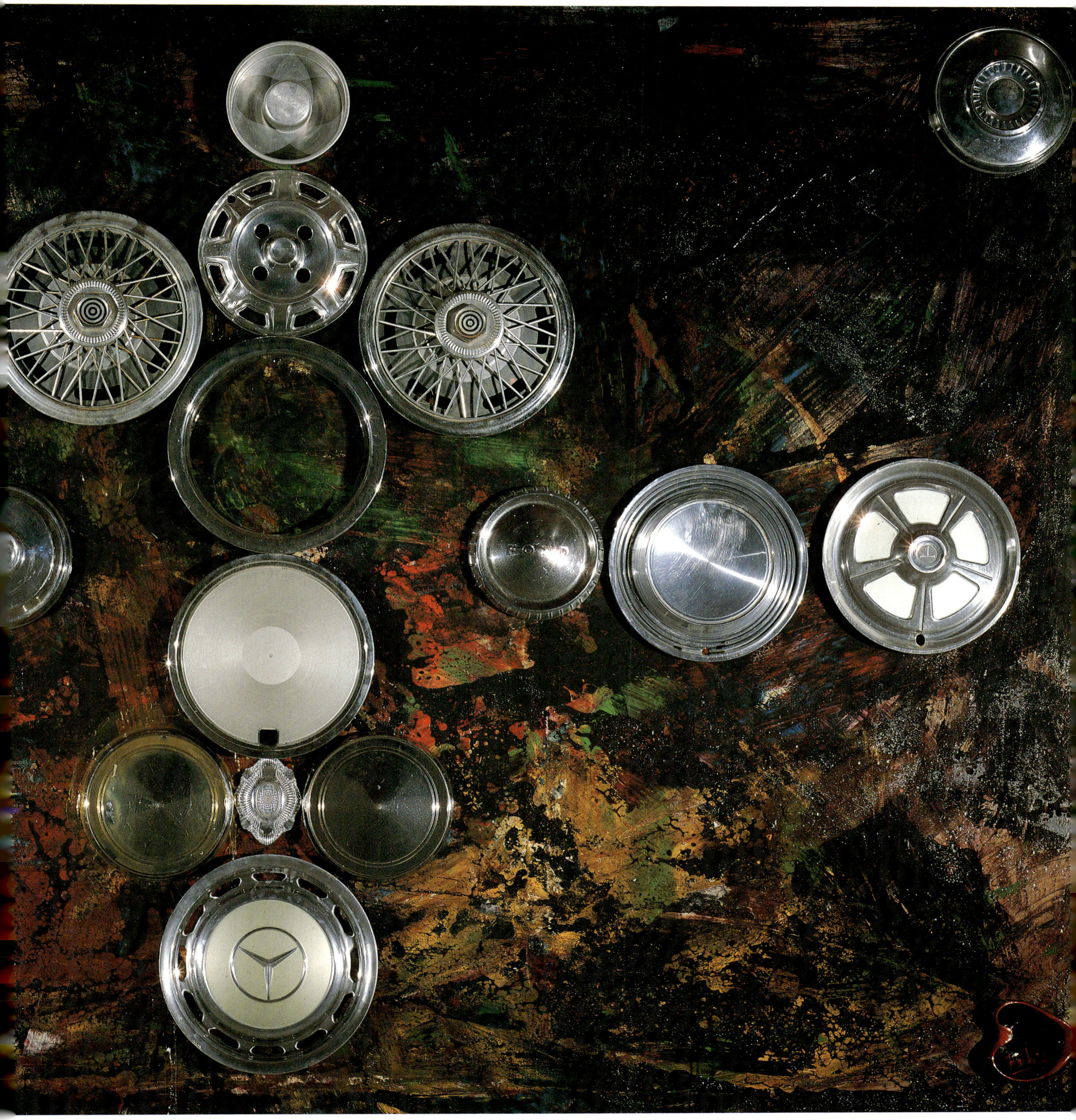

Plate 25
Knowing Known the Poison Gundy
Acrylic paint, varnish, on canvas
200 x 300 cm
1989
Collection of Allen, Allen & Hemsley, Sydney

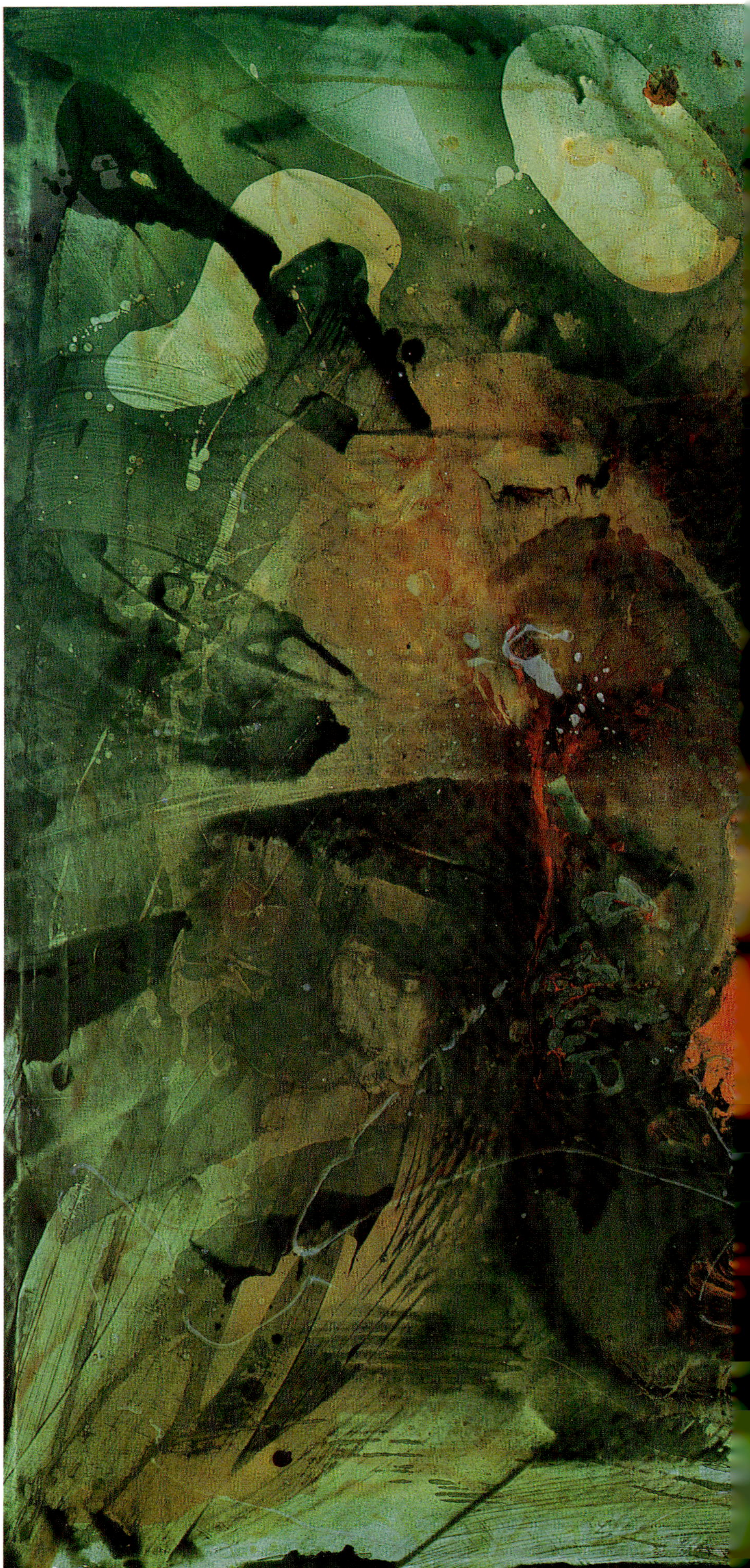

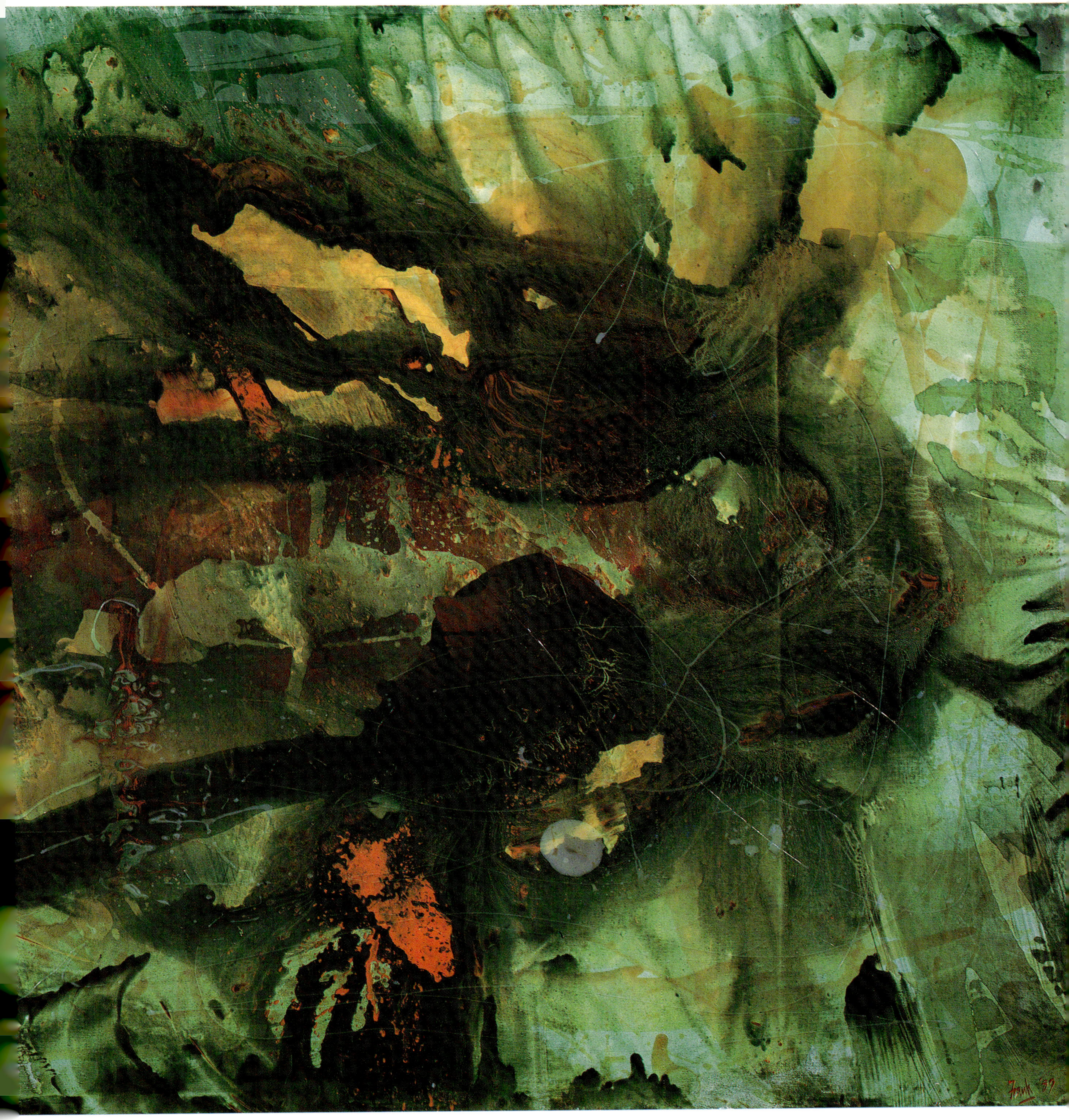

Plate 26
Art
Printed acrylic mink
230 x 190 cm
1989

Following page:
Plate 27
Art with Flowers
Printed vinyl Contact on canvas
230 x 190 cm
1989

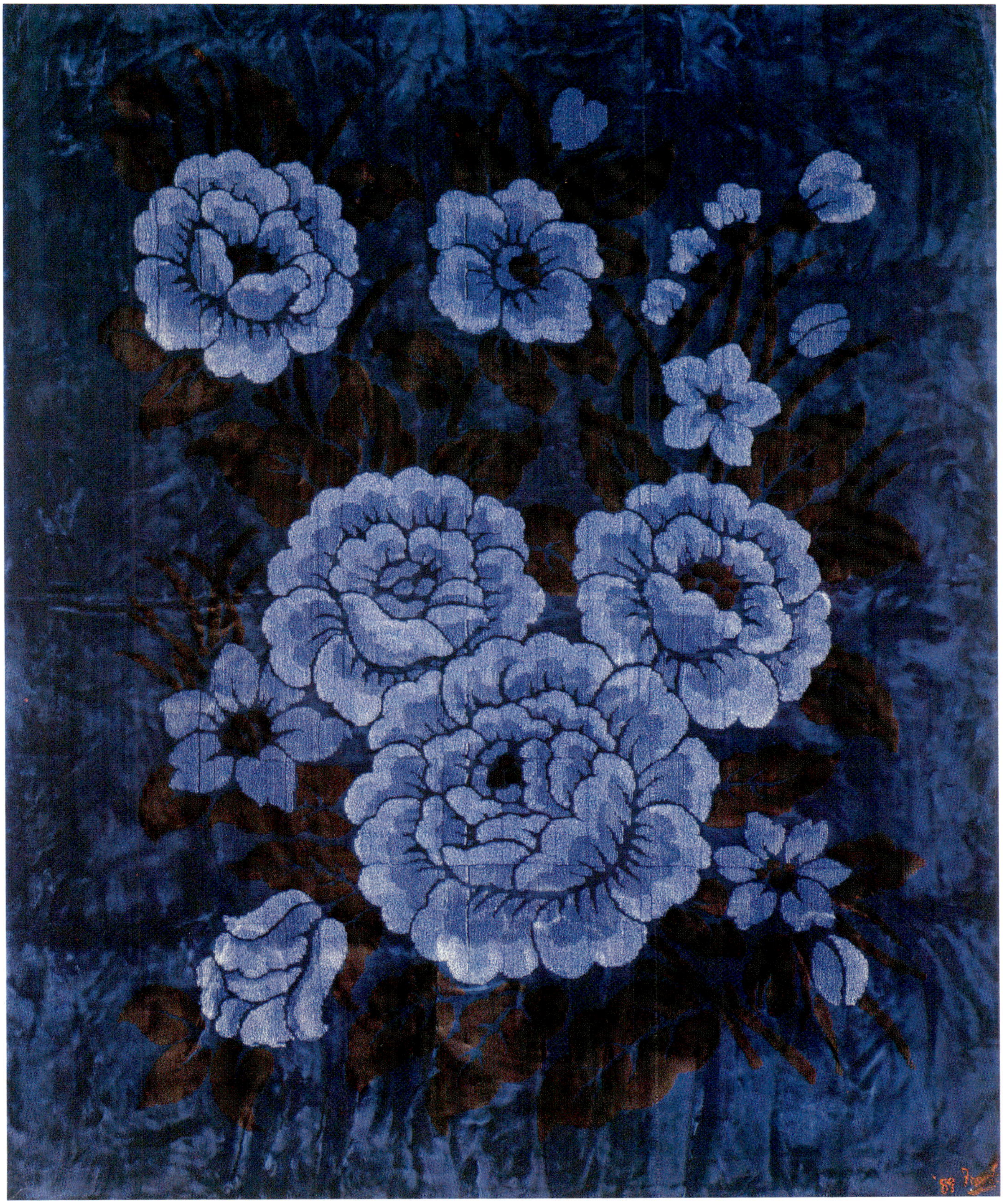

Plate 28
Classicism
Spanish printed synthetic mink (Santonja, dib # 298)
216 x 191 cm
1990

Following page:
Plate 29
Culture/Europa
Printed vinyl Contact on canvas
230 x 180 cm
1990

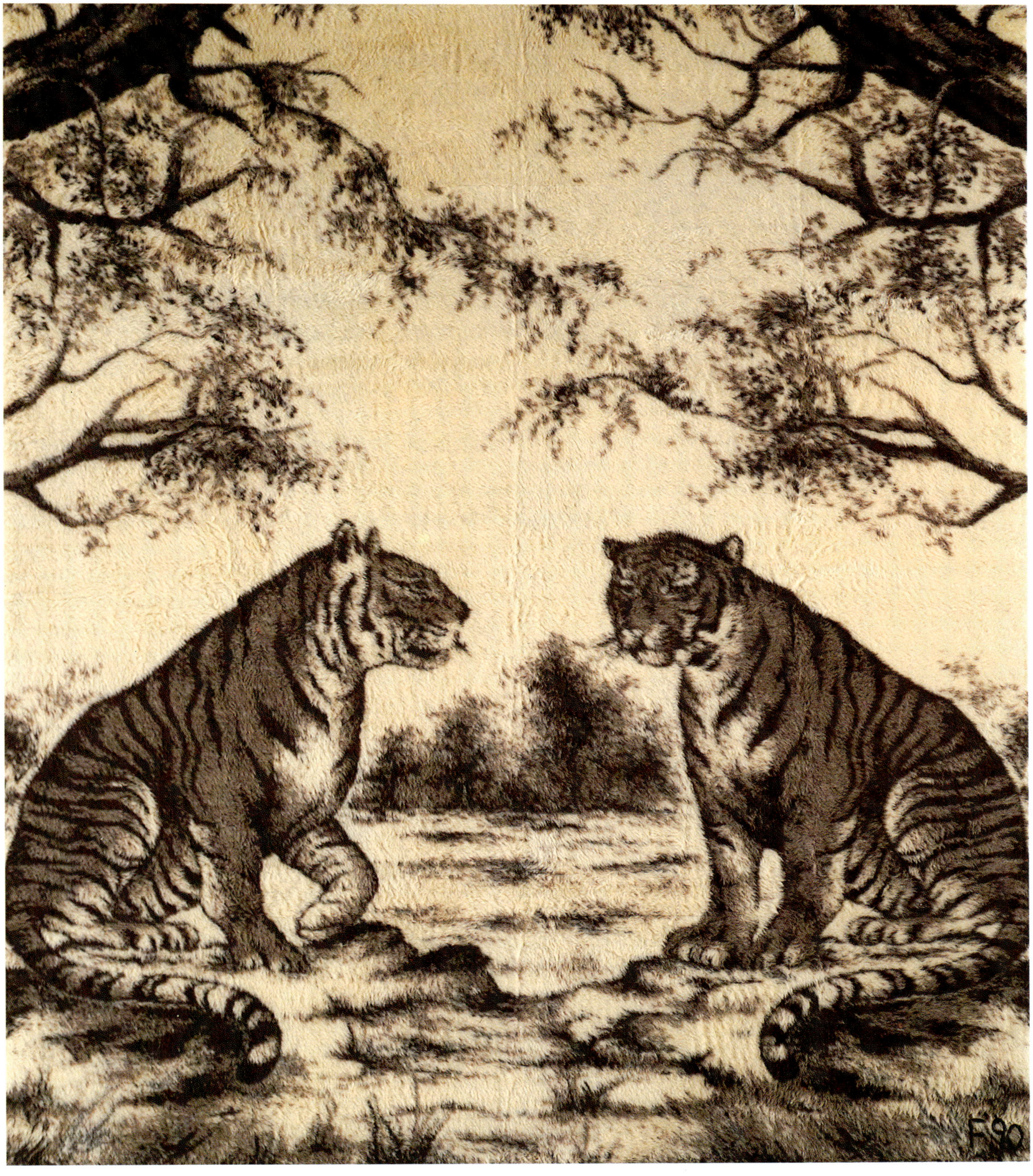
F90

Plate 31
The Bad Daddy Painting
Acrylic paint, oil paint, on canvas (with round hole)
230 x 180 cm
1990

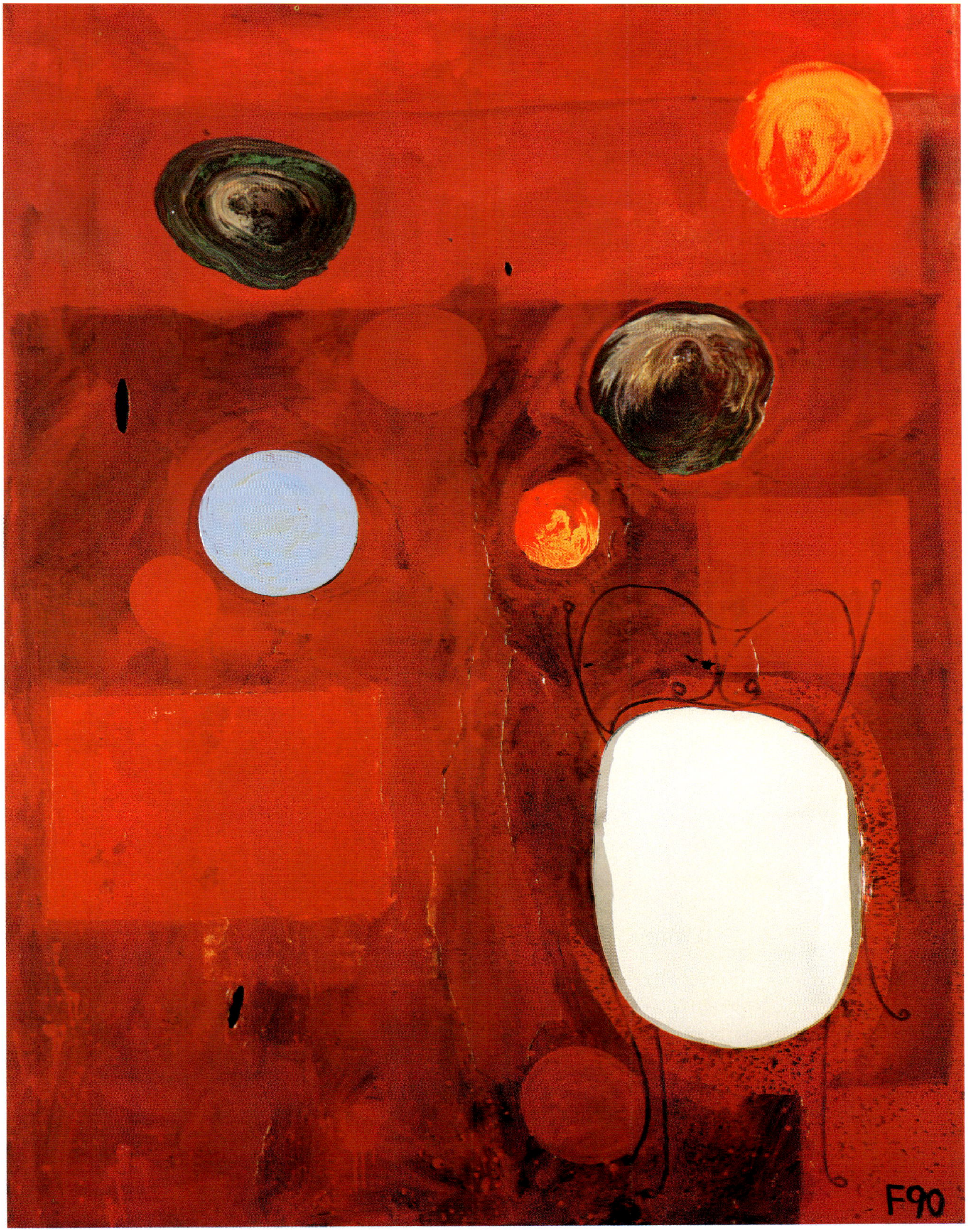
F90

Plate 32
Erotophobia
Varnish on printed vinyl Contact on canvas
200 x 300 cm
1990

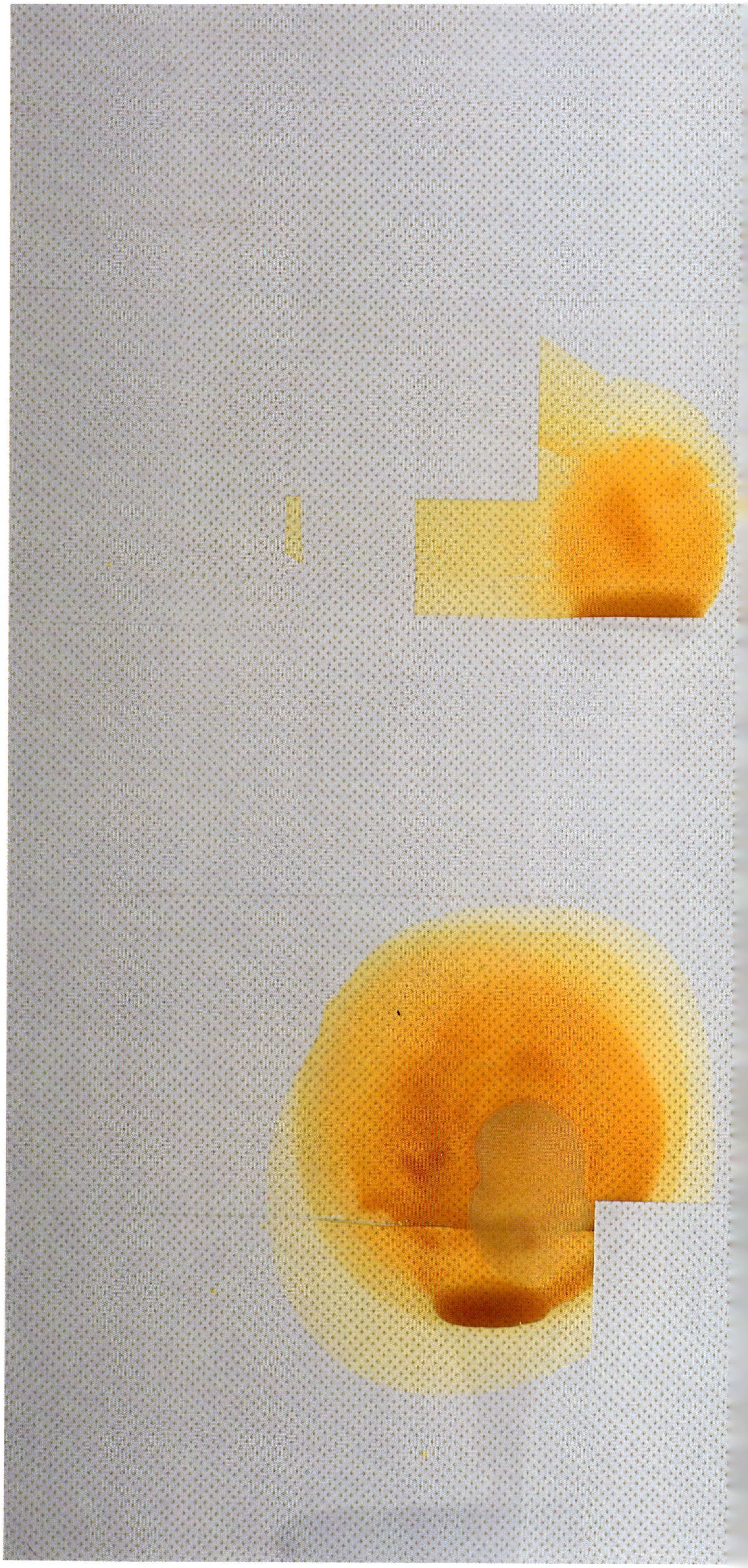

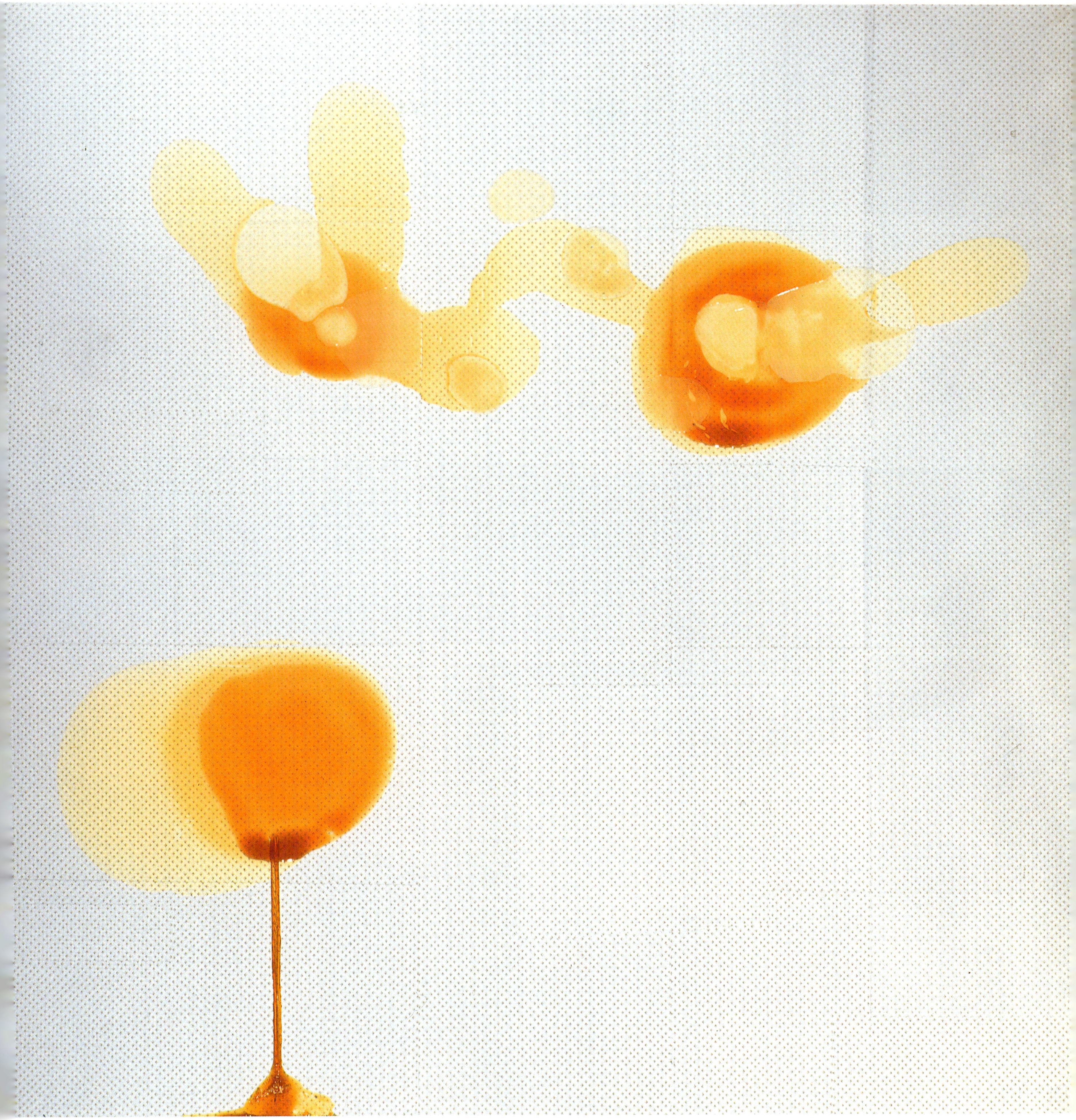

Plate 33
Poking up Daisies
Enamel paint on printed cotton
150 x 120 cm
1990

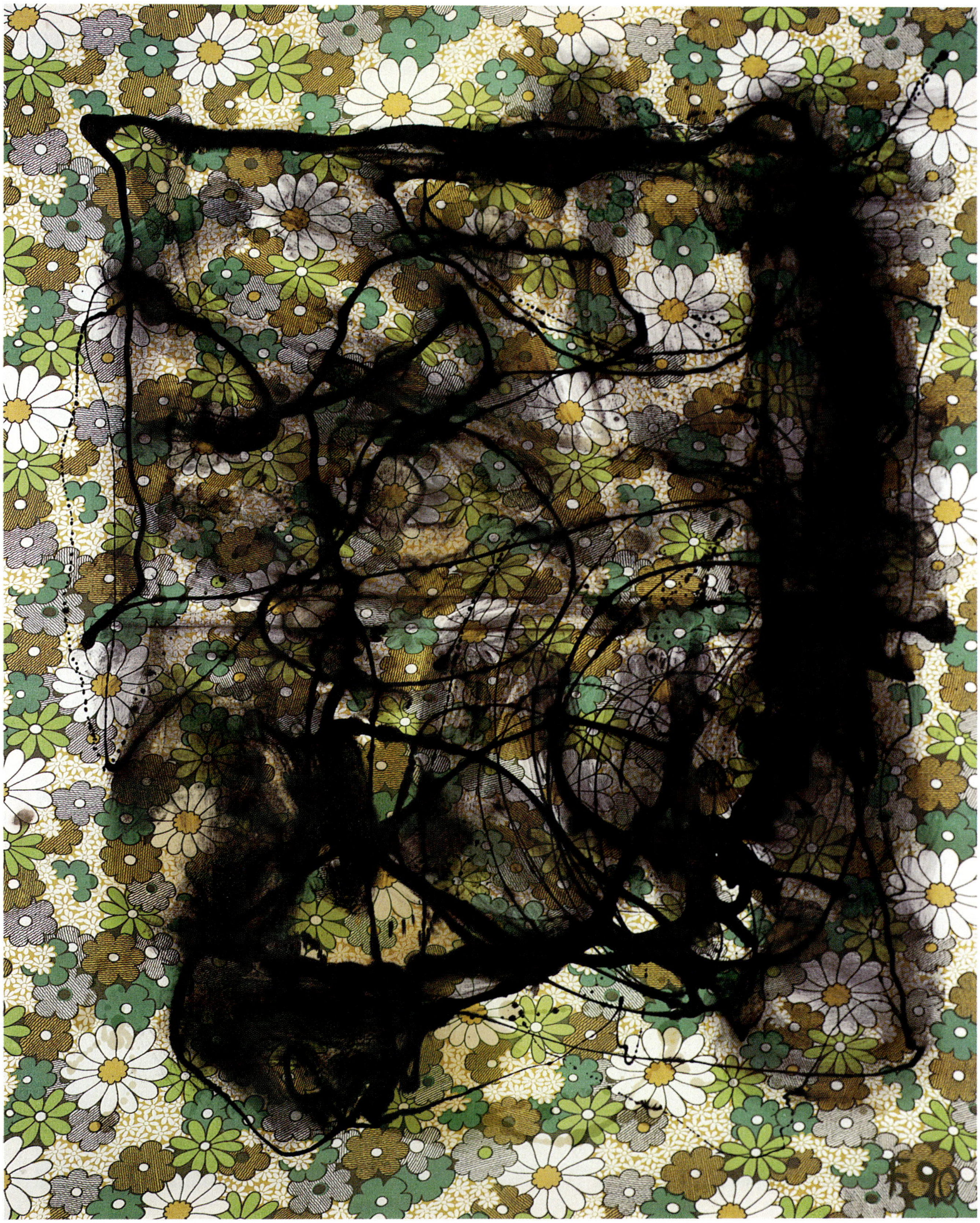

Plate 34
I Love You
Acrylic paint, oil paint, varnishes on canvas
200 x 300 cm
1990
Private collection, Melbourne

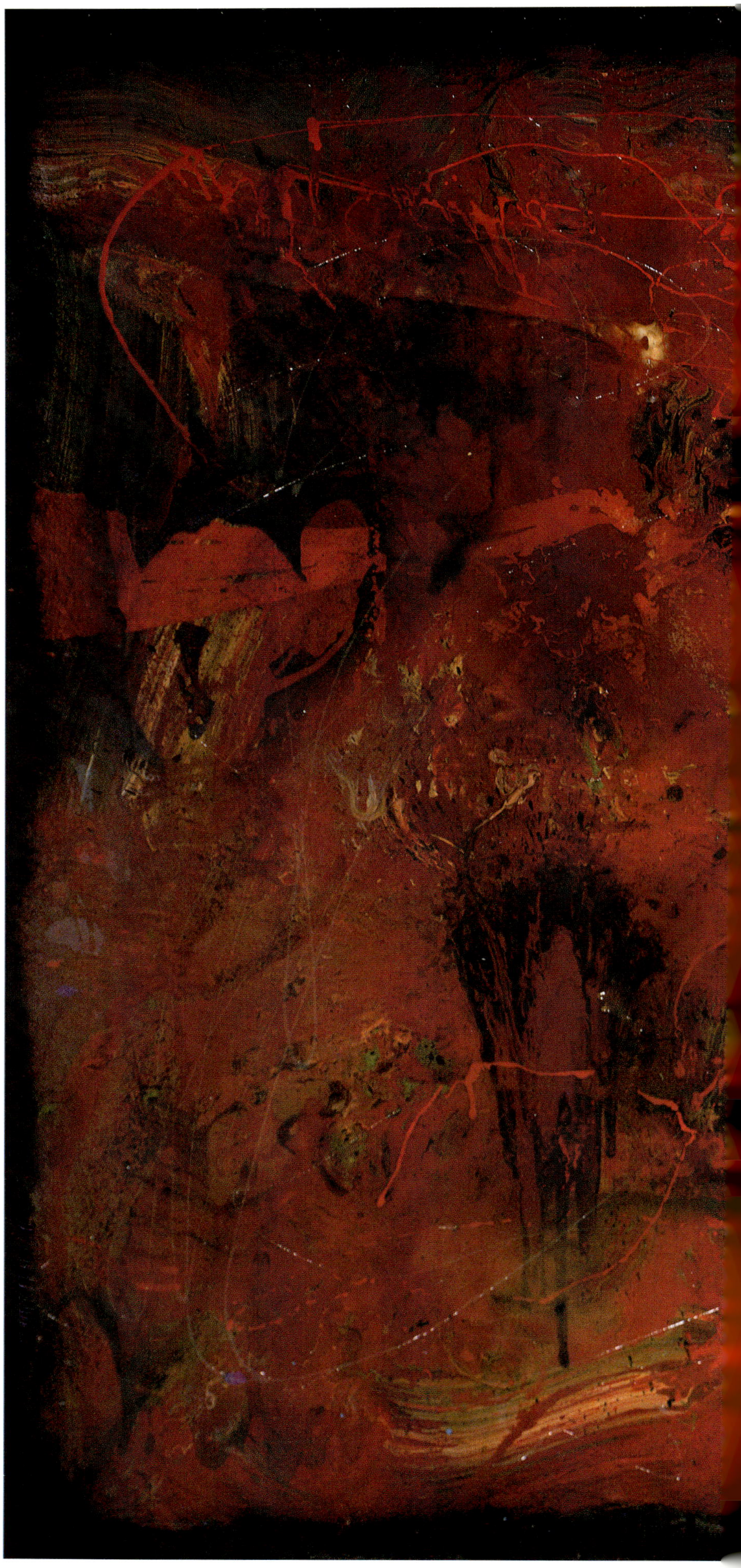

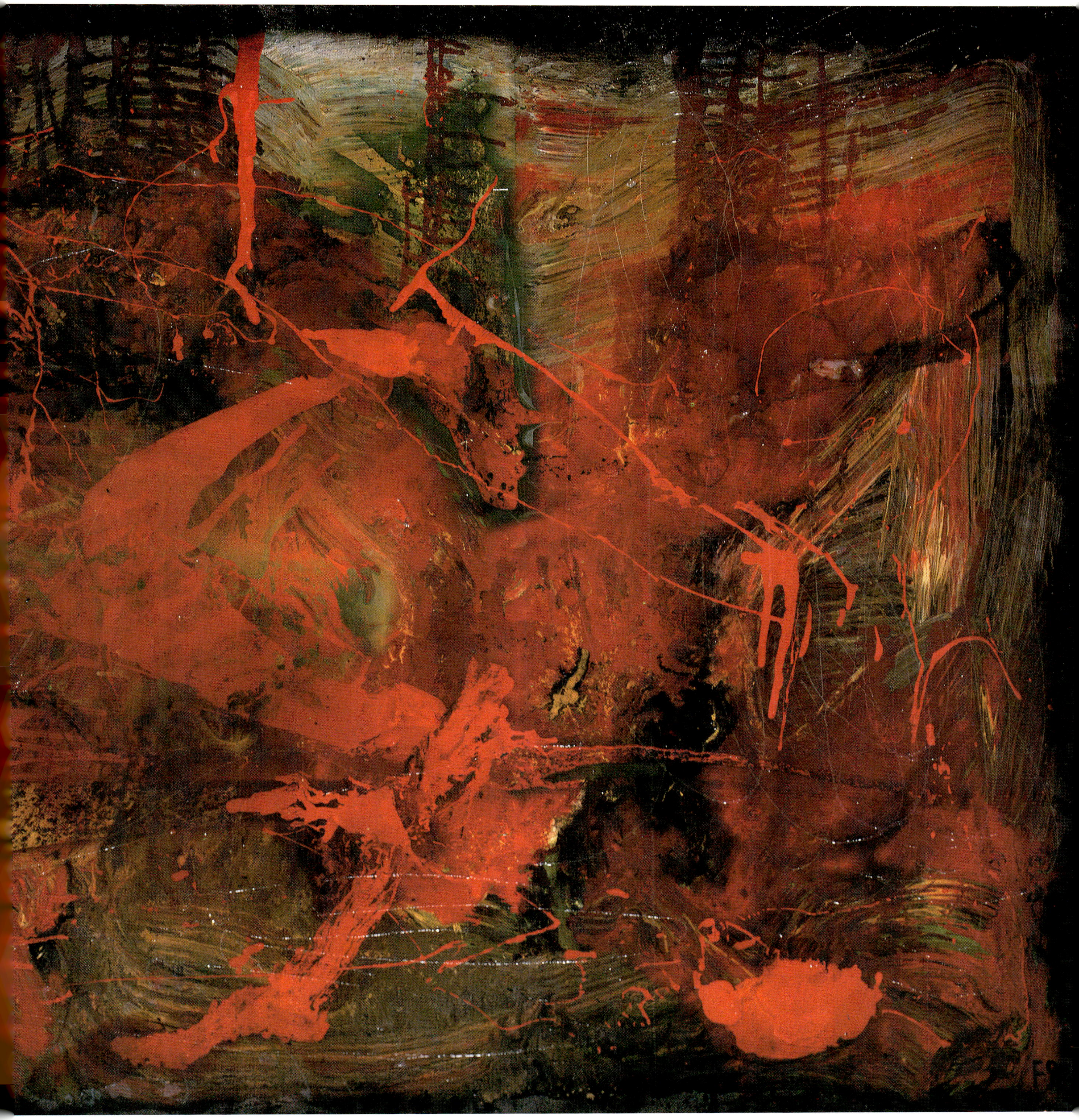

Plate 35

The Apparition of the Head of John the Baptist in Formal Florid Goa

Italian printed synthetic cotton on jute

223 x 180 cm

1990

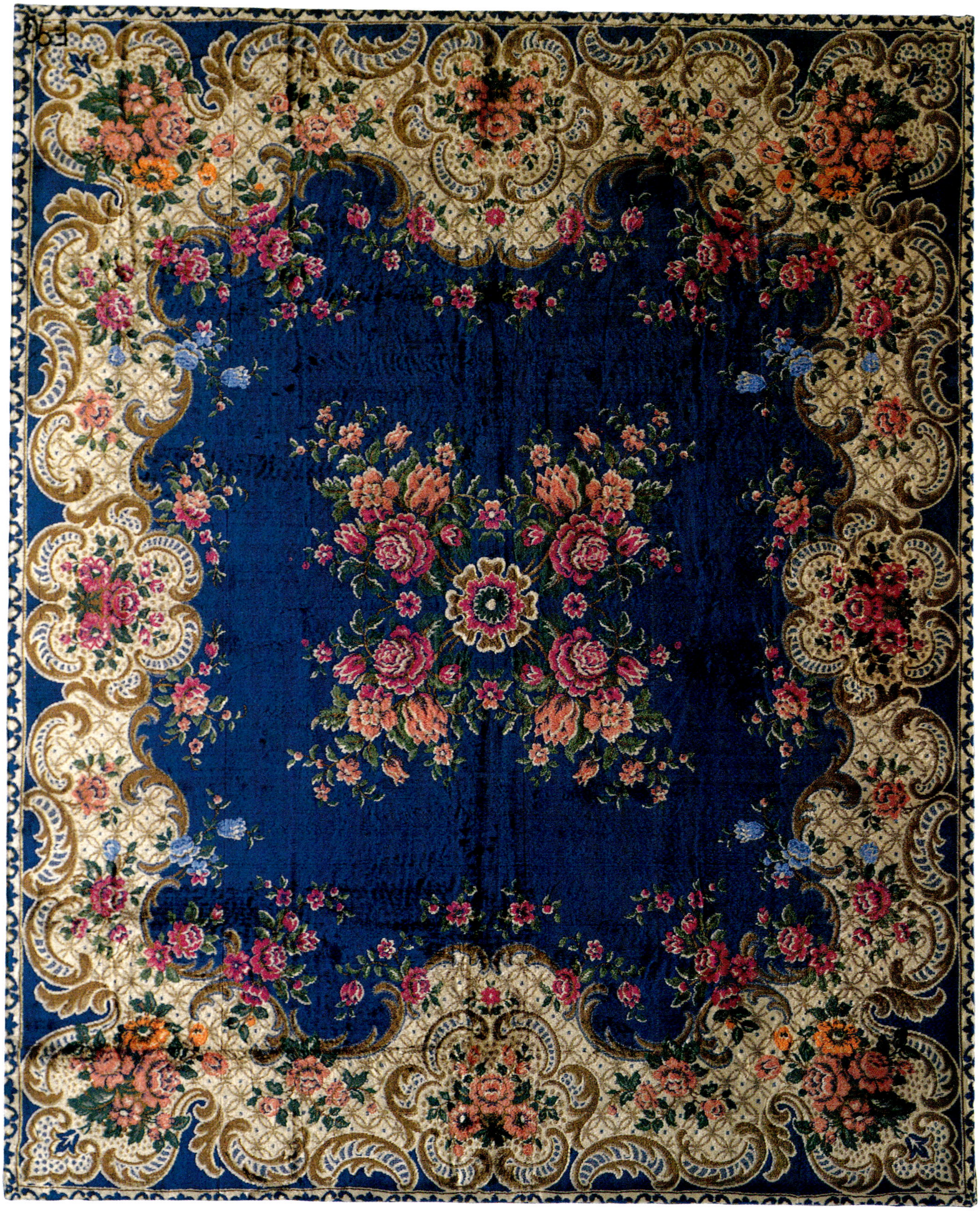

Plate 37
One Hundred Little Arseholes all Paying Homage to a True Master
Acrylic paint, roller print on canvas
260 x 200 cm
1991

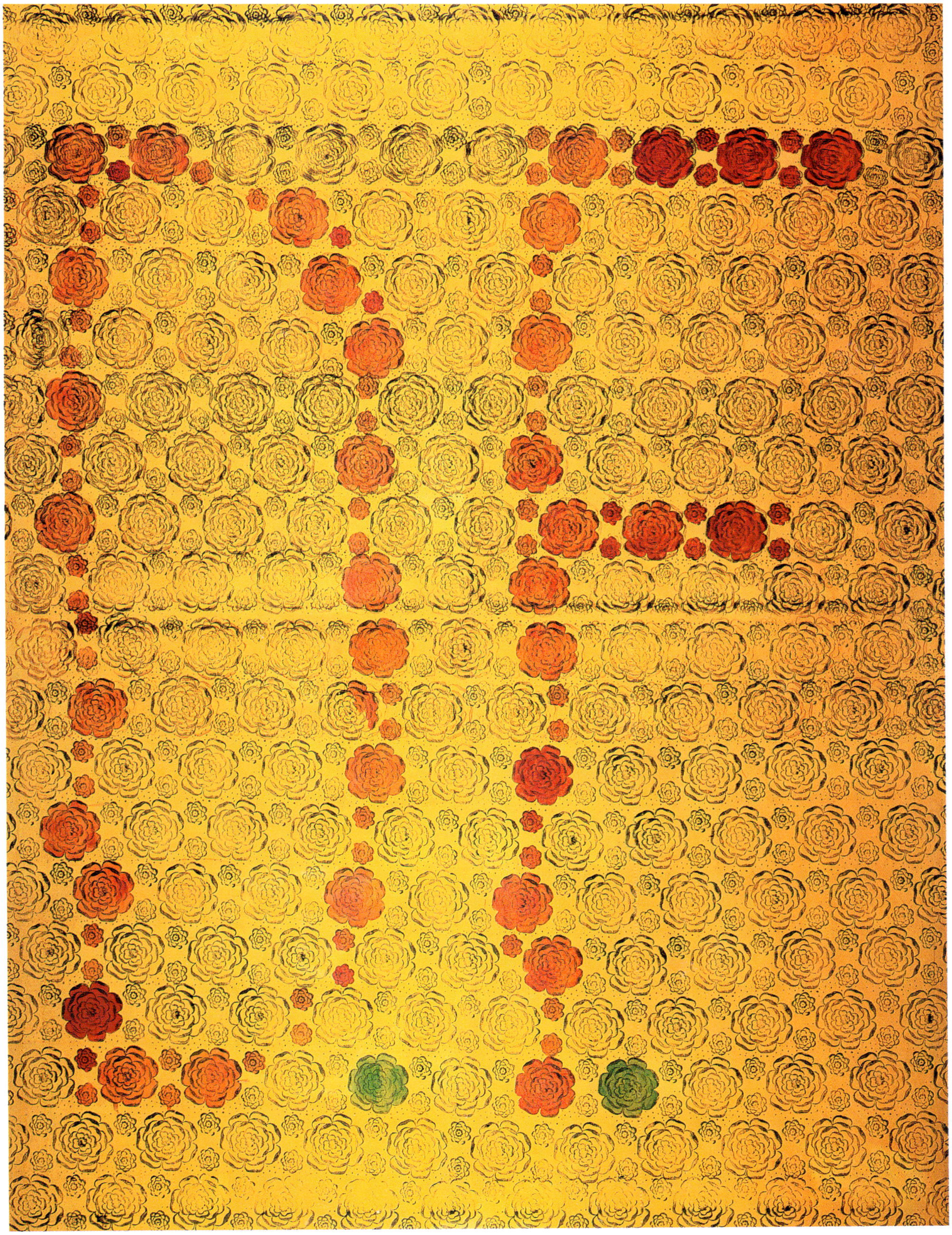

Plate 38
Saddam Saddam He's My Man
Acrylic paint on canvas
260 x 200 cm
1991

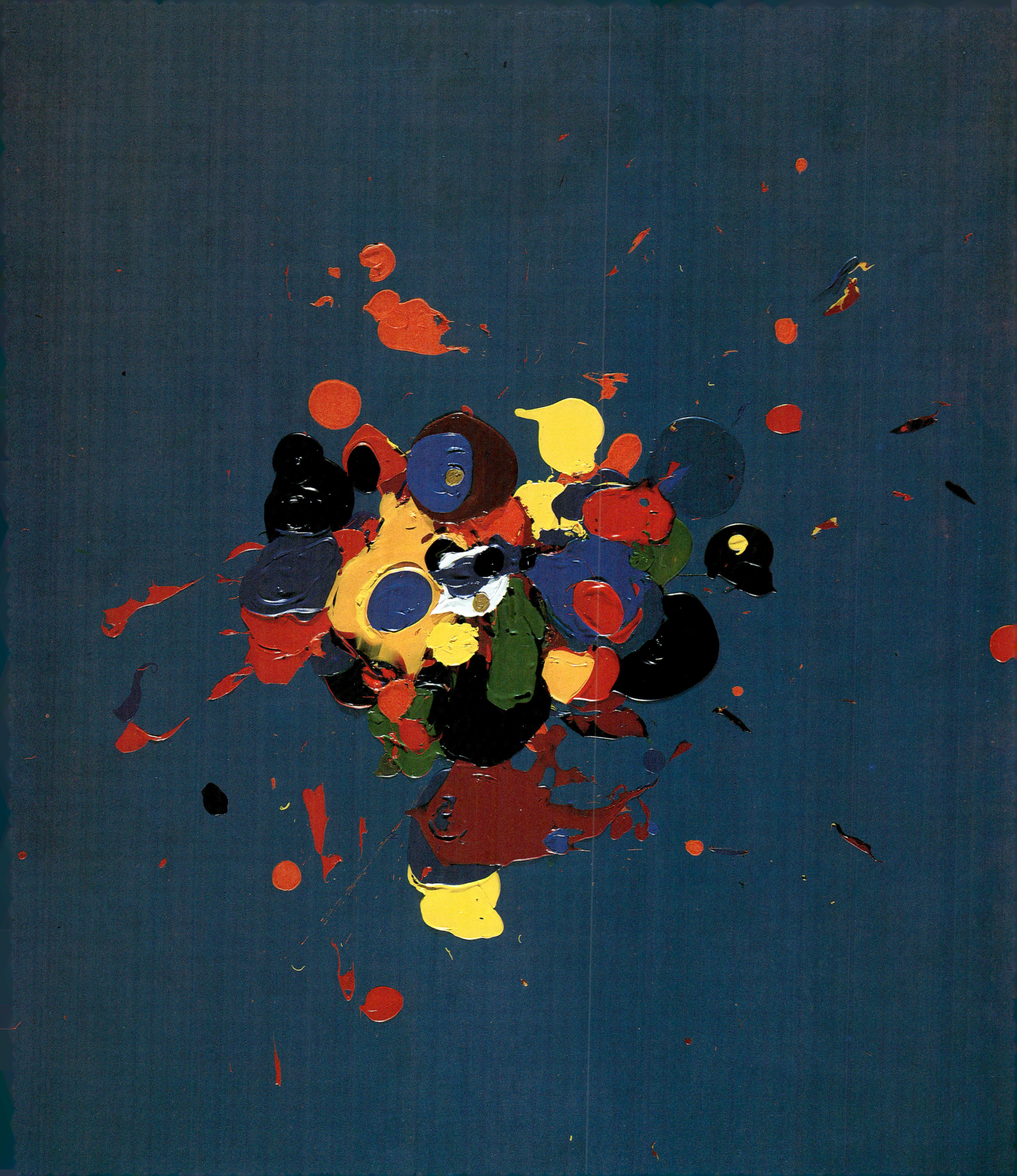

Plate 39

Venture Venture Nothing Gained, into the Artist's Arms without Refrain. With only Disgust Disgust, it is only Me you can Trust. Listen Hard, Listen Long, Listen Listen, but not too Long

Acrylic paint on canvas

260 x 200 cm

1991

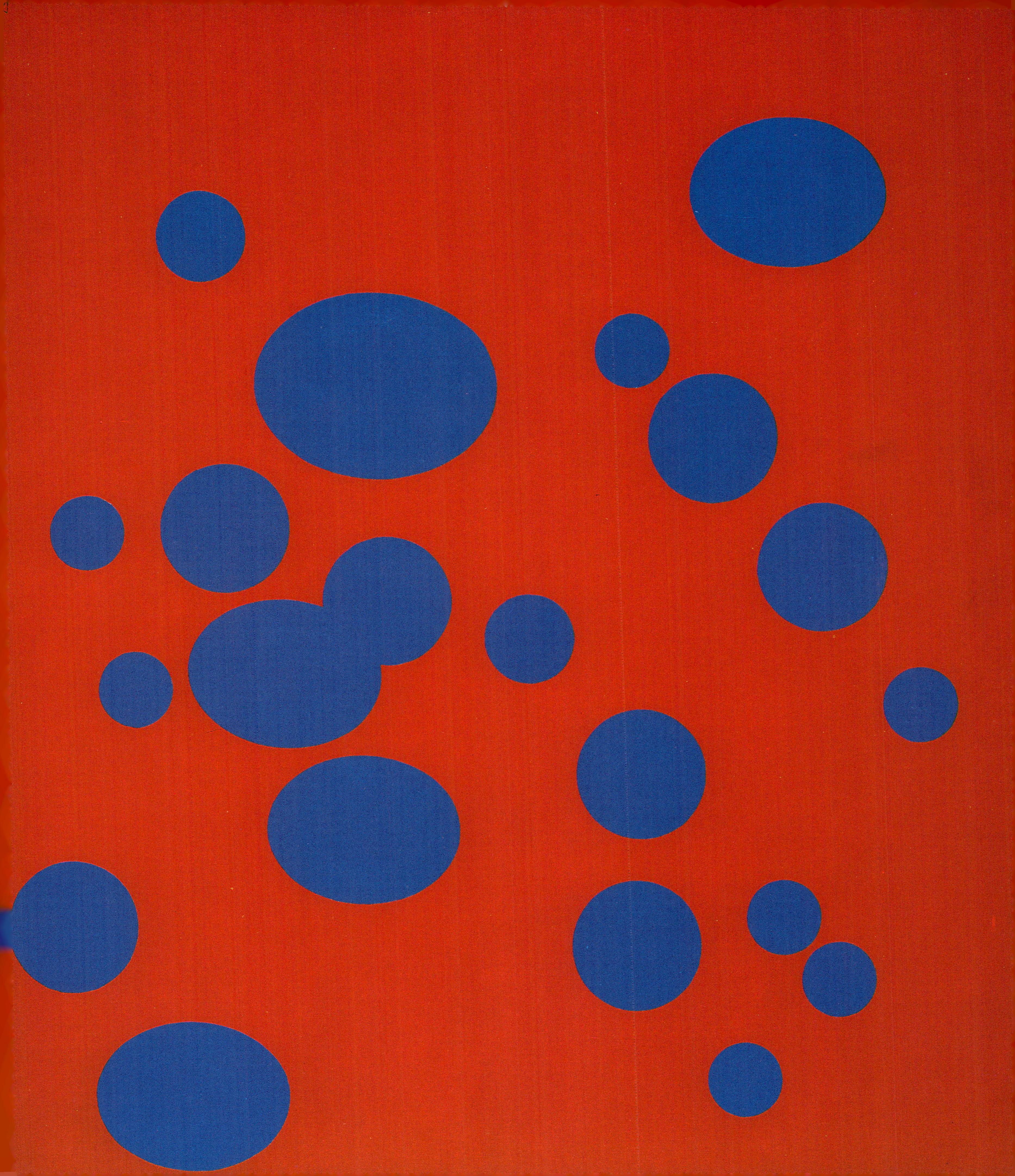

Plate 40
The Artist's Fairy Floss Sold on the Merry-Go-Round of Life
(Sucker Dealer)
Sucker Dealer and the Righteous Anus
Acrylic paint on canvas
240 x 200 cm
1991

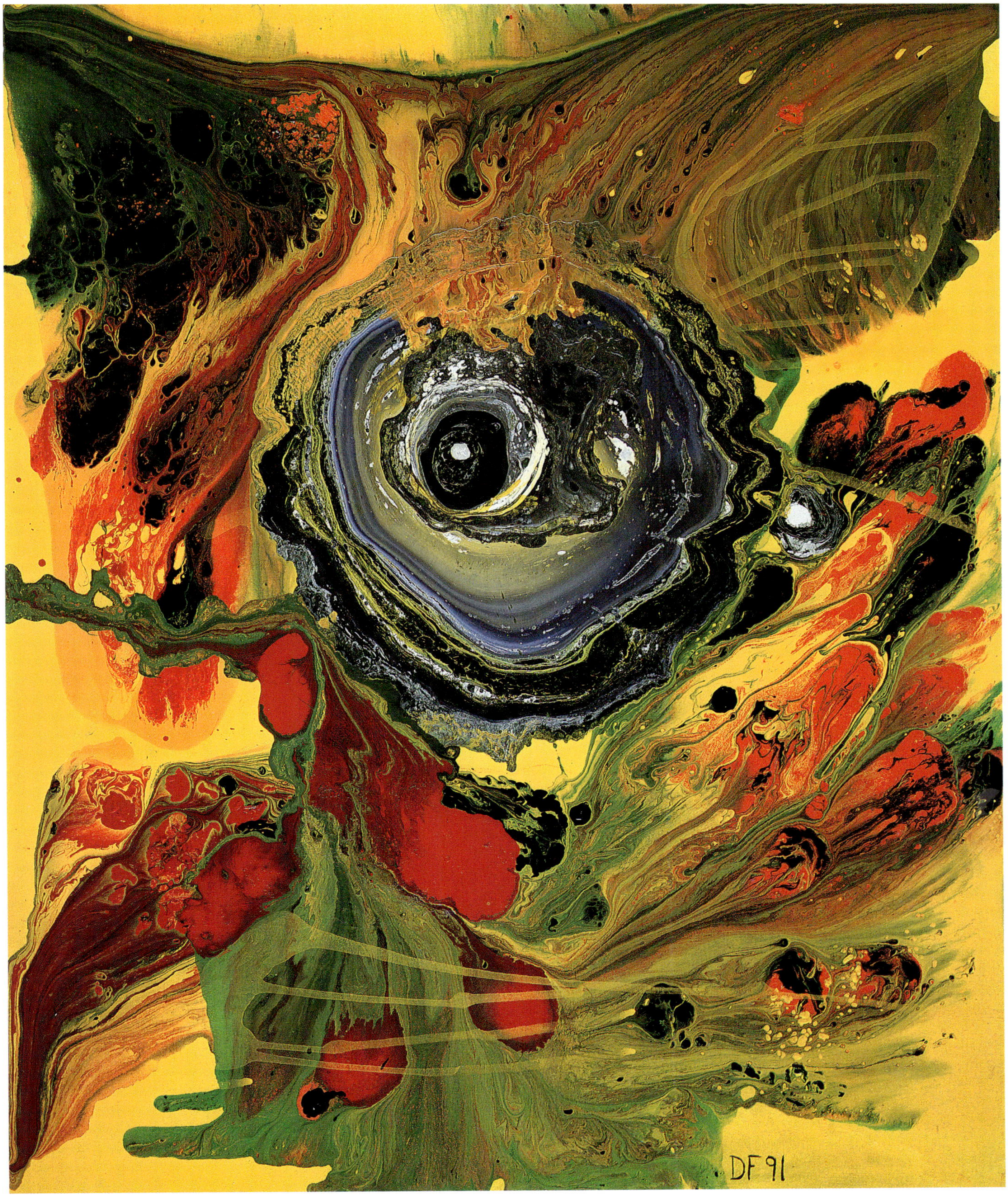
DF 91

Plate 41
Cilla Black
Acrylic paint on canvas
240 x 200 cm
1991

Following page:
Plate 42
The Beached Sperm Whale and his Affection to the Disinfected Onlooker, an Art Moral
Pencil, acrylic wash on paper
182 x 356 cm
1985

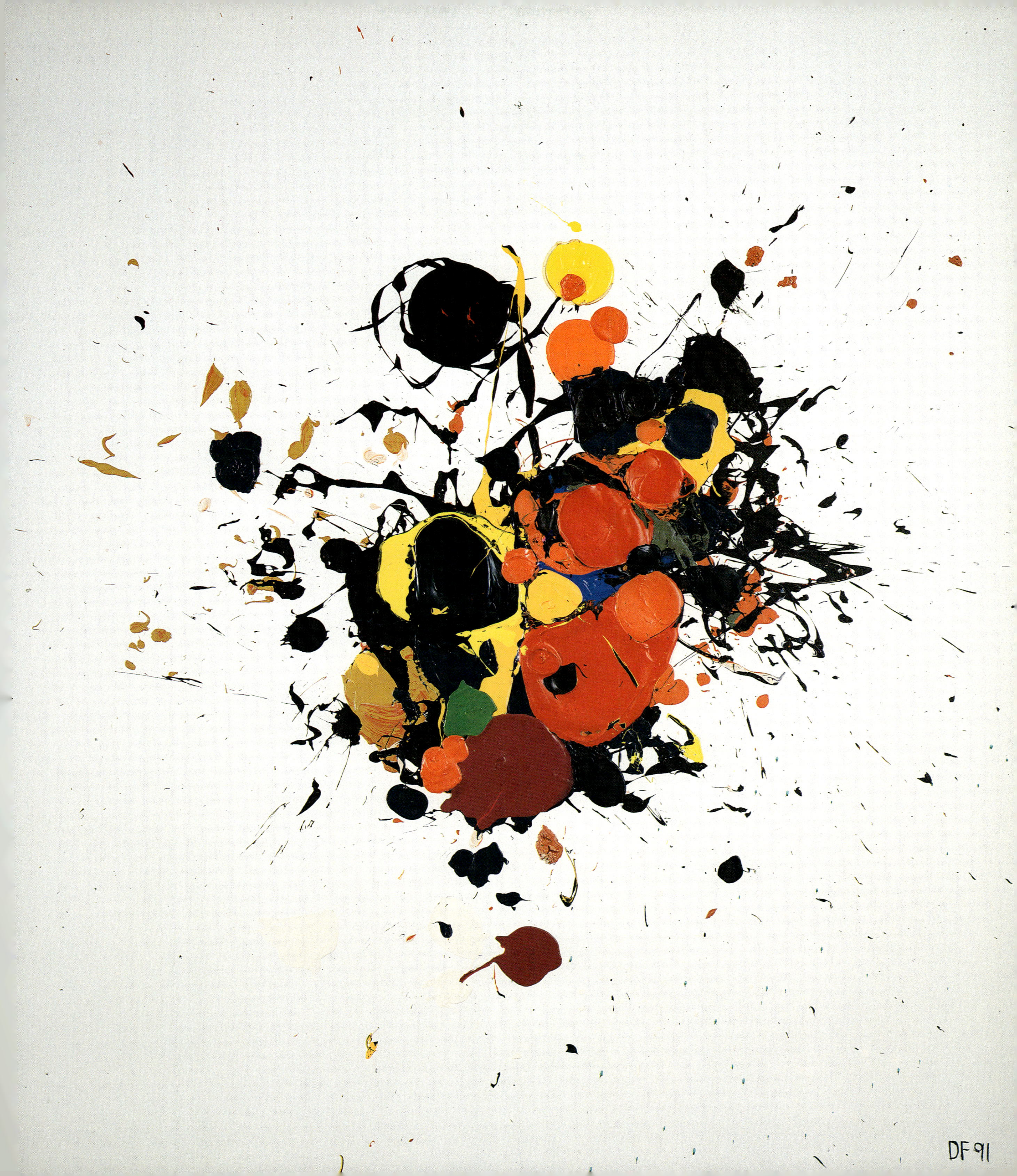
DF 91

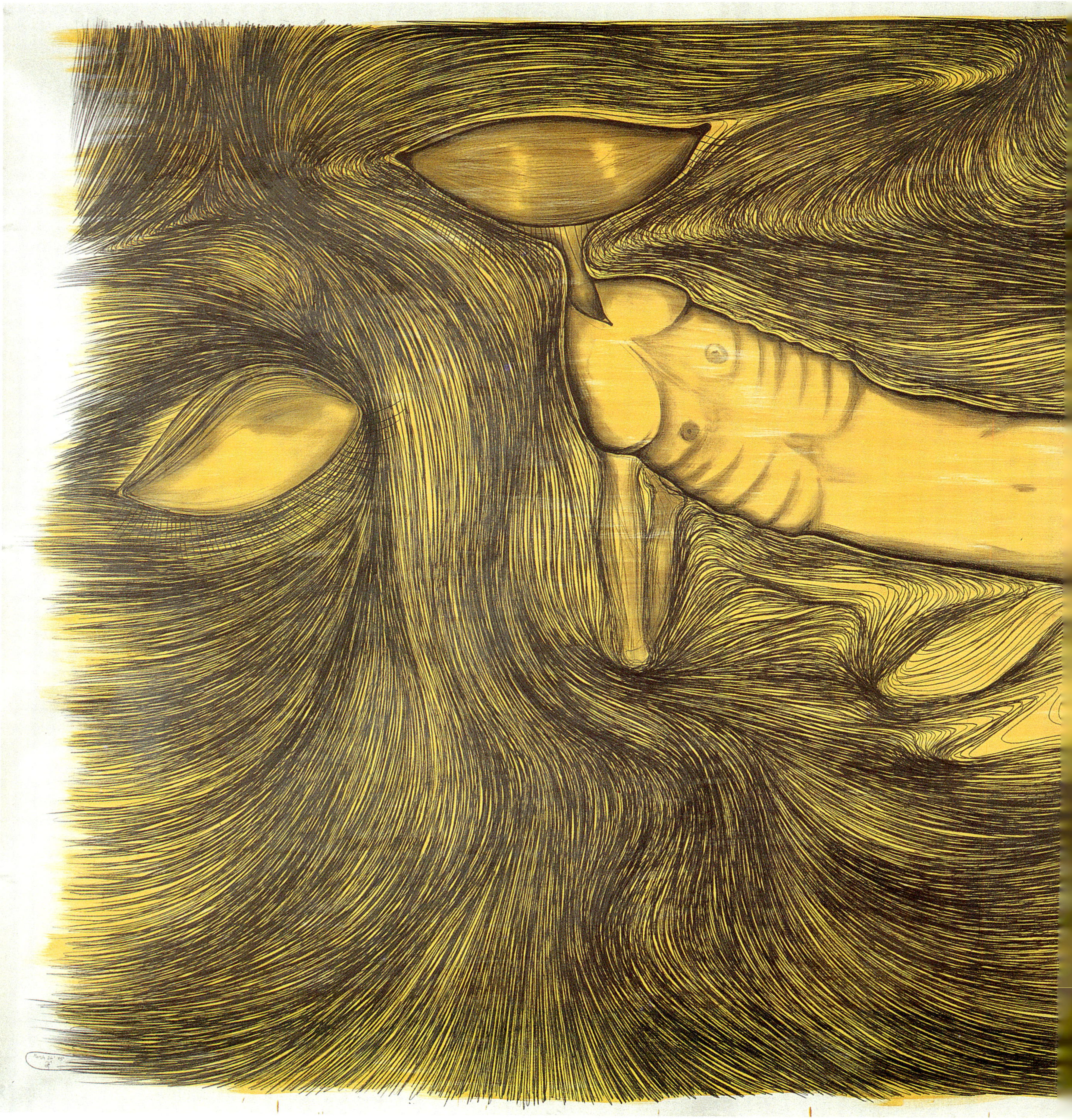

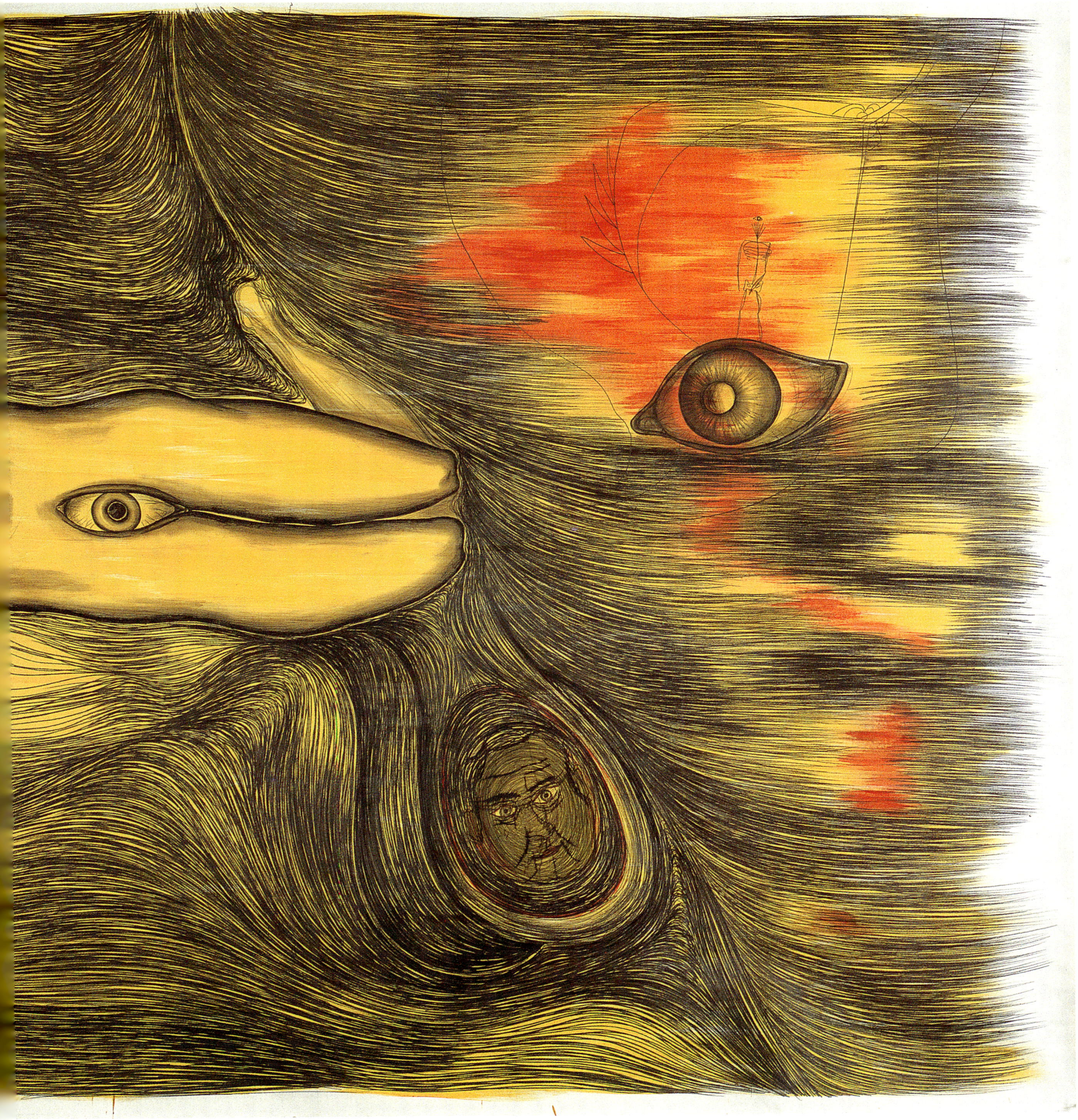

Plate 43
I
Pencil, acrylic wash, on paper
182 x 248 cm
1985

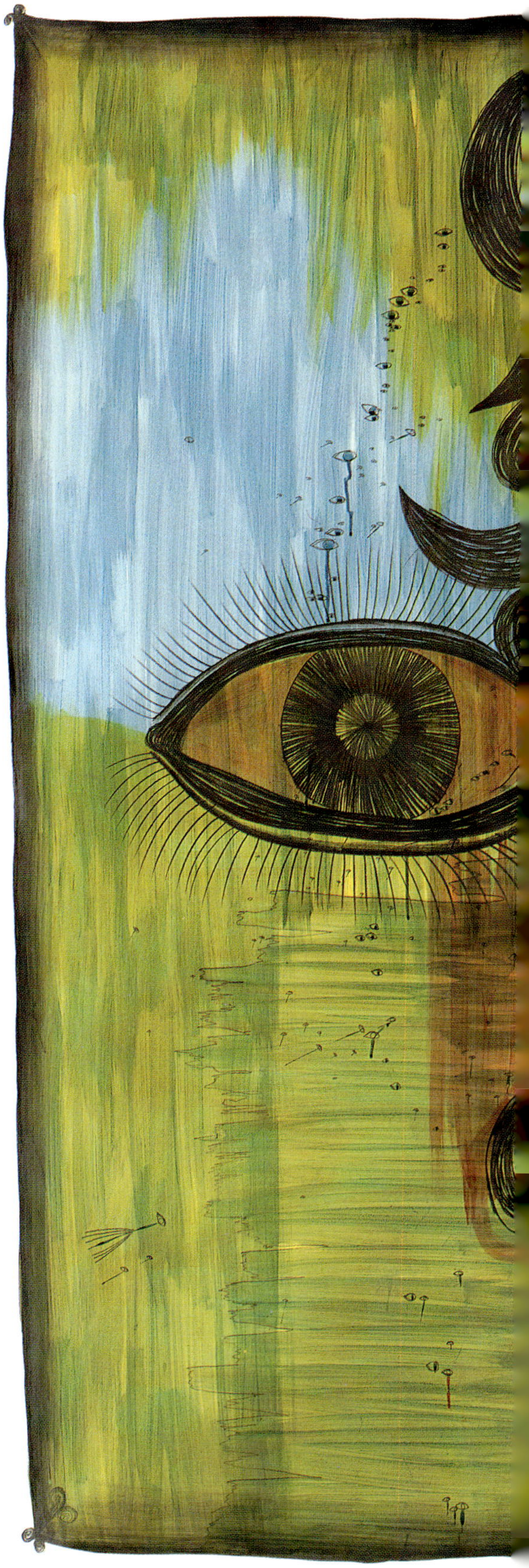

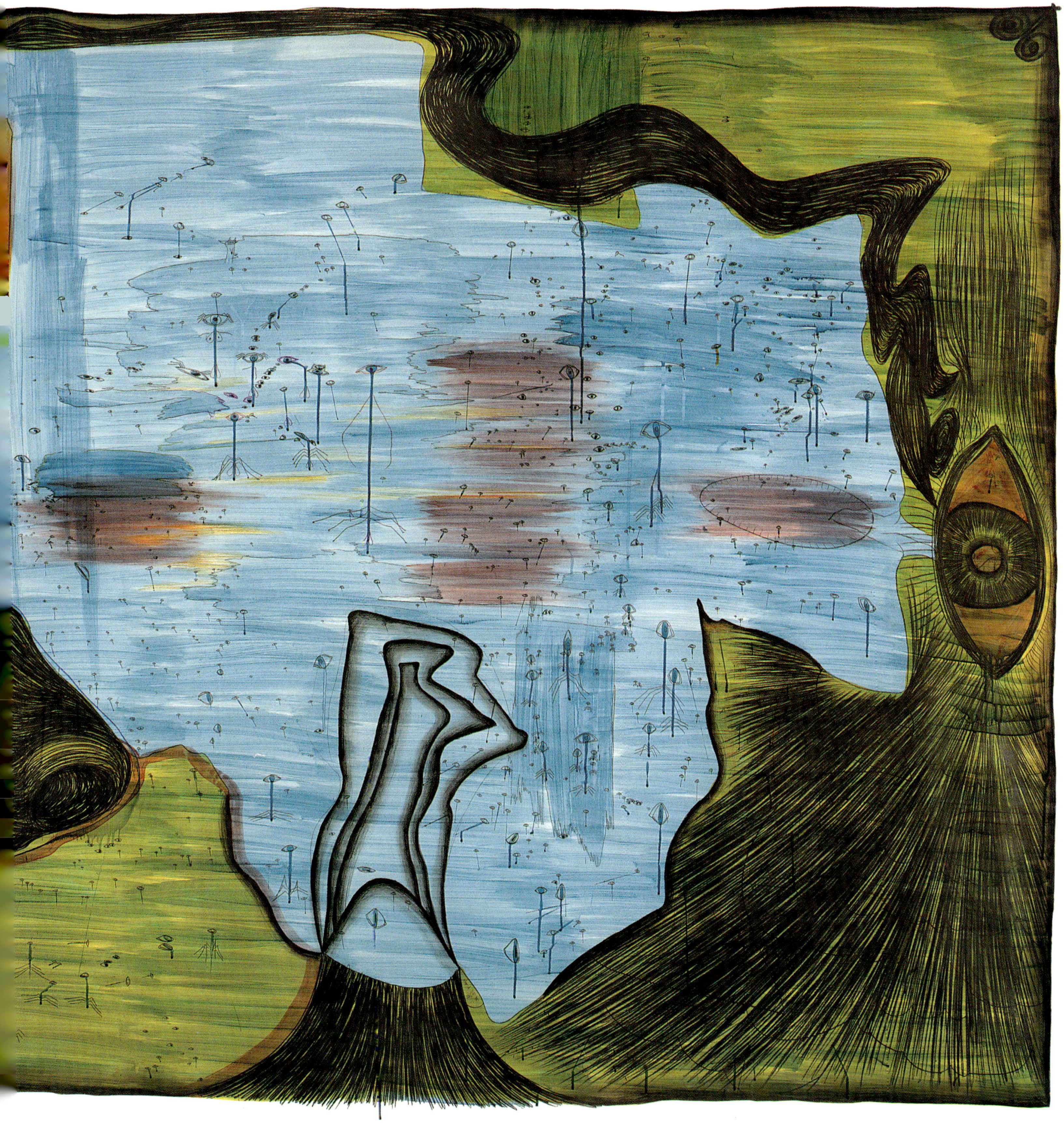

Plate 44

The Demon Artist's Portrait with a Question of Siamese Success

Pencil, acrylic wash on paper

182 x 320 cm

1984

Private collection, New York

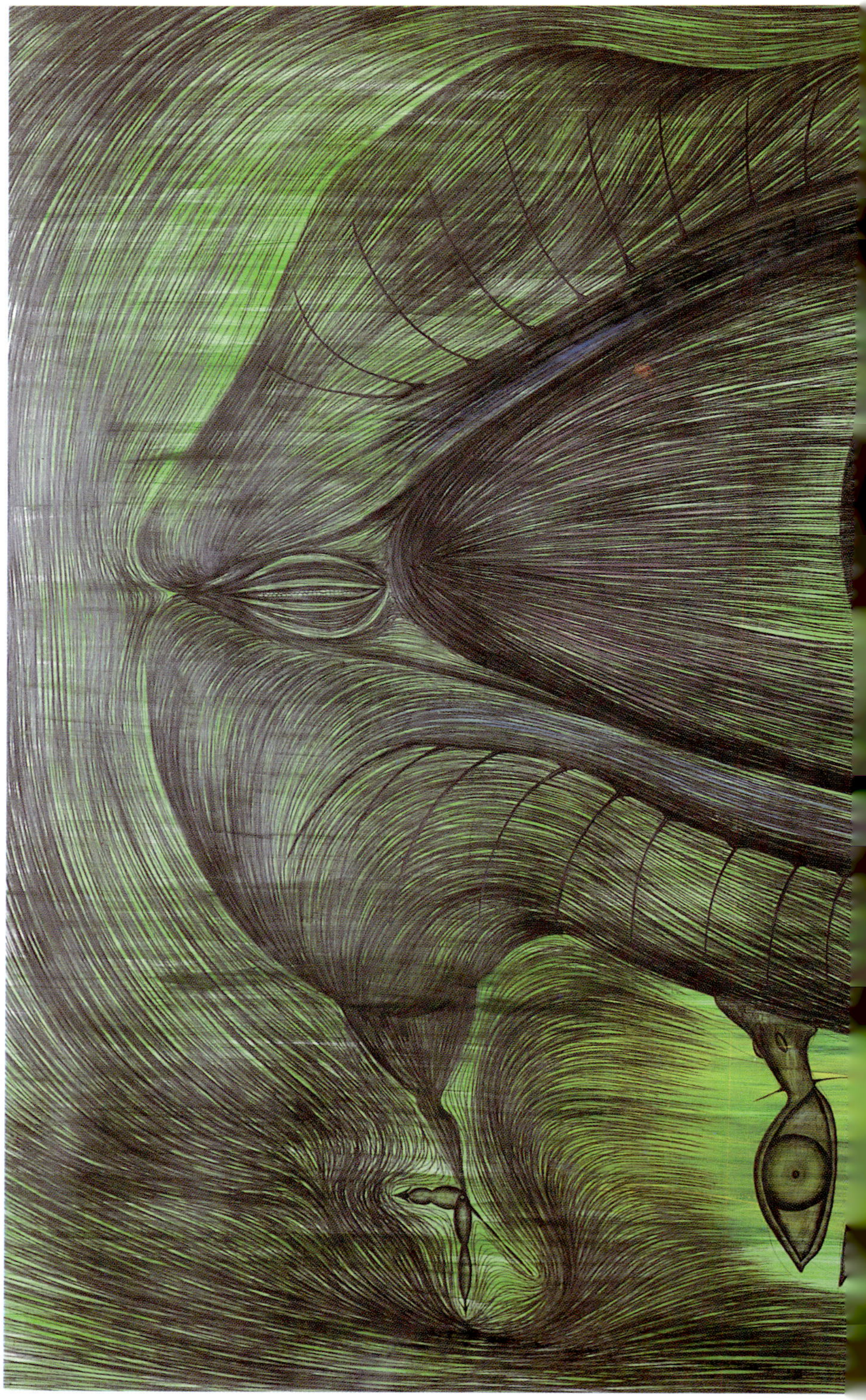

Following page:

Plate 45

The Deformed Artist with no Excuse — the Creature from Self-Portraits — the Clam

Pencil, acrylic wash, on paper

182 x 343 cm

1985

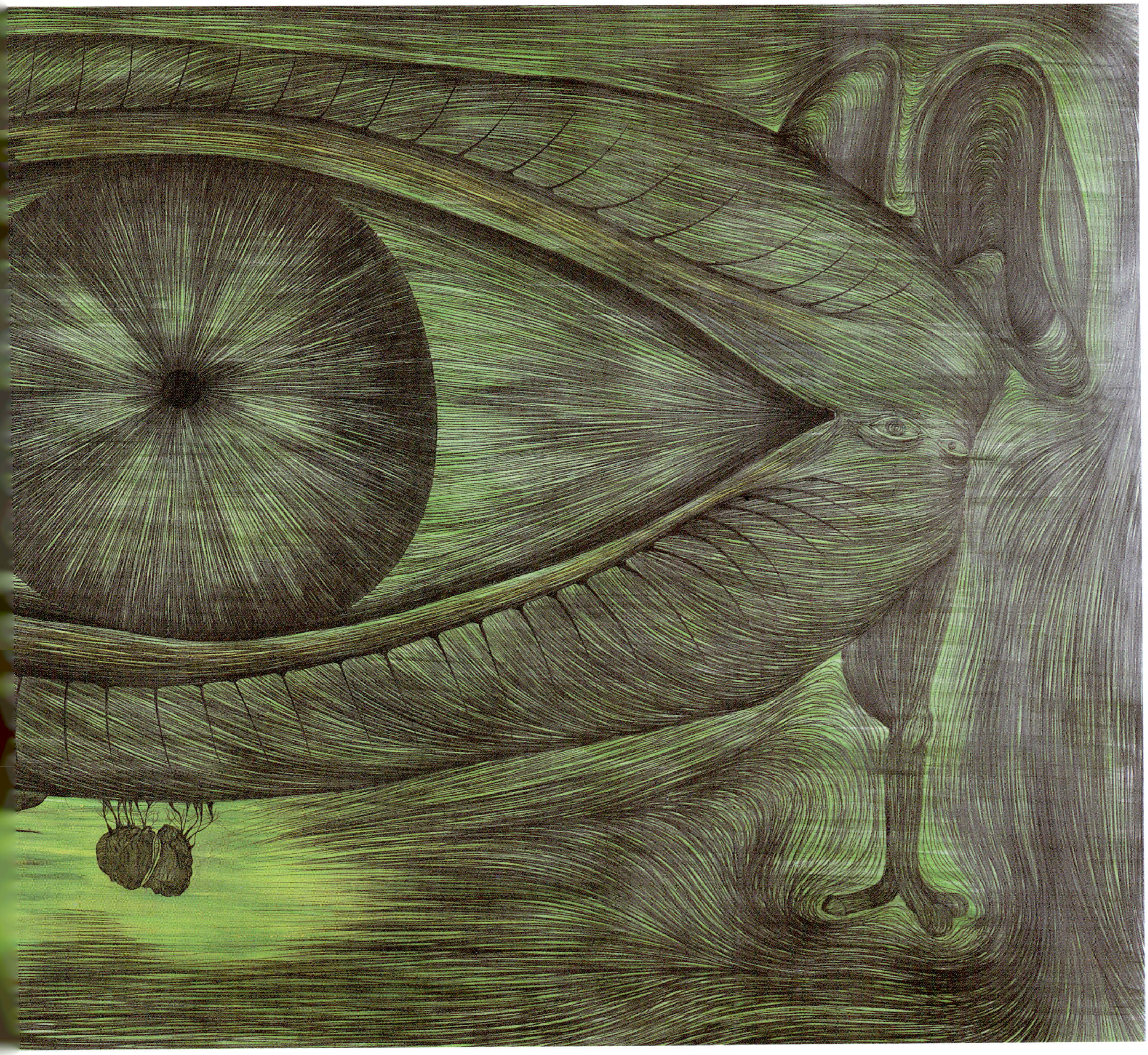

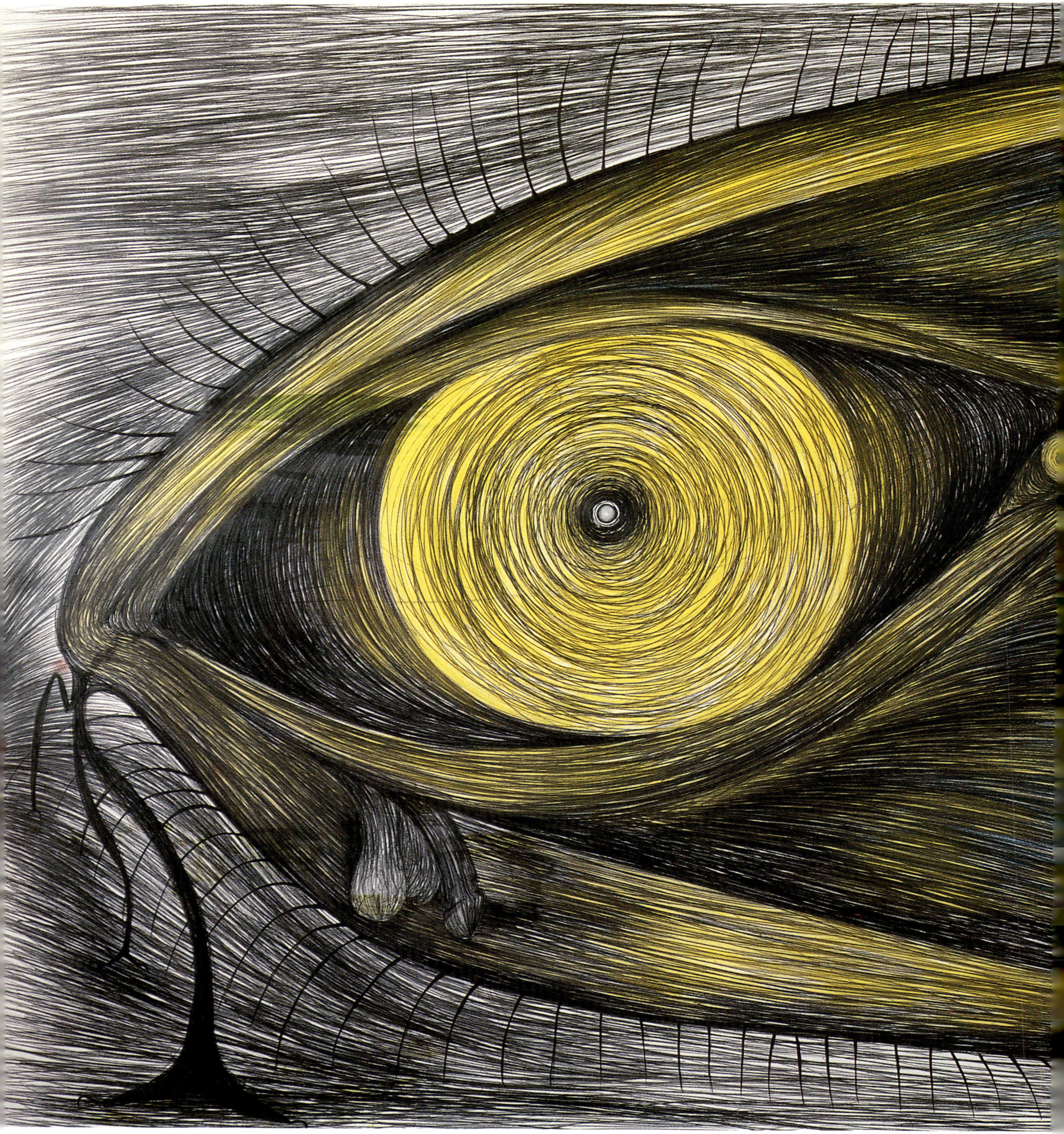

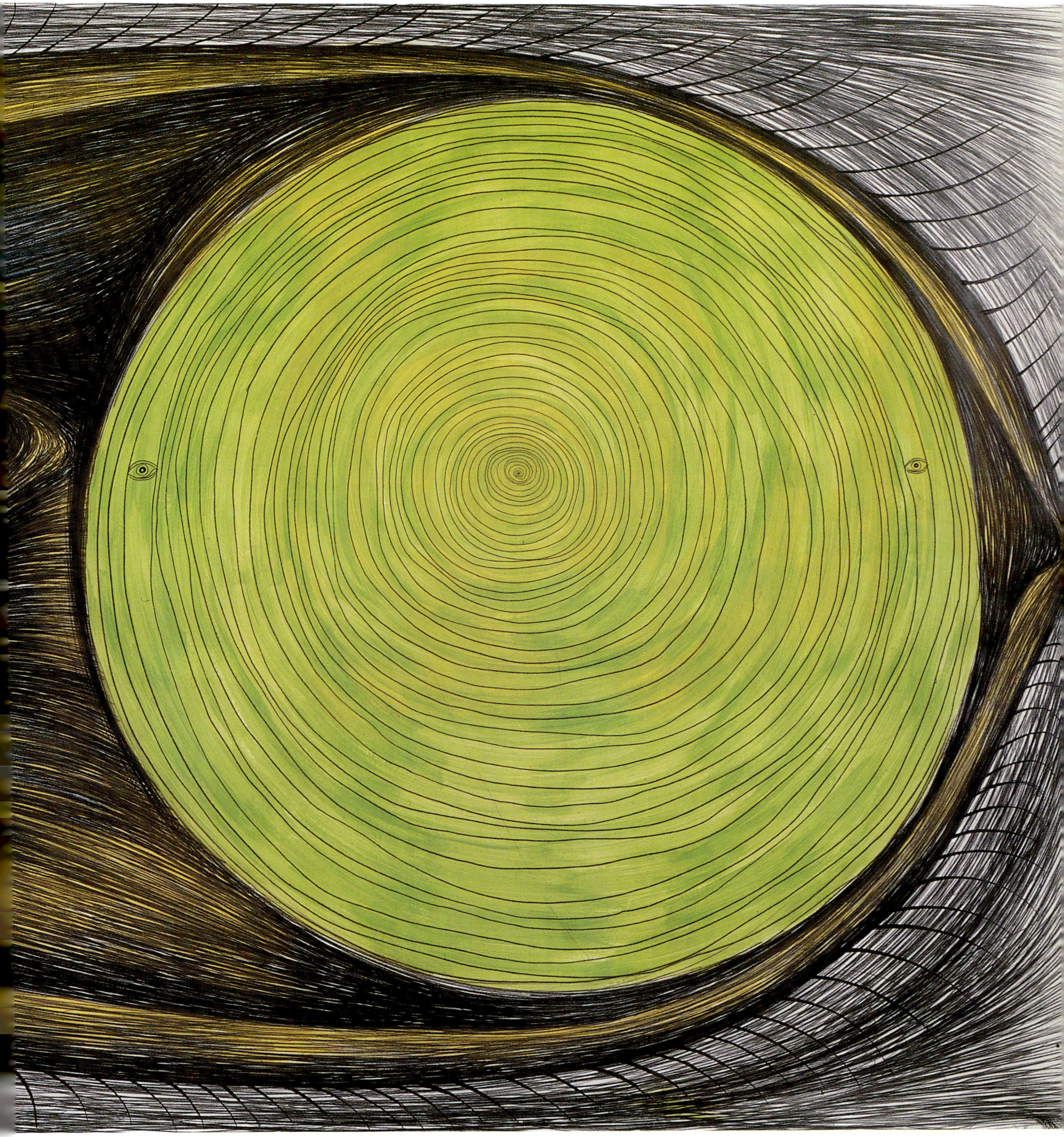

The Black and White Figures

Figure 1
Immortality, The Garden, Foulling the Bed
Pencil on paper
(together 5 drawings) 150 x 525 cm
(each drawing, 150 x 105 cm)
1981
Private collection, Bologna, Italy
Illustrated, part 3, part 4, part 5

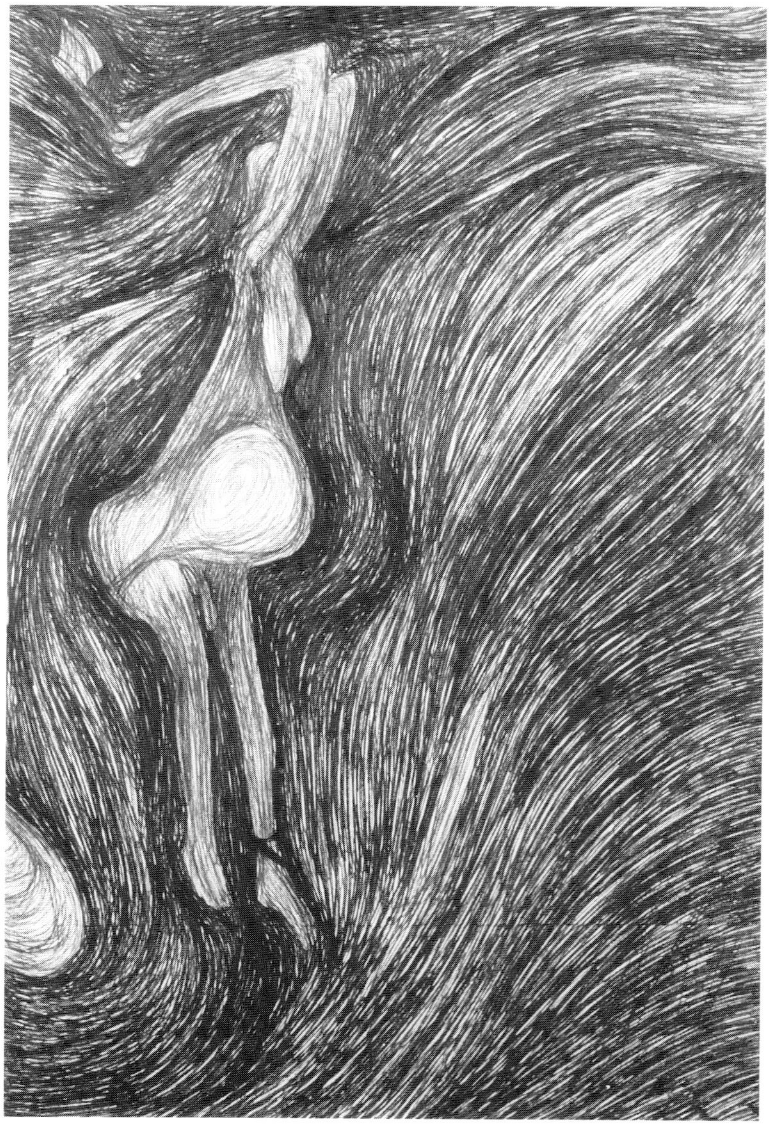

Following page:
Figure 2
Limp Trees that have no Wooden Ships when Migrated
Pencil on paper
269.5 x 669 cm
1982

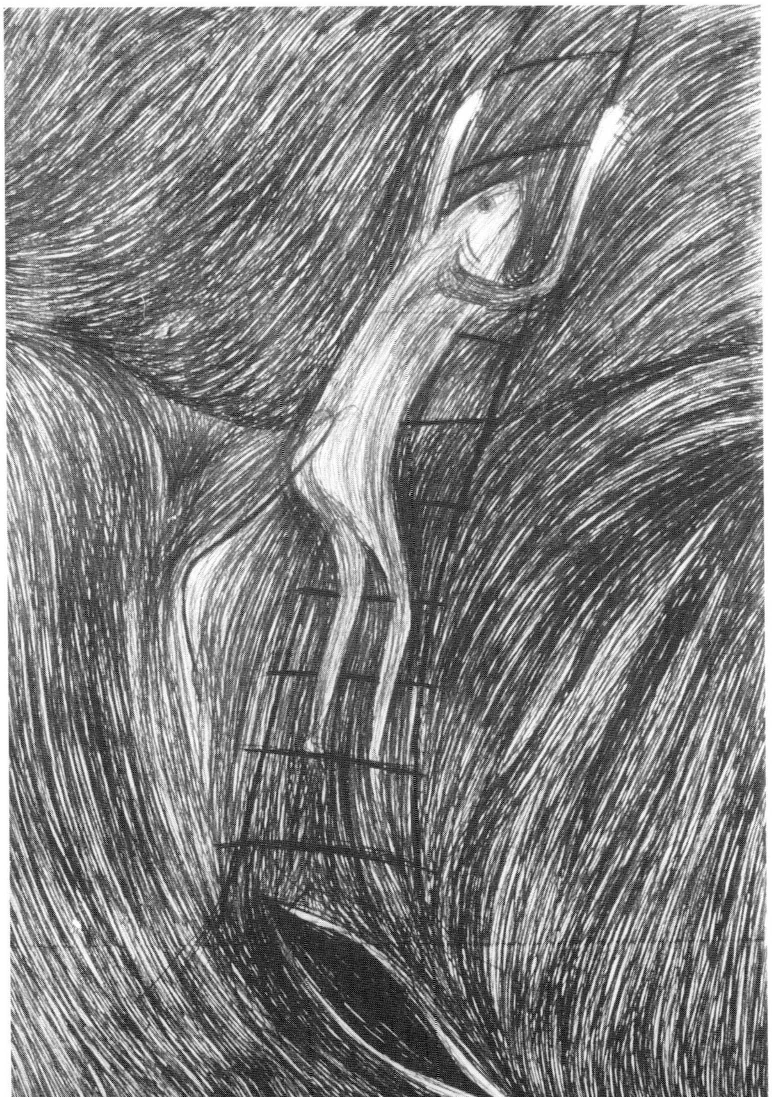

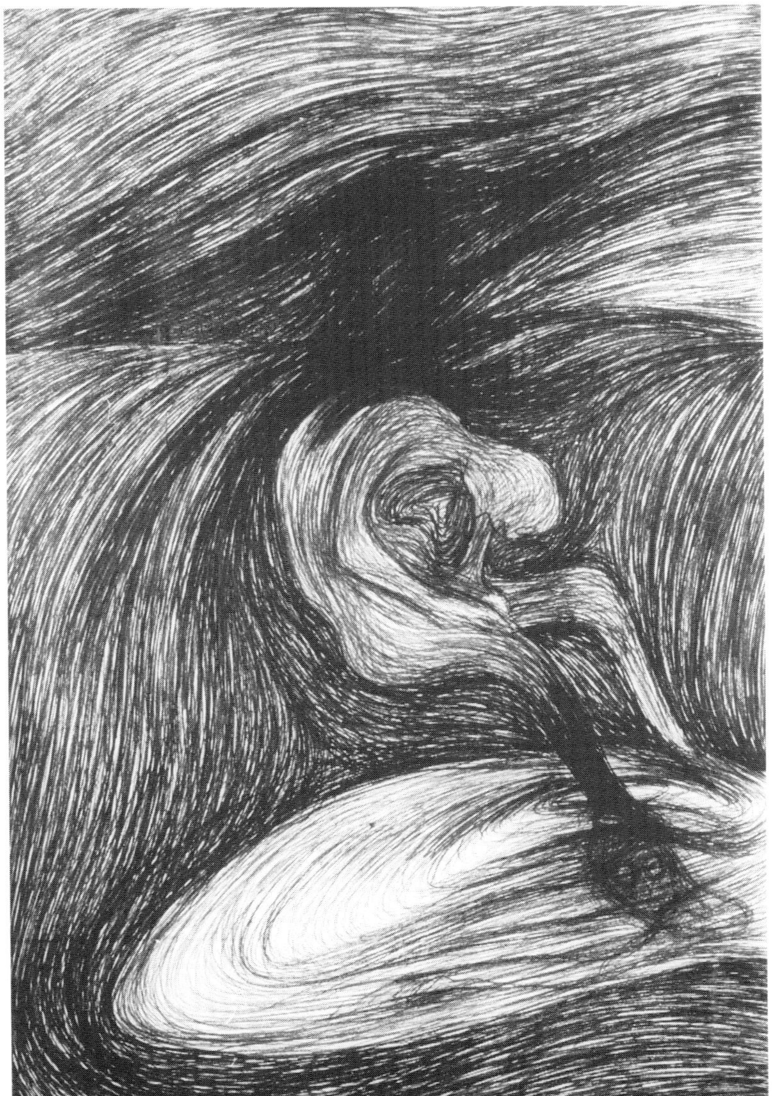

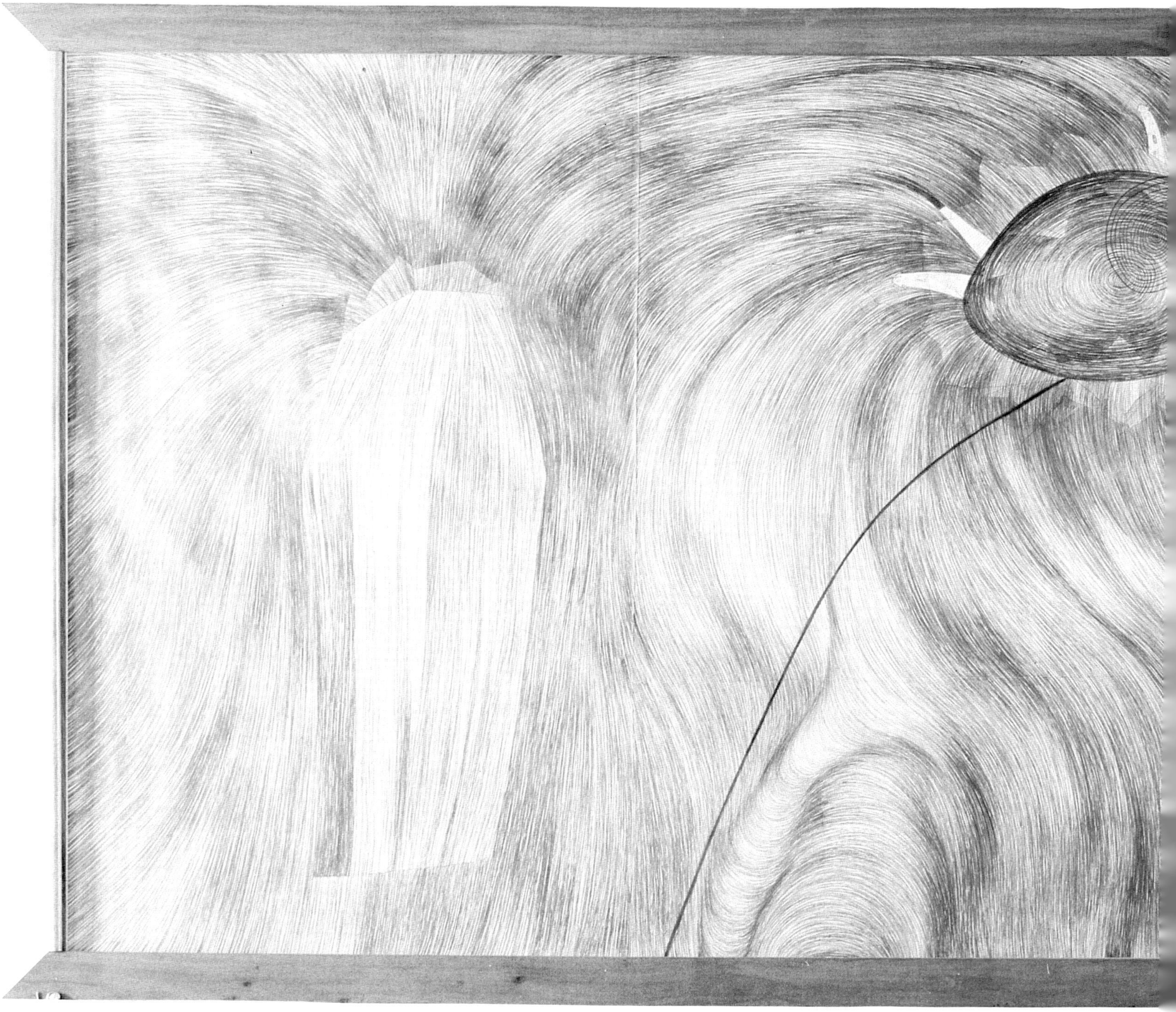

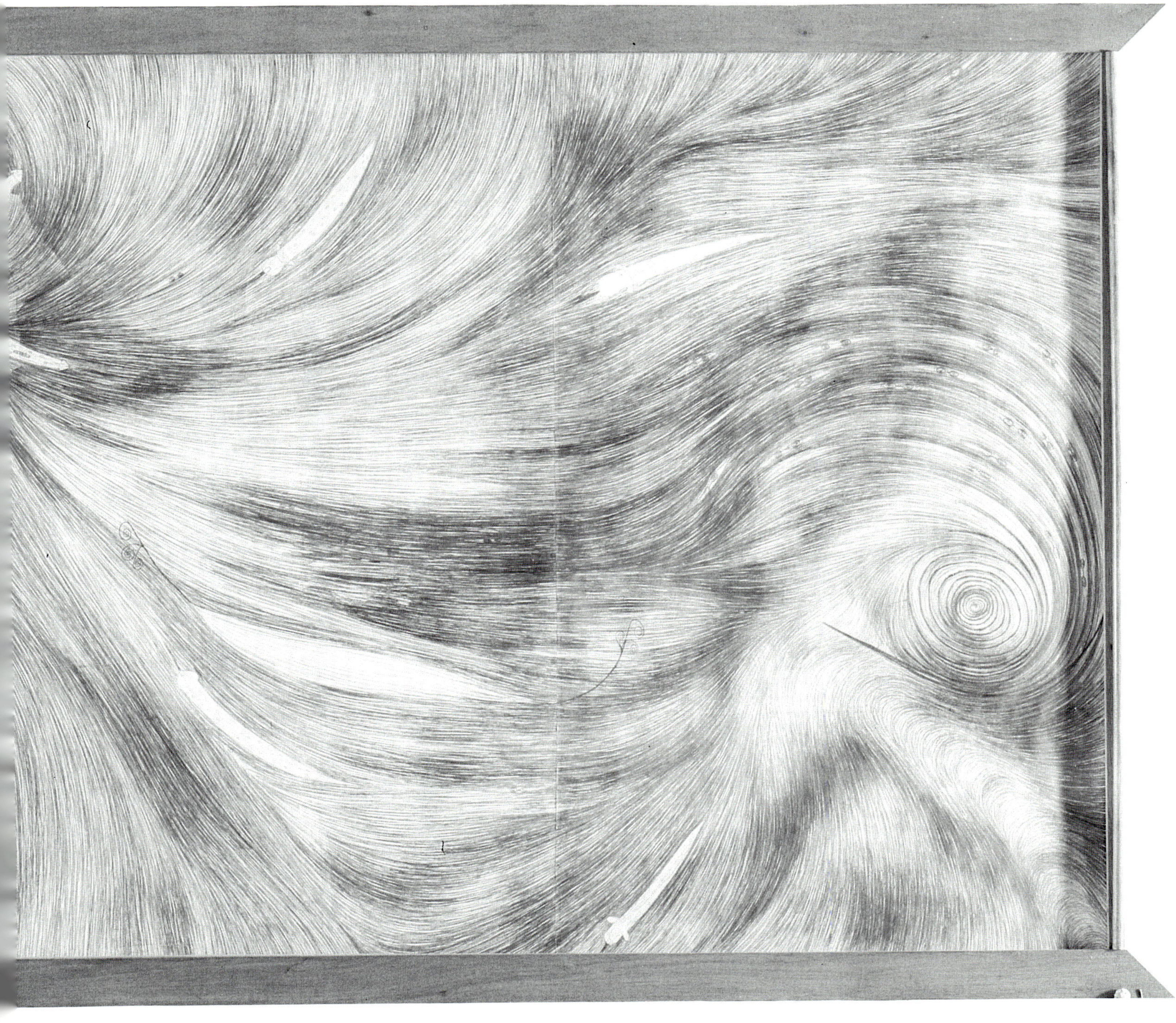

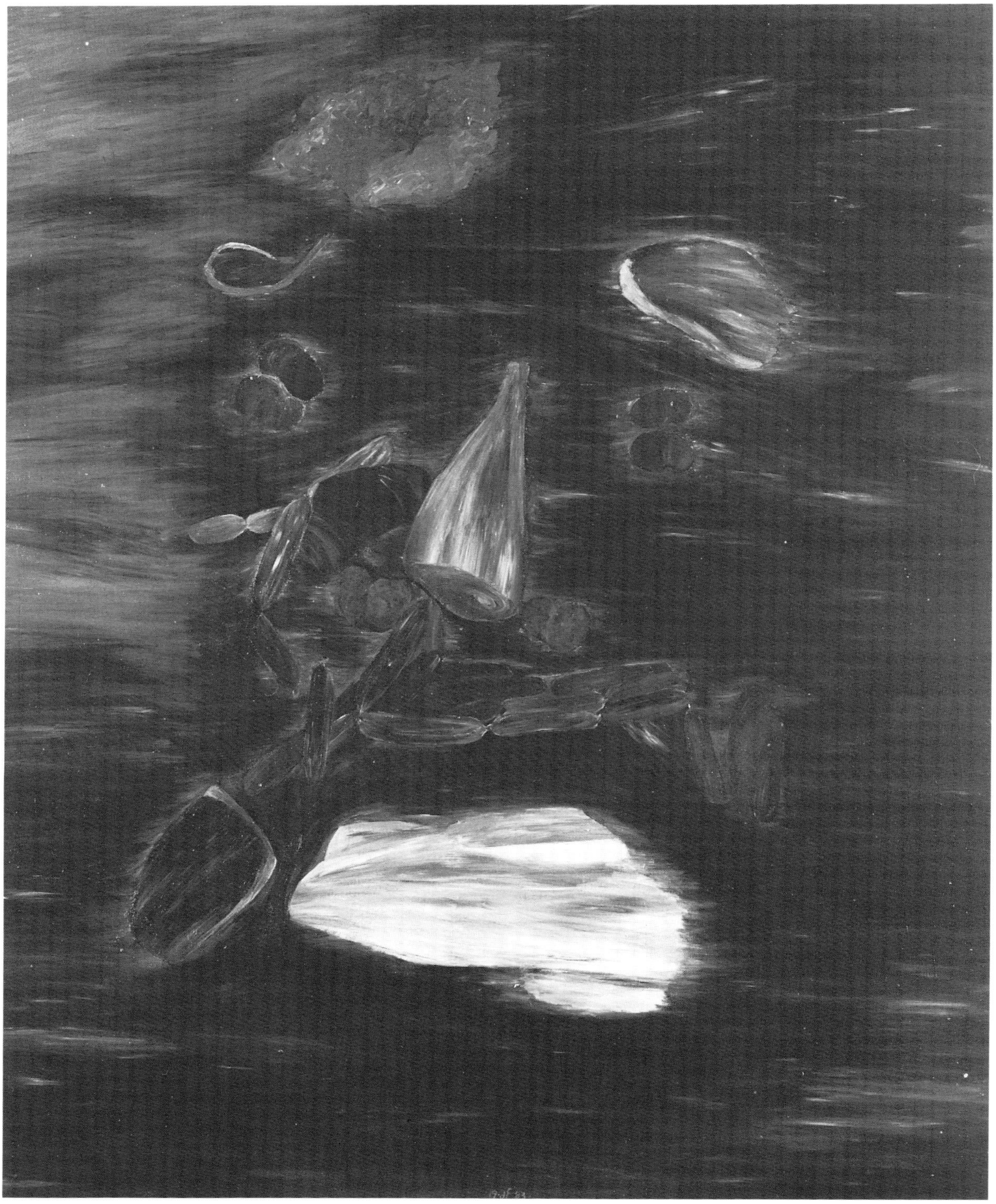

Figure 3
The Fleshy Islands and Red Tide Self-Portrait
Acrylic on canvas
120 x 100 cm
1983

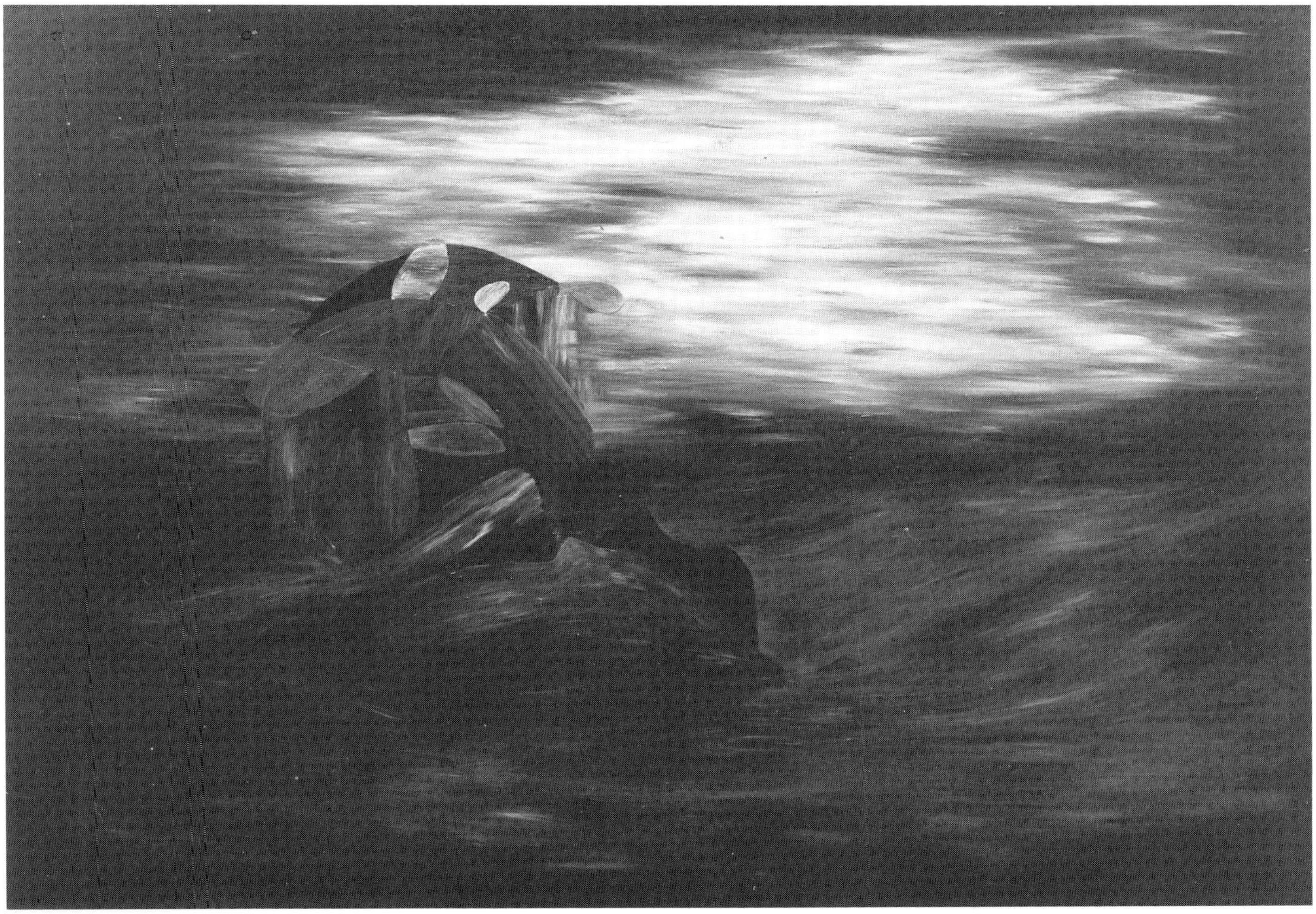

Figure 4
The Island Structure and the Sugar Recollections
Acrylic paint on canvas
125 x 185 cm
1983
Private collection, Sydney

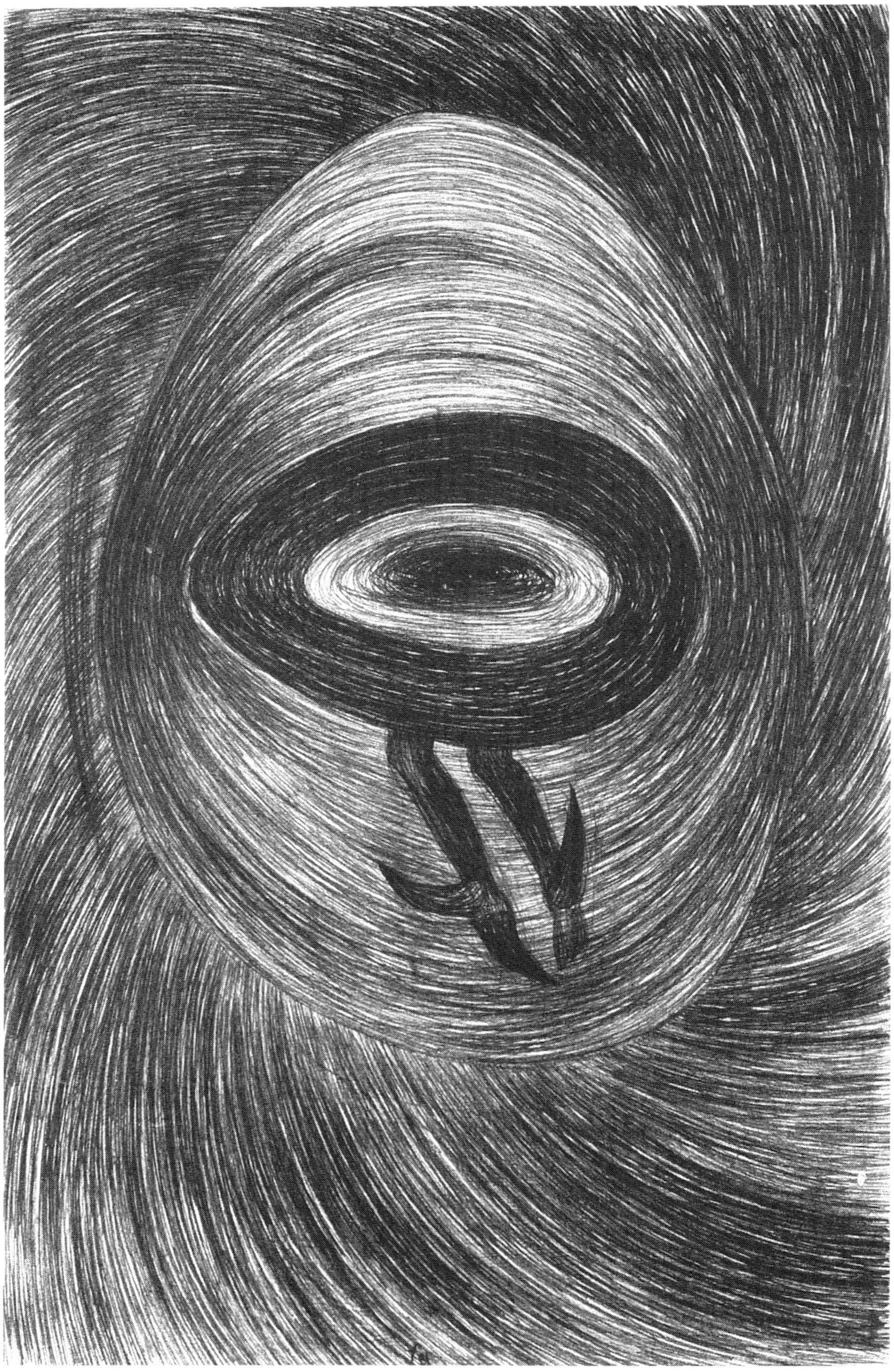

Figure 5
Better Lead Heels than Stung
Pencil on paper
150 x 100 cm
1982
Private collection, Munich, Germany

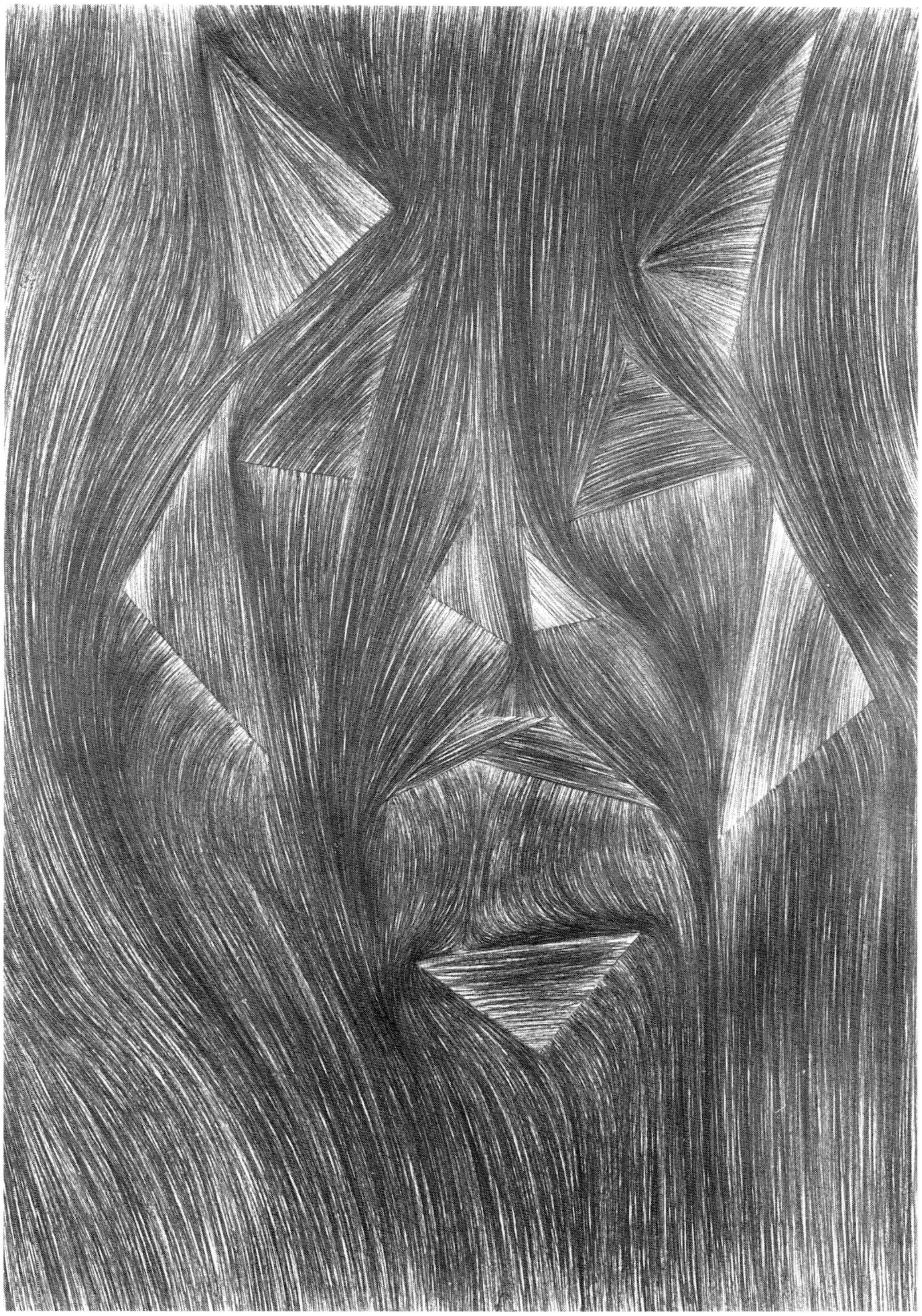

Figure 6
The Found Air and the Mother's Floating Face
Pencil on paper
134 x 94 cm
1982

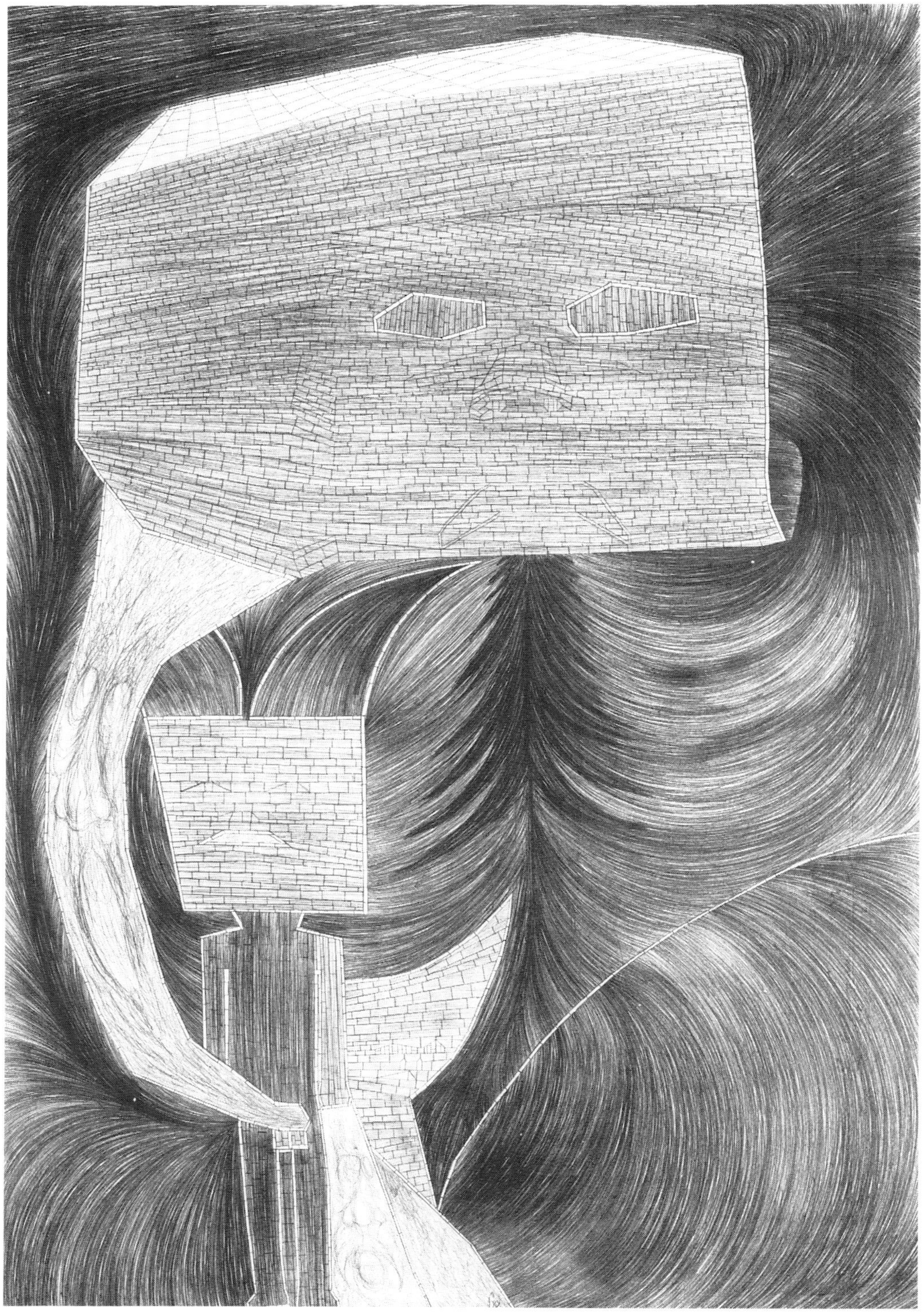

Figure 7
The Longing Expulsion and Self-Portrait
Pencil on paper
188 x 134 cm
1982

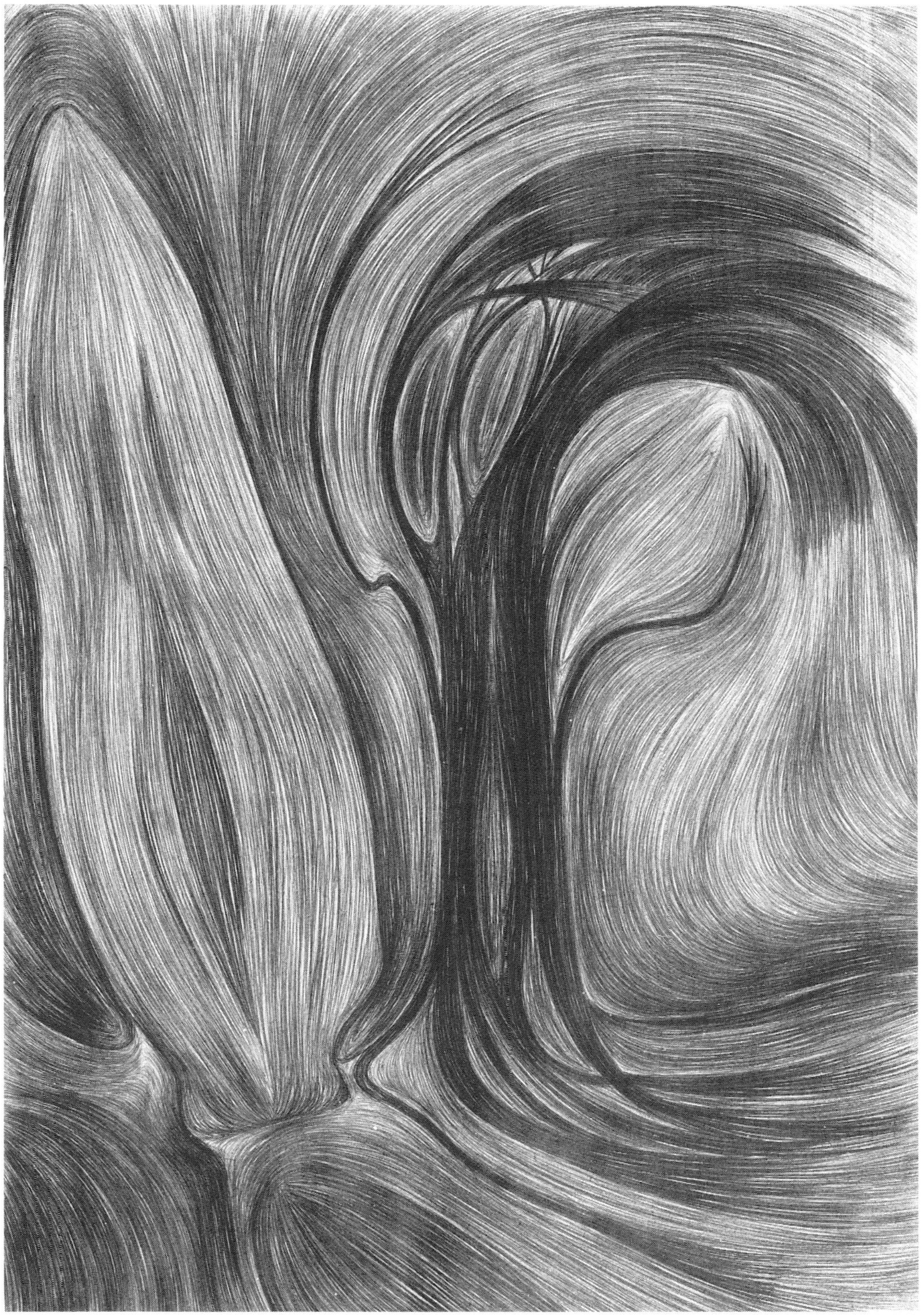

Figure 8
The Sameness in Face and Fear of the Pine
Pencil on paper
188 x 134 cm
1982

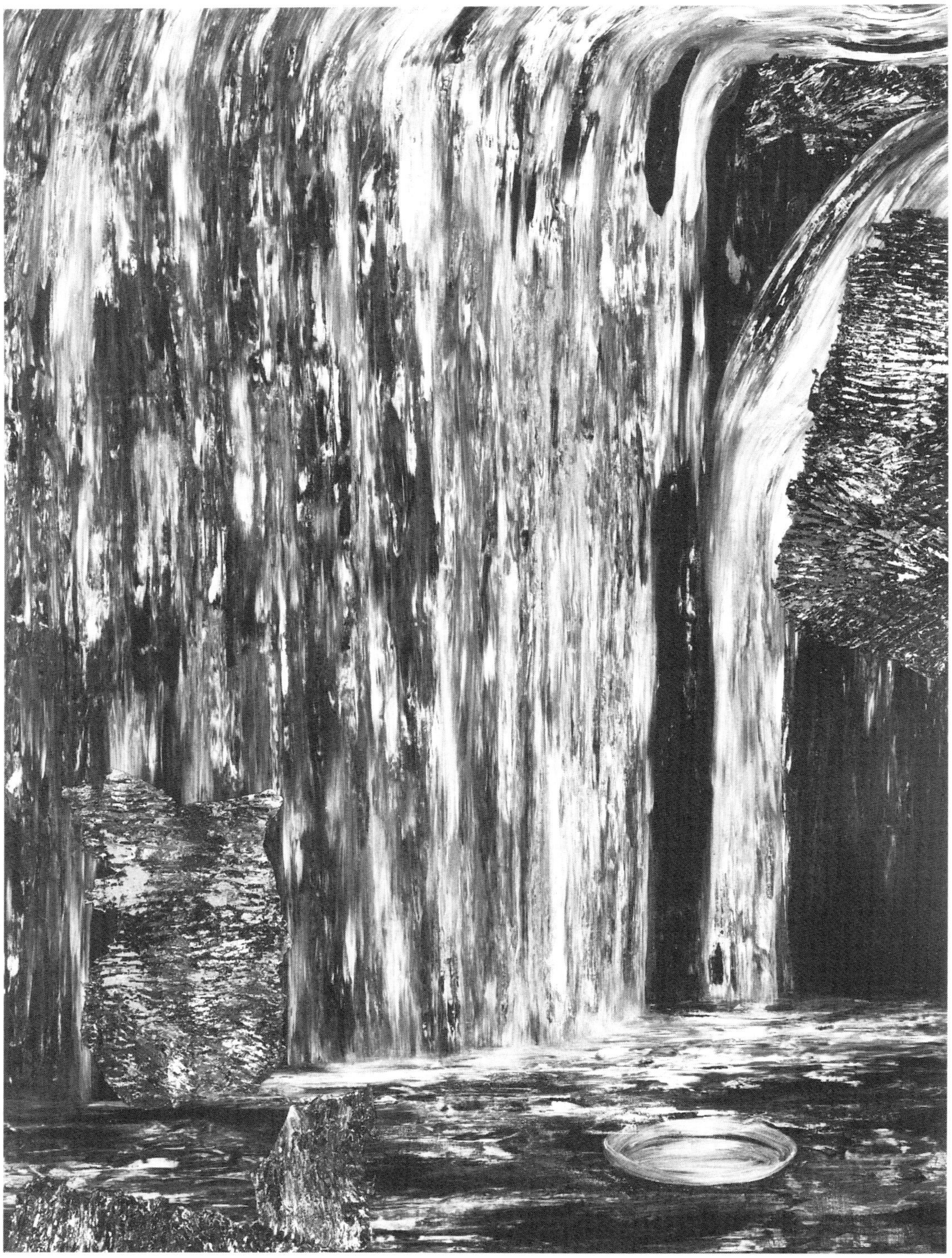

Figure 9
The Studio Falls (The Sleeping after the Light)
Acrylic on canvas
240 x 180 cm
1984
Private collection, New York

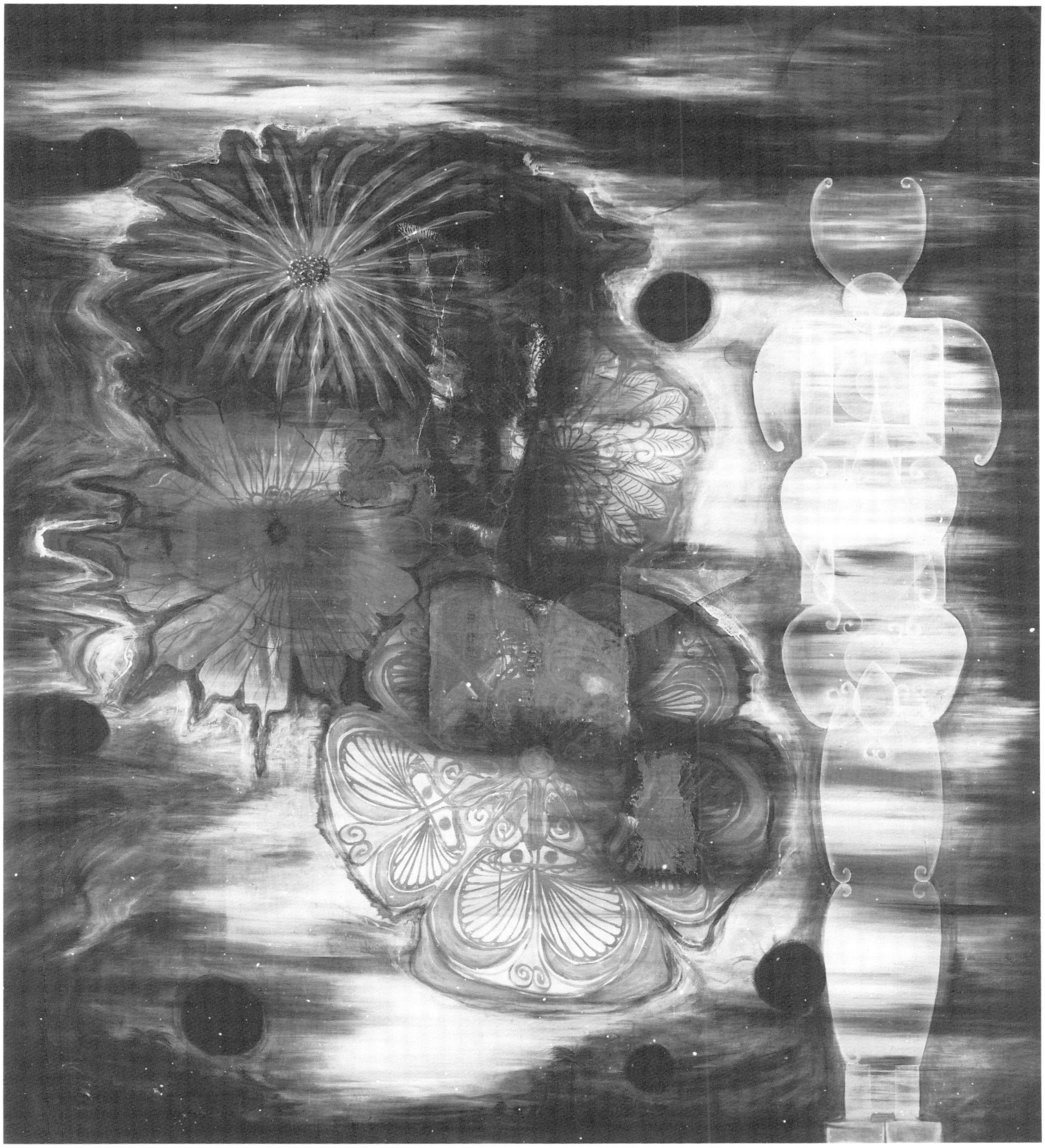

Figure 10
The Four Flowers of Death in the Tropics with an Oscar to Pat
Acrylic paint on canvas
200 x 180 cm
1986
Private collection, New York

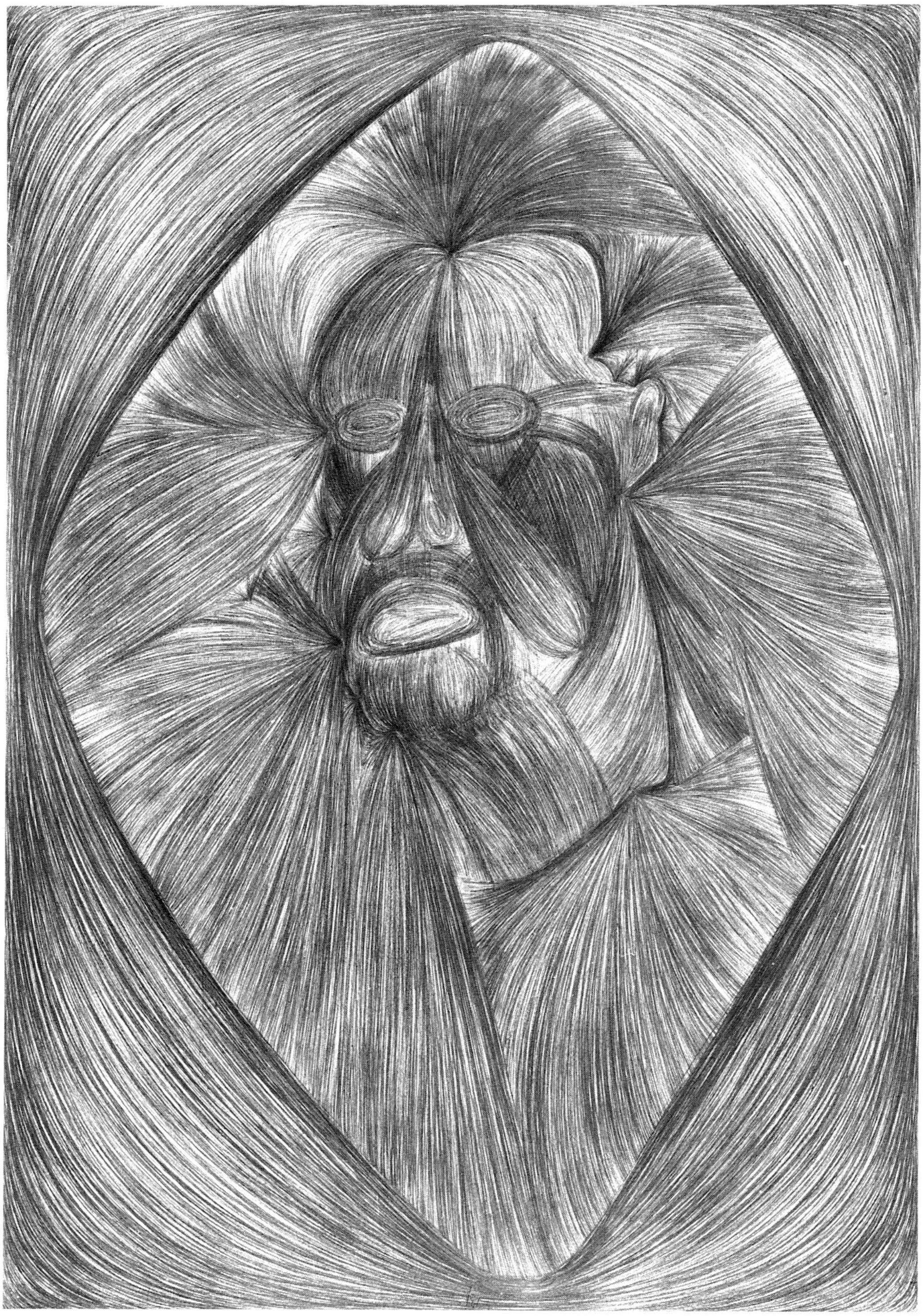

Figure 11
Self-Portrait as Pitiful Light and Mountain Peaks
Pencil on paper
188 x 134 cm
1982

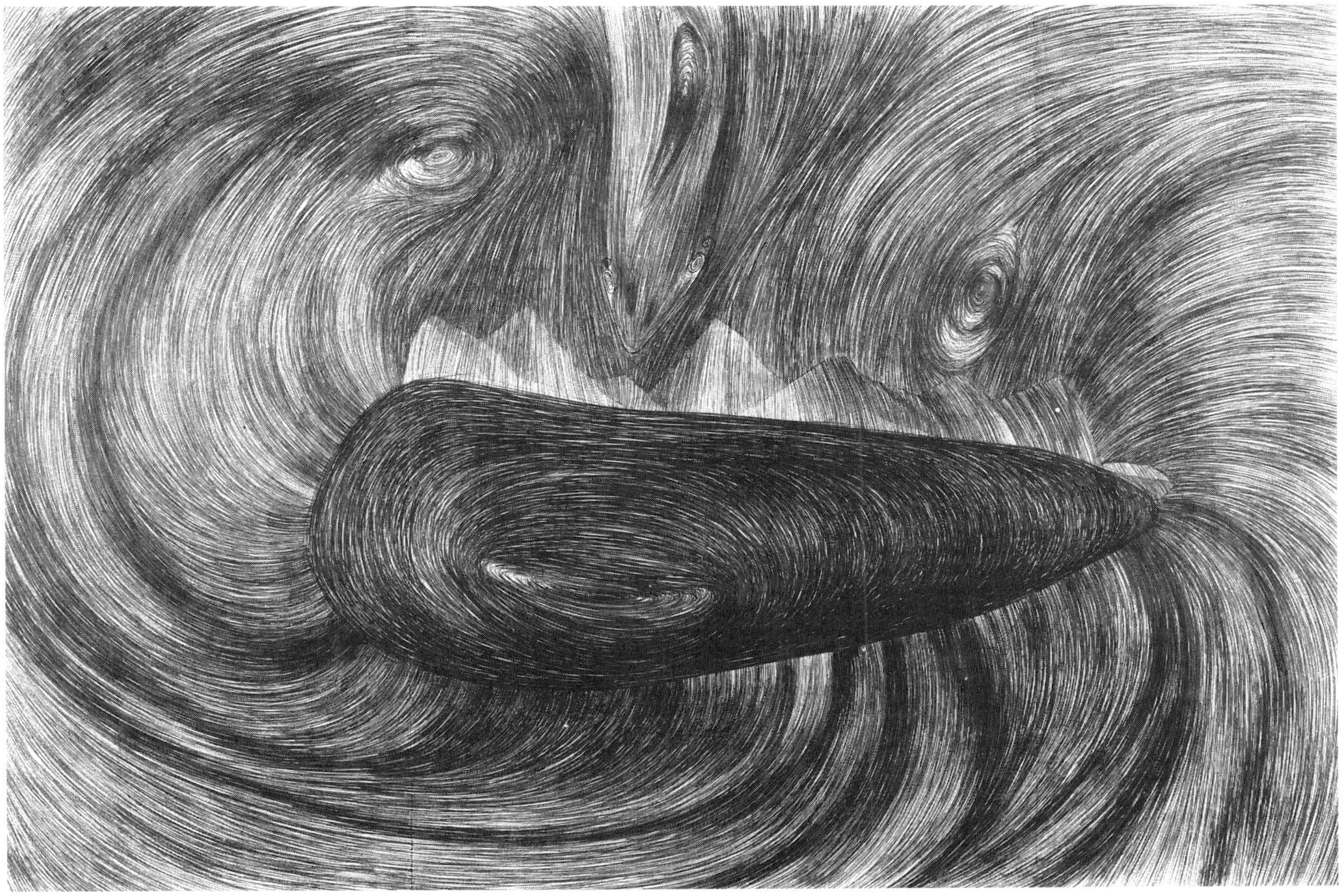

Figure 12
The Sinclair House Beats the Peak Sunsets
Pencil on paper
180 x 268 cm
1982
Collection of Naracoorte Regional Gallery, Australia

Following page:
Figure 13
The Hierophant's Cancerous Oats
Pencil on paper
188 x 268 cm
1982

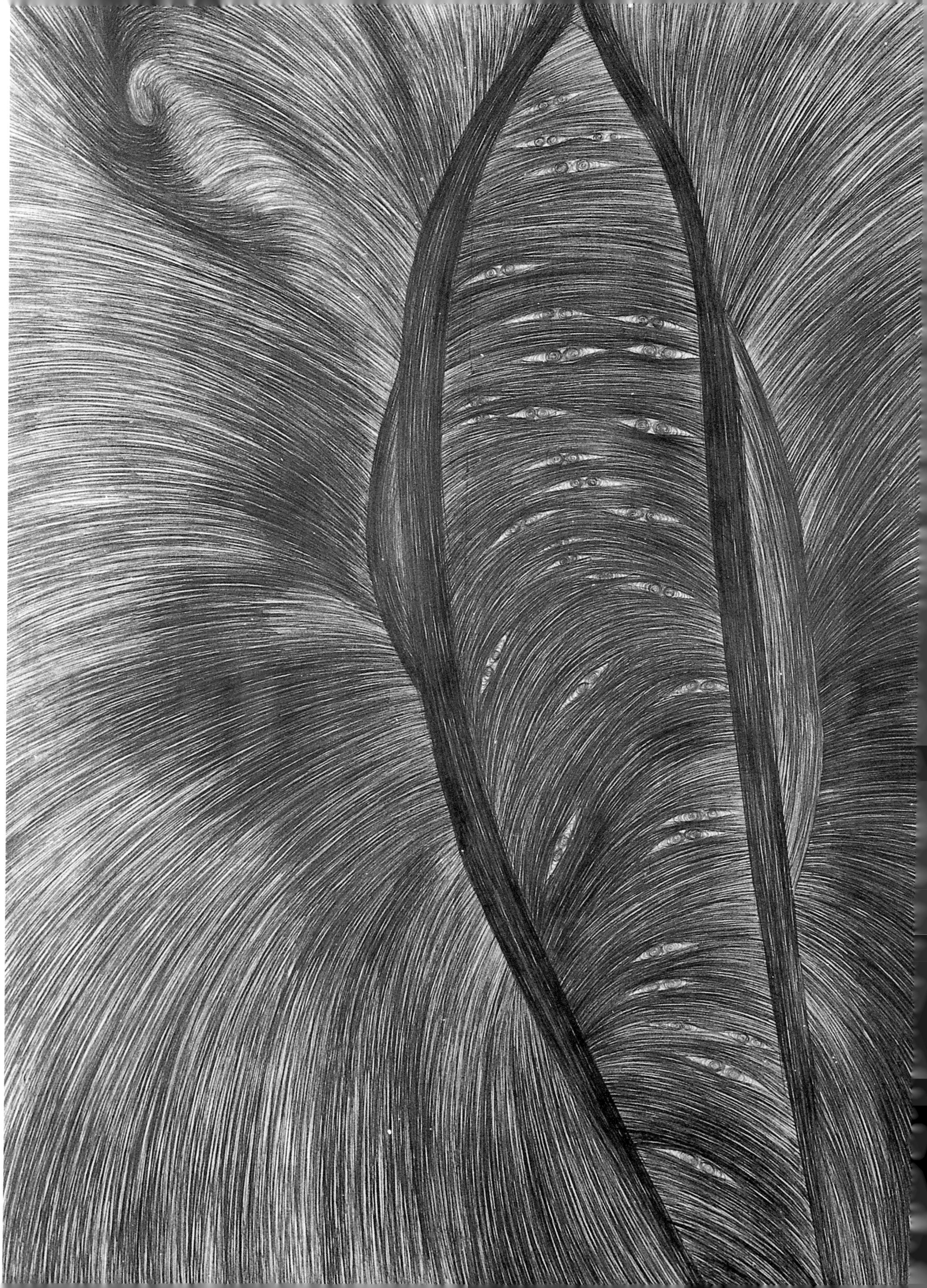

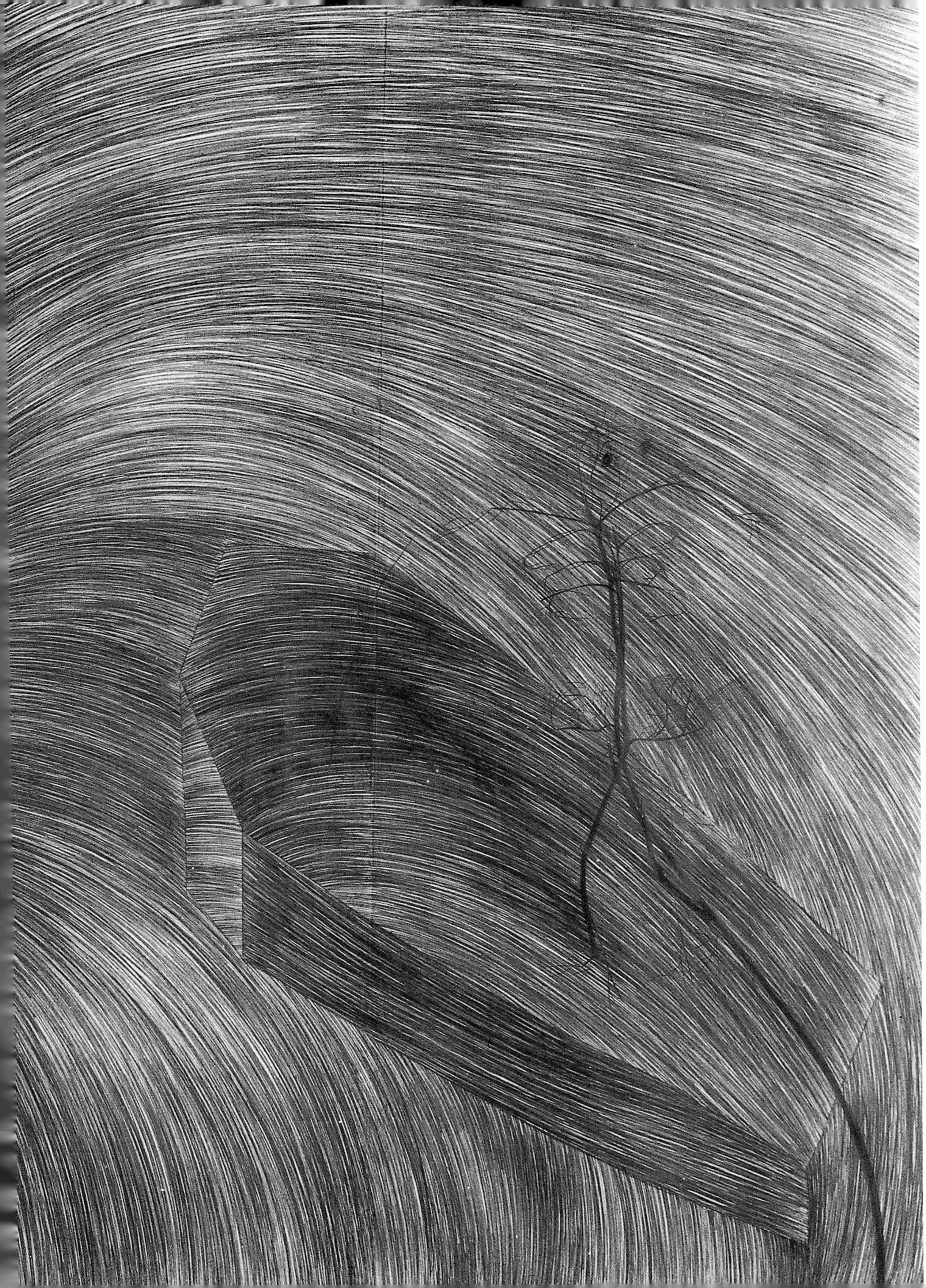

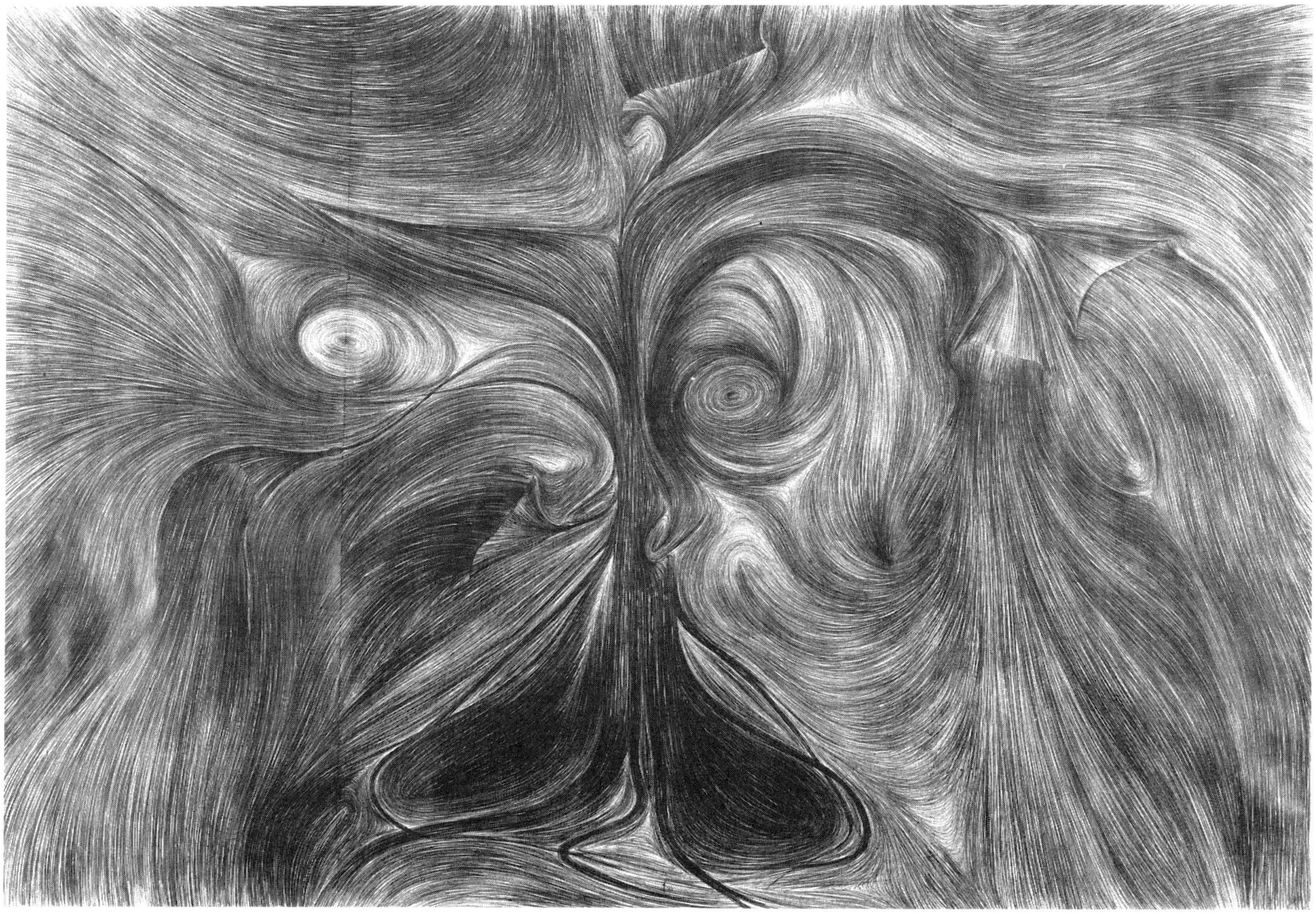

Figure 14
The Appealing Eyes of the Blacksmith Facing the Tyrant
Pencil on paper
188 x 268 cm
1982
Collection of National Gallery of Victoria, Melbourne

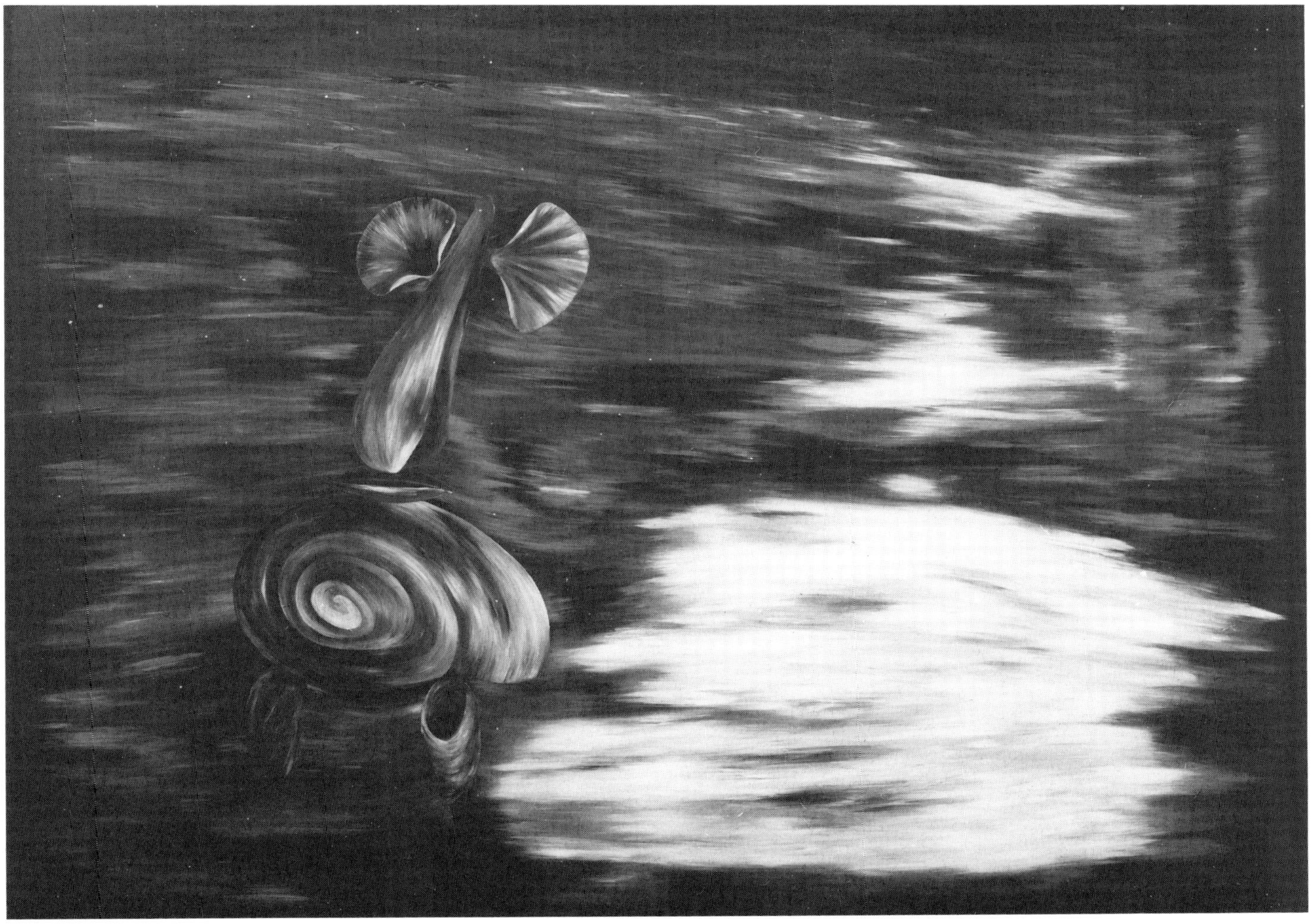

Figure 15
The Tide at the Watershed and the Lemon Peel
Acrylic paint on canvas
200 x 278 cm
1984
Private collection, Milan, Italy

Following page:
Figure 16
Self-Portrait at 21 with Milk Maids
Pencil on paper
157 x 290 cm
1983
Collection of National Gallery of New Zealand, Wellington

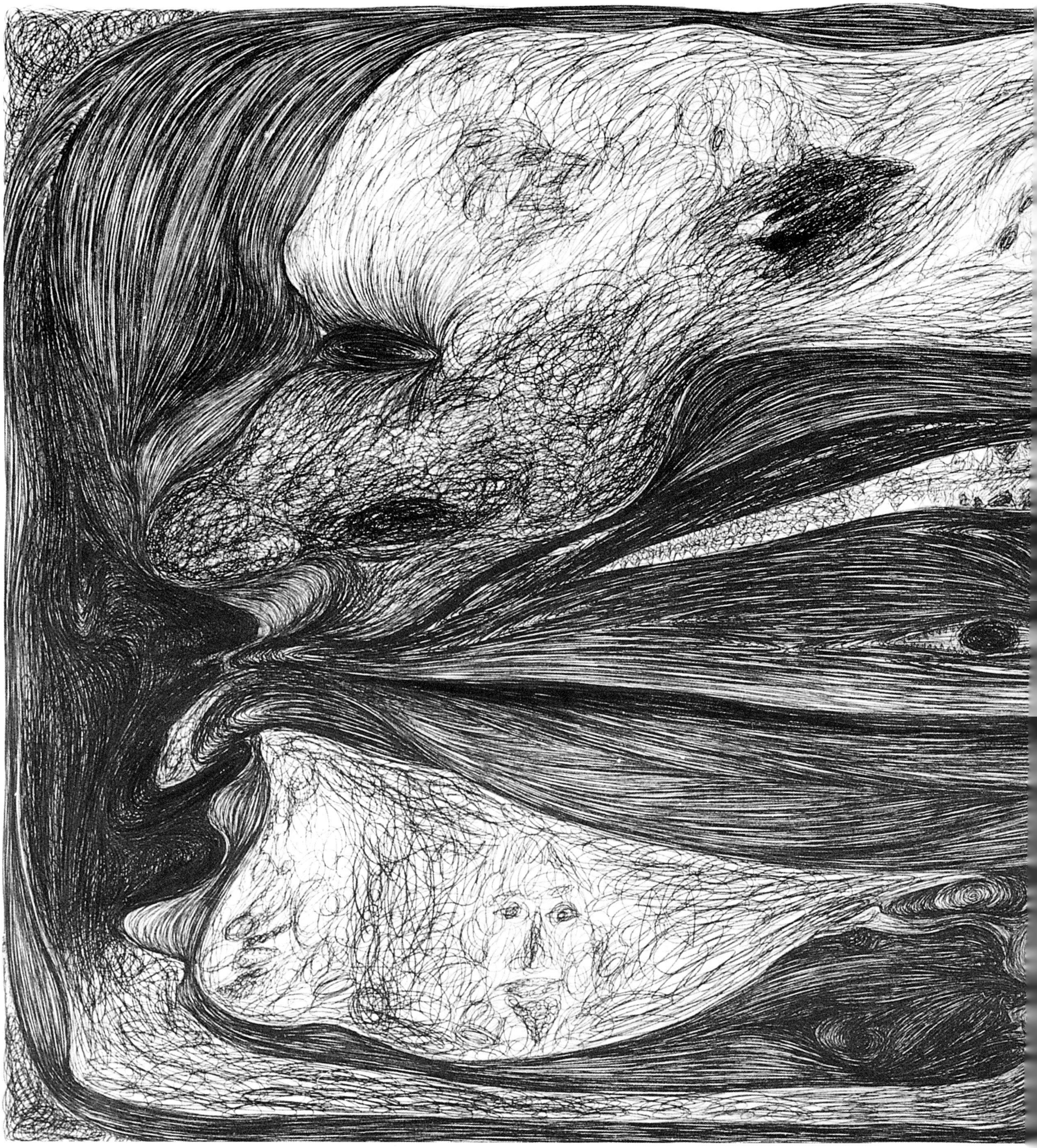

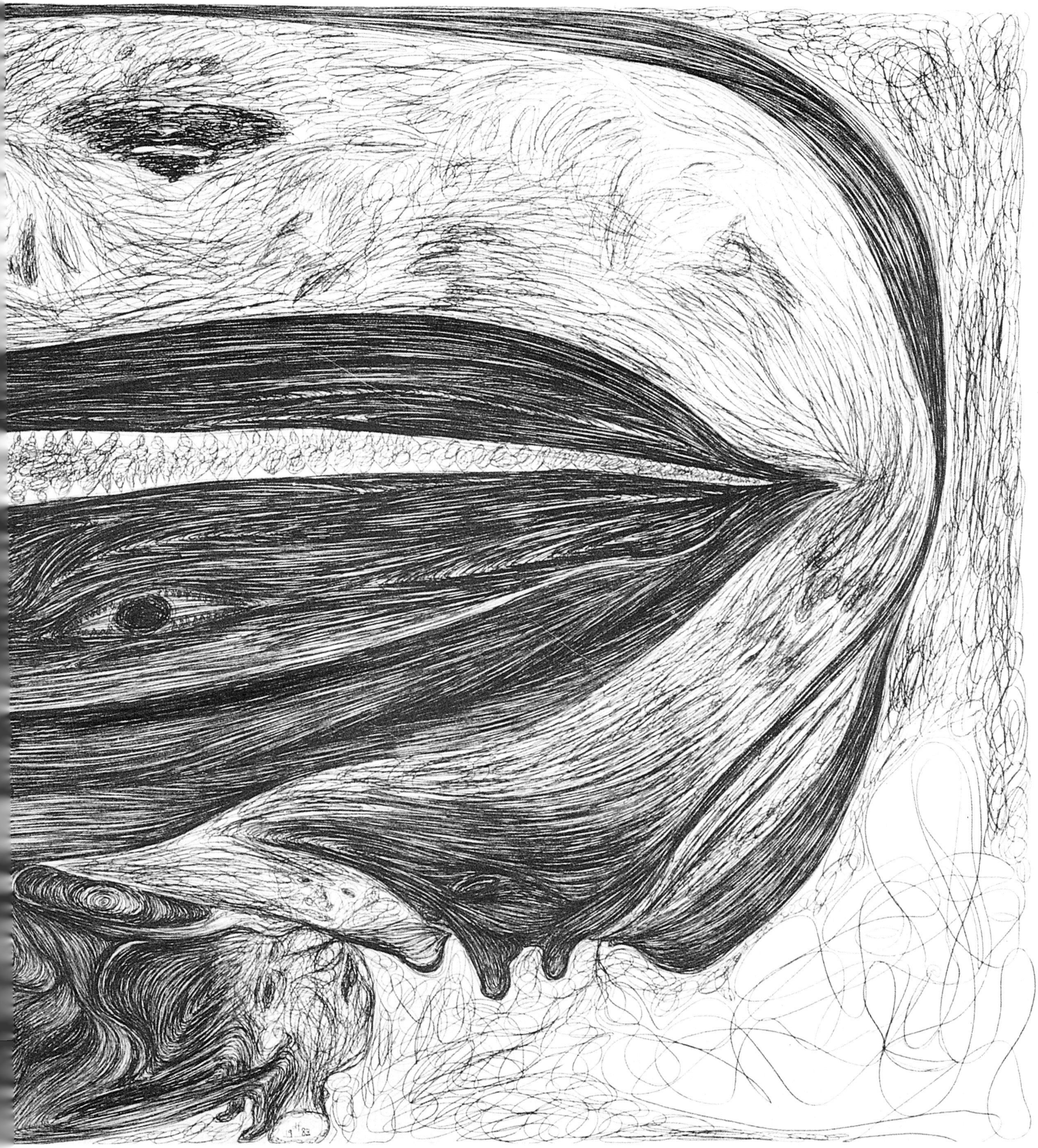

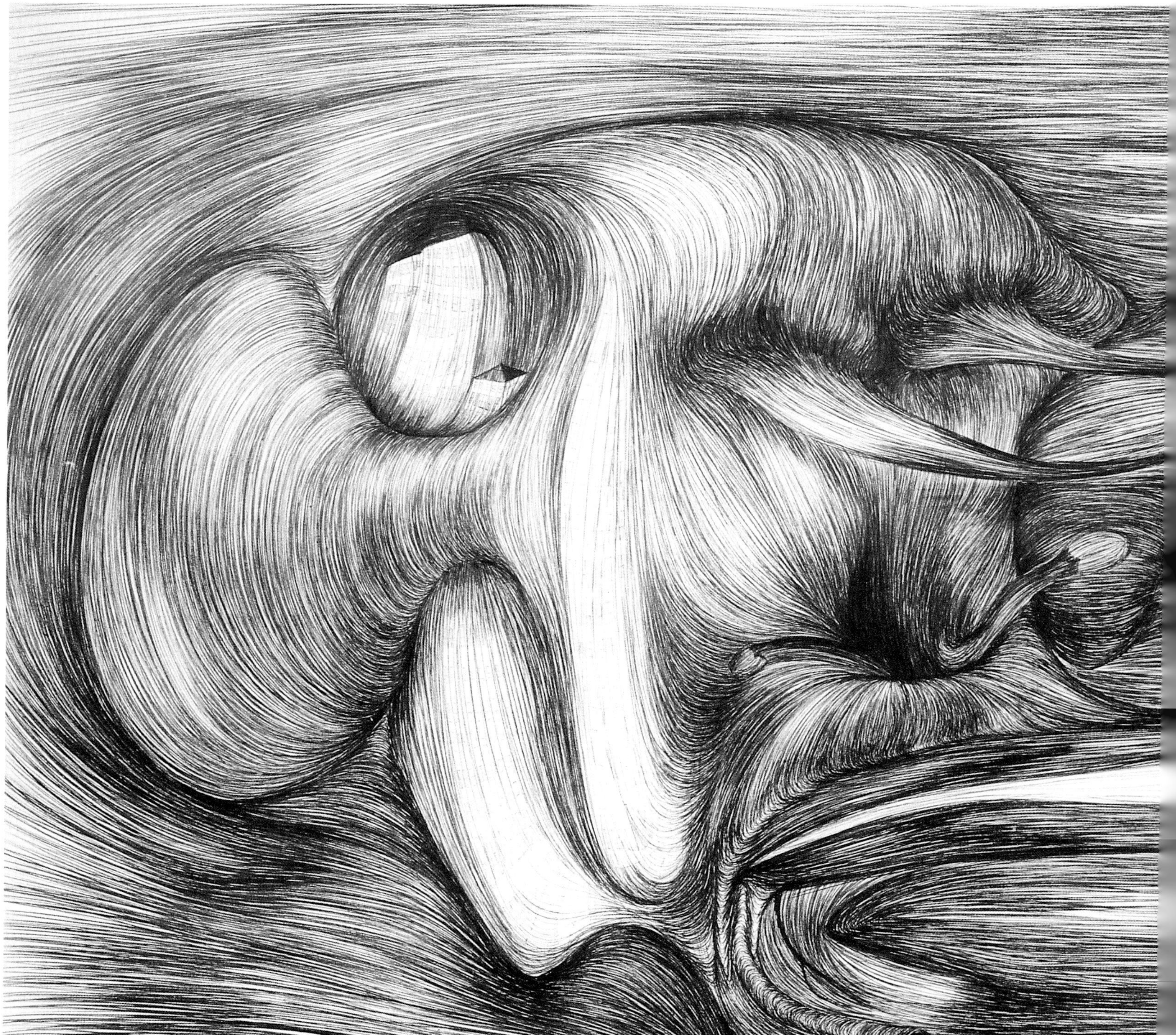

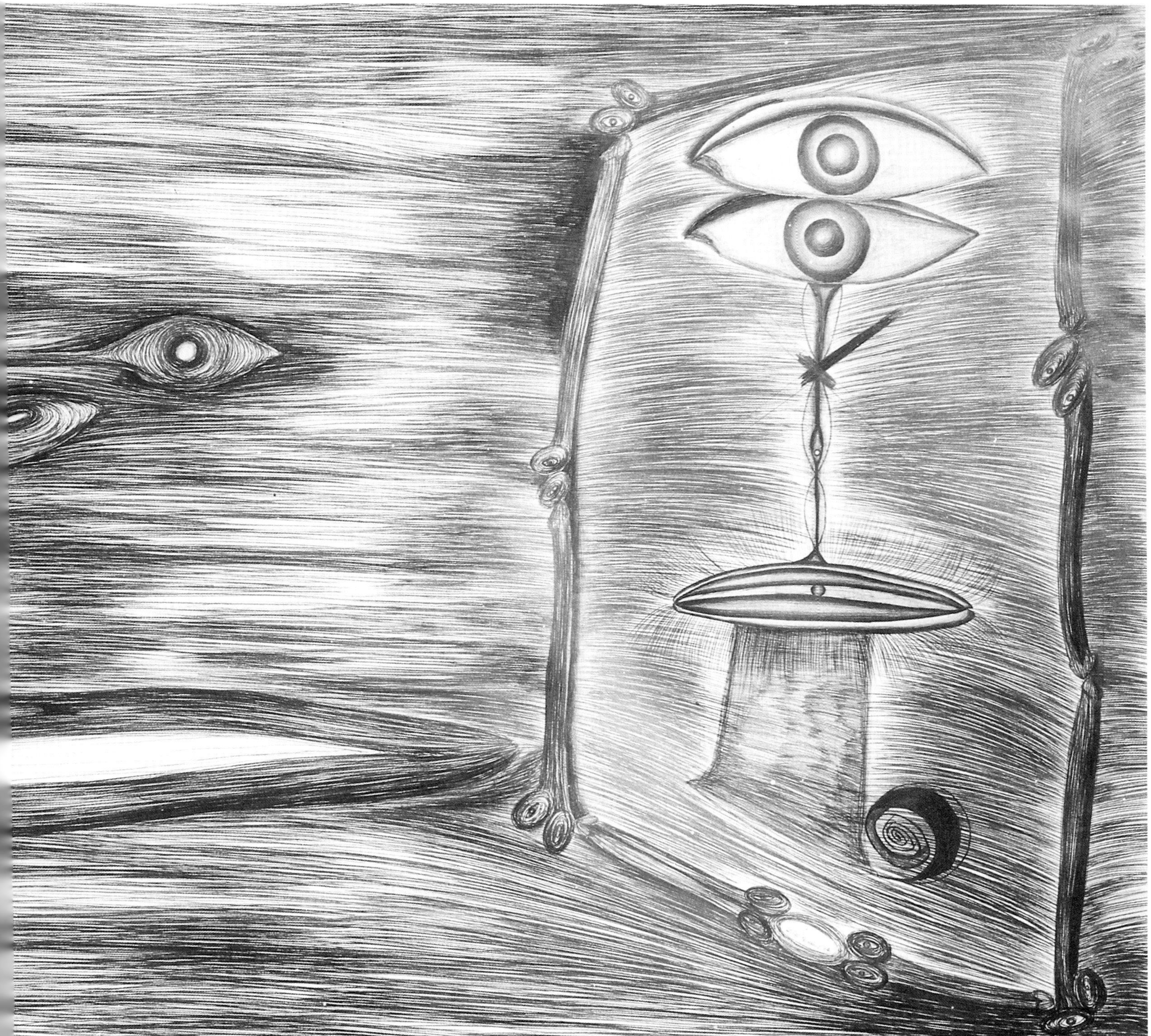

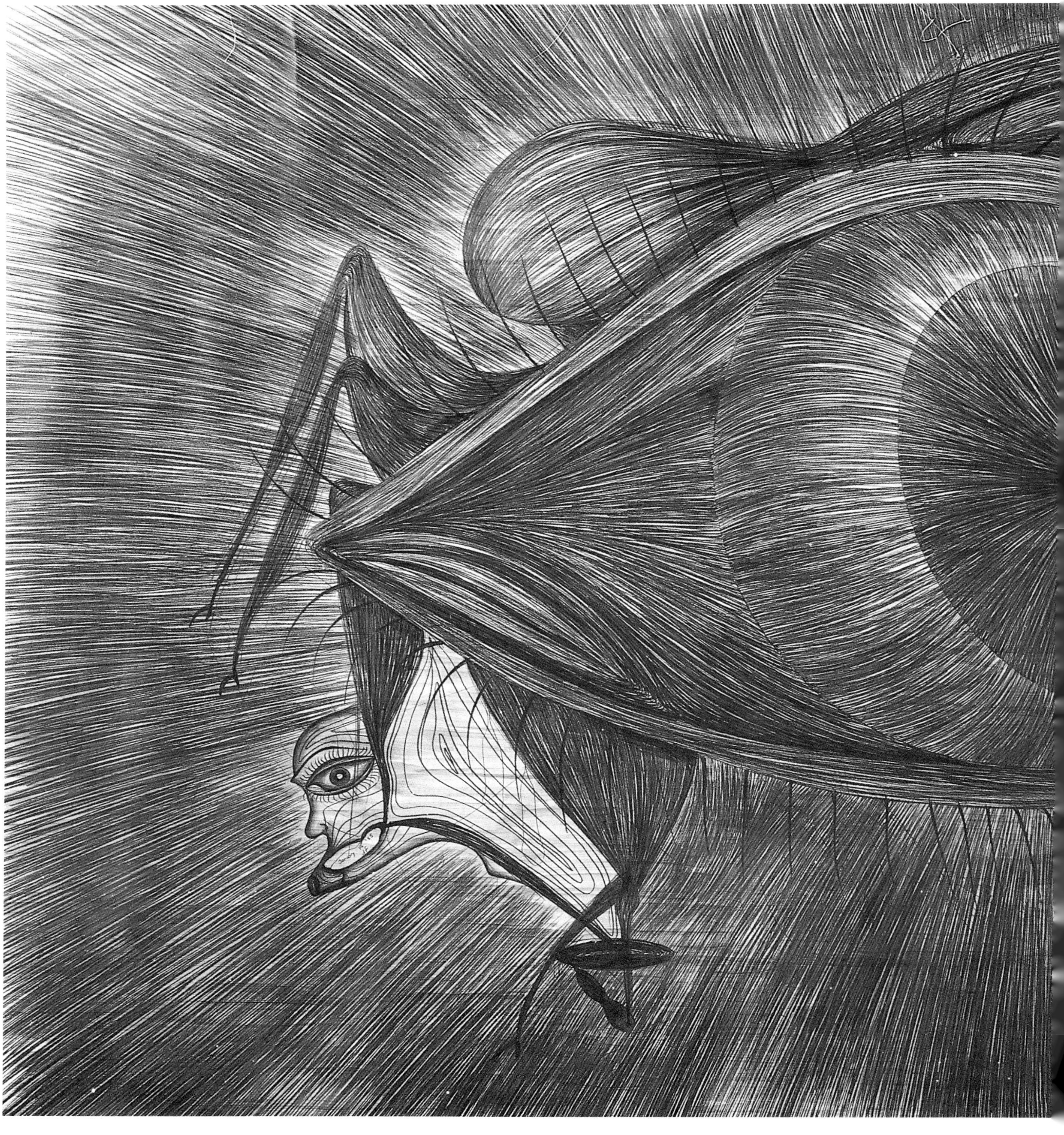

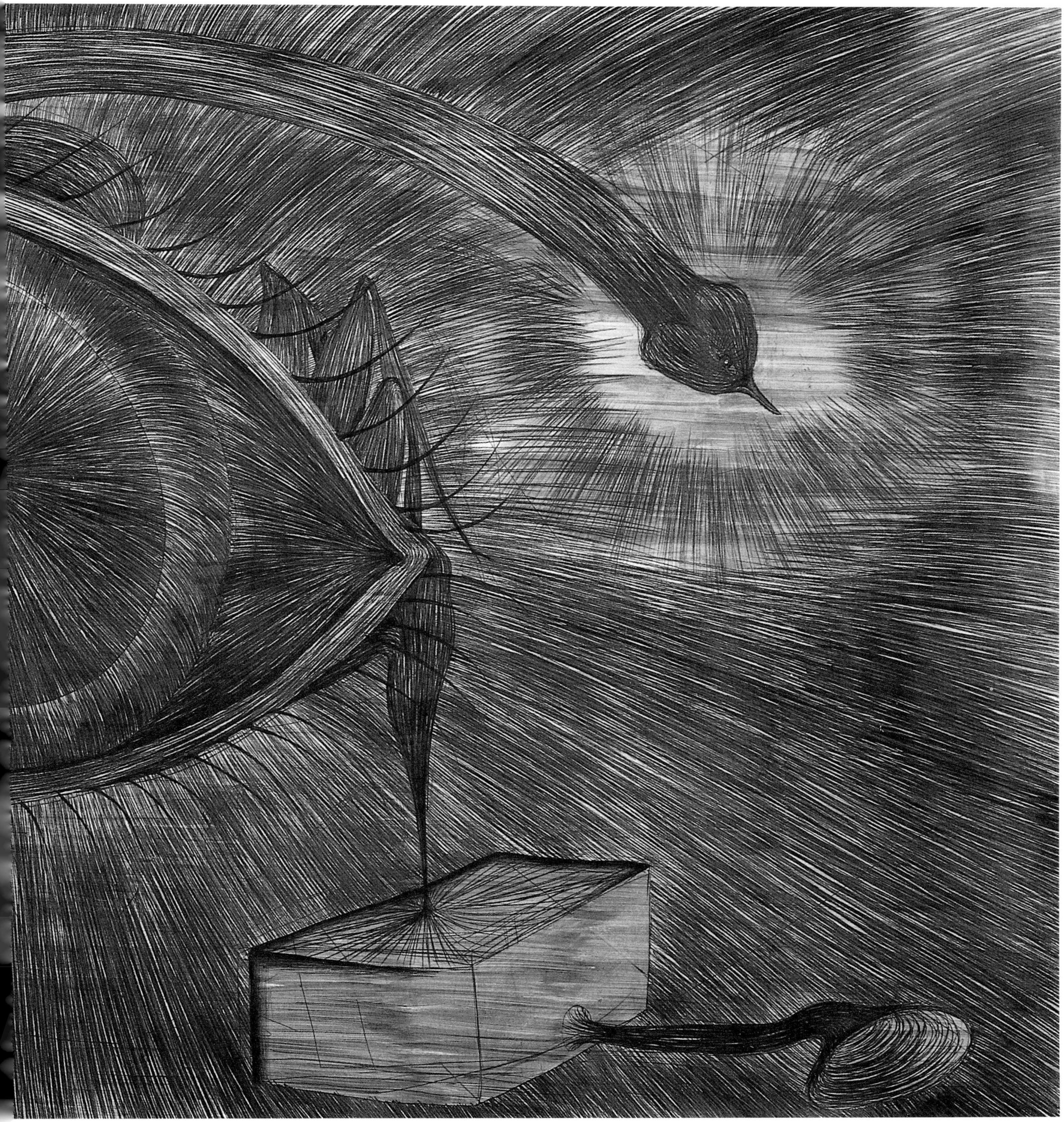

Pages 178–179
Figure 17
Self-Portrait to the Peered at the Yellow Sea
Pencil on paper
182 x 382 cm
1984
Private collection, Antwerp, Belgium

Pages 180–181
Figure 18
The Secret Camouflage and the Black Flag Conspiracy — Self-Portrait with Art
Pencil, acrylic wash on paper
182 x 340 cm
1984
Collection of Queensland Art Gallery, Brisbane

Figure 19
The Critic's Bladder (Portrait of Paul Foss)
Pencil and mixed media on paper
275 x 297 cm
1992

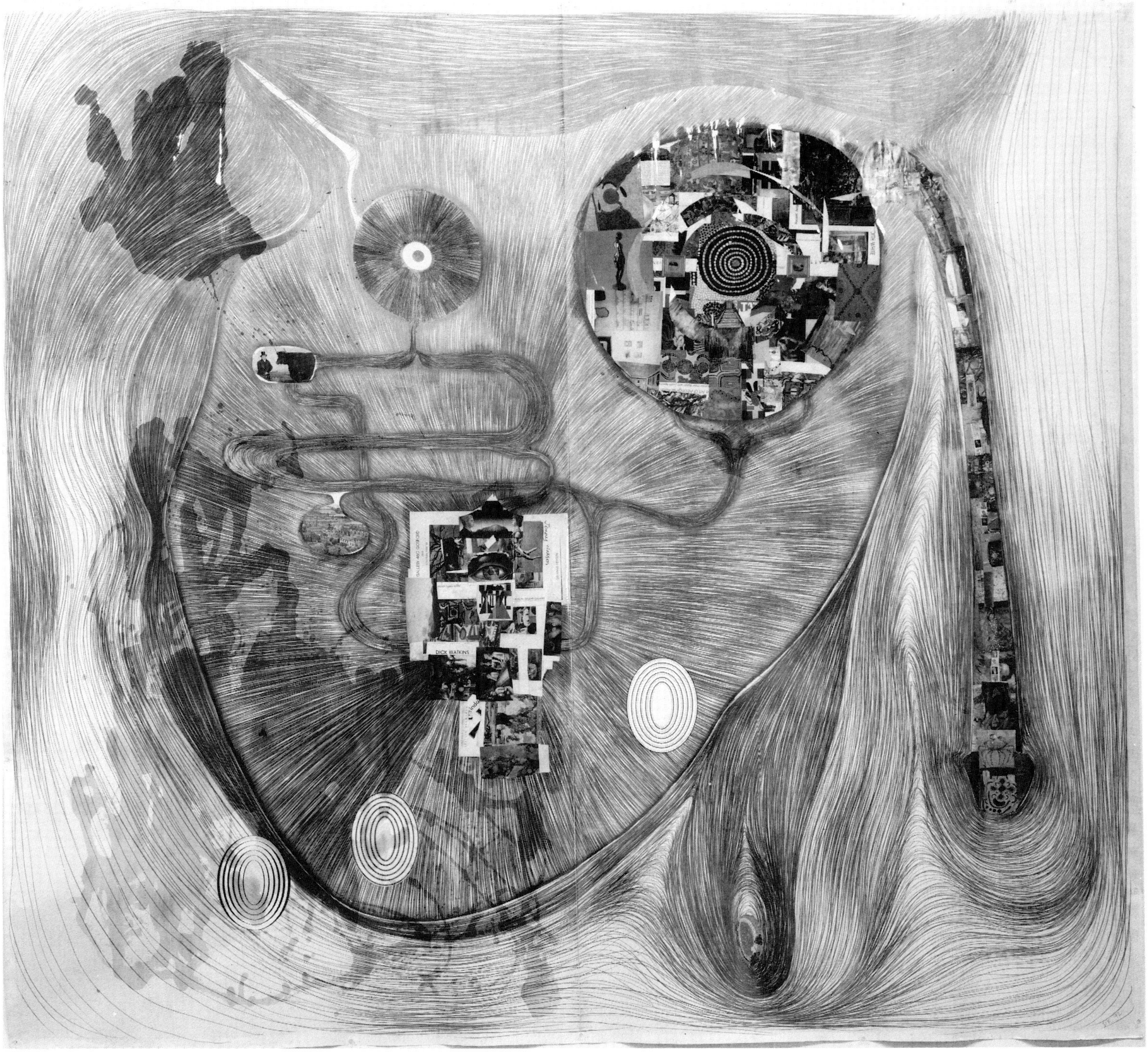
DICK WATKINS

Figure 20
Self-Portrait at being Crowned the Father of Contemporary Australian Drawing with 25 Flies
Pencil on paper
291 x 306 cm
1984

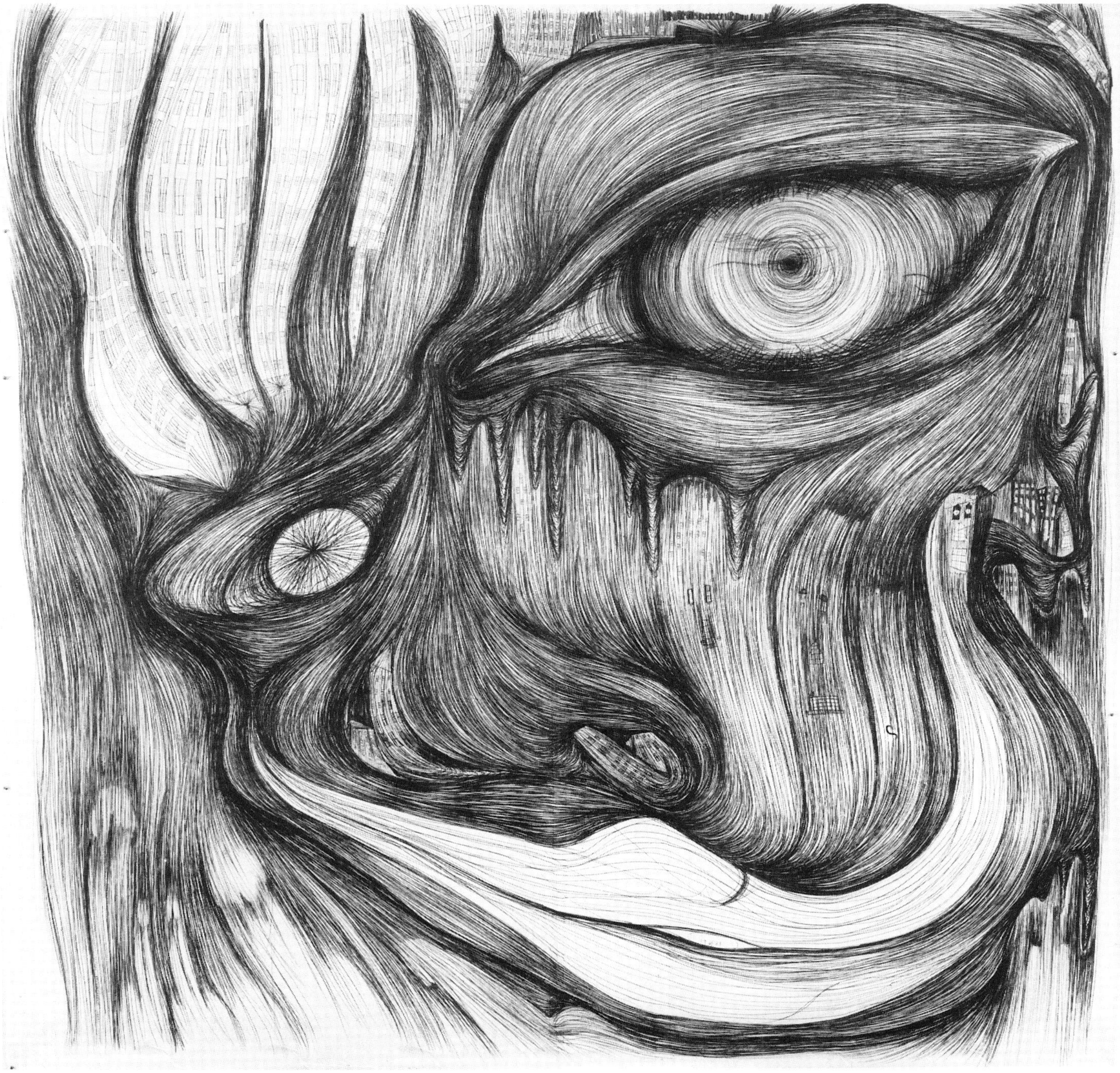

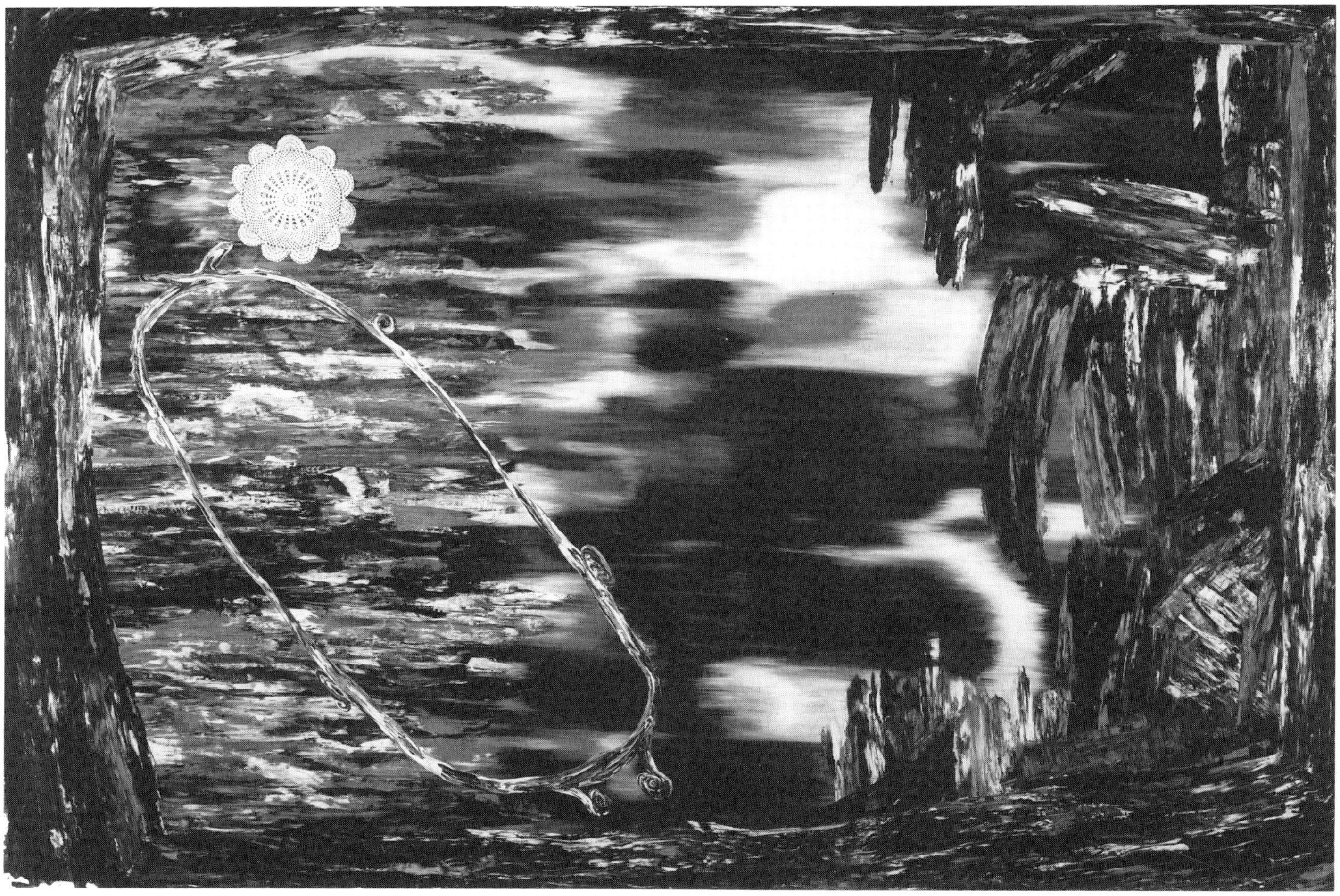

Figure 21
And the Painting of the Painting that was Justly so Afraid it Stuck to the Frame of the Inner Light and the Guiding Light of the Virgin Painting (The Studio Eye)
Acrylic on canvas
200 x 305 cm
1984

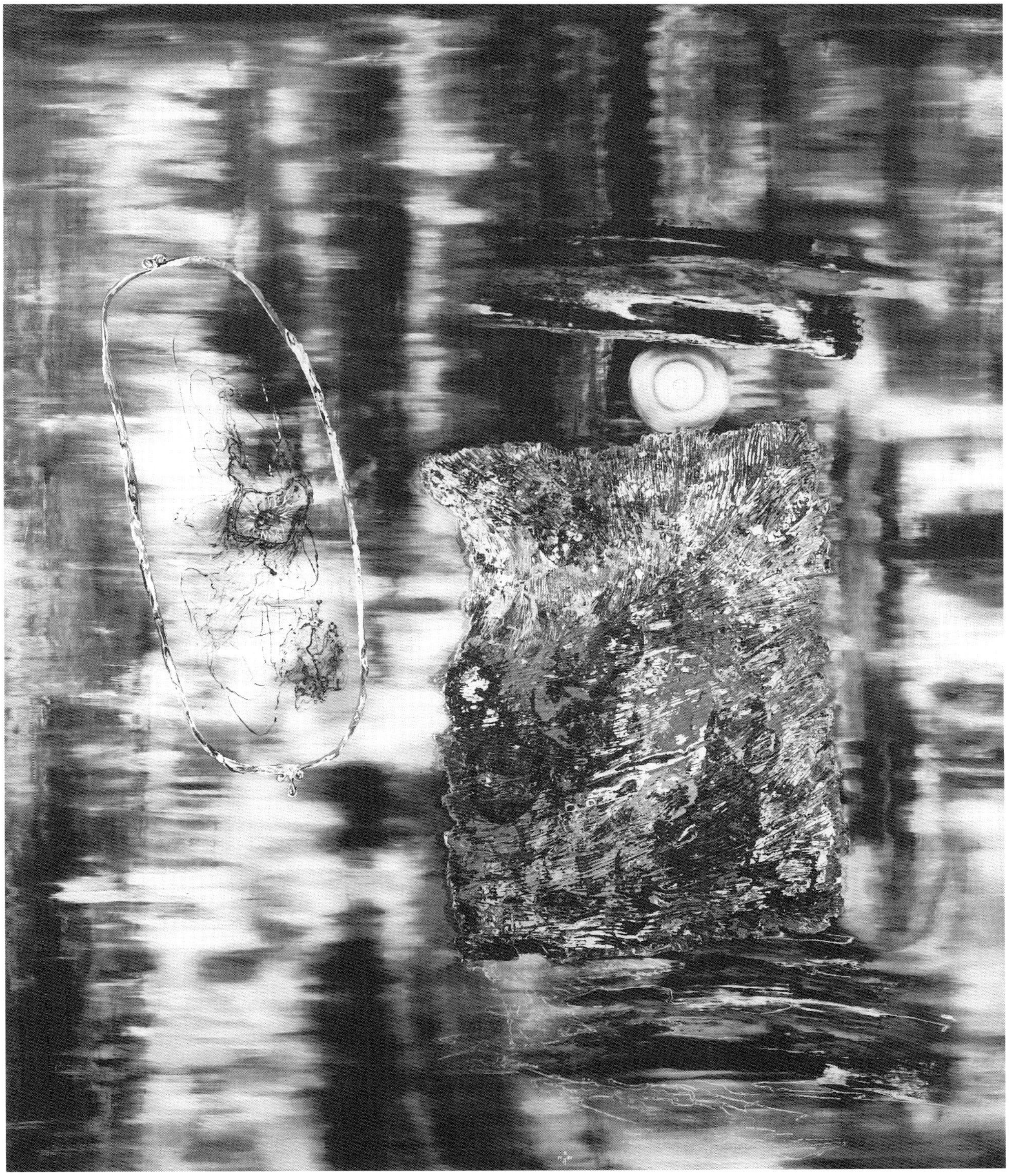

Figure 22
The Wounded Painting that Tempted to Look into the Mirror behind the Artist's Back — Why Women are not Artists
Acrylic paint on canvas
200 x 179 cm
1985

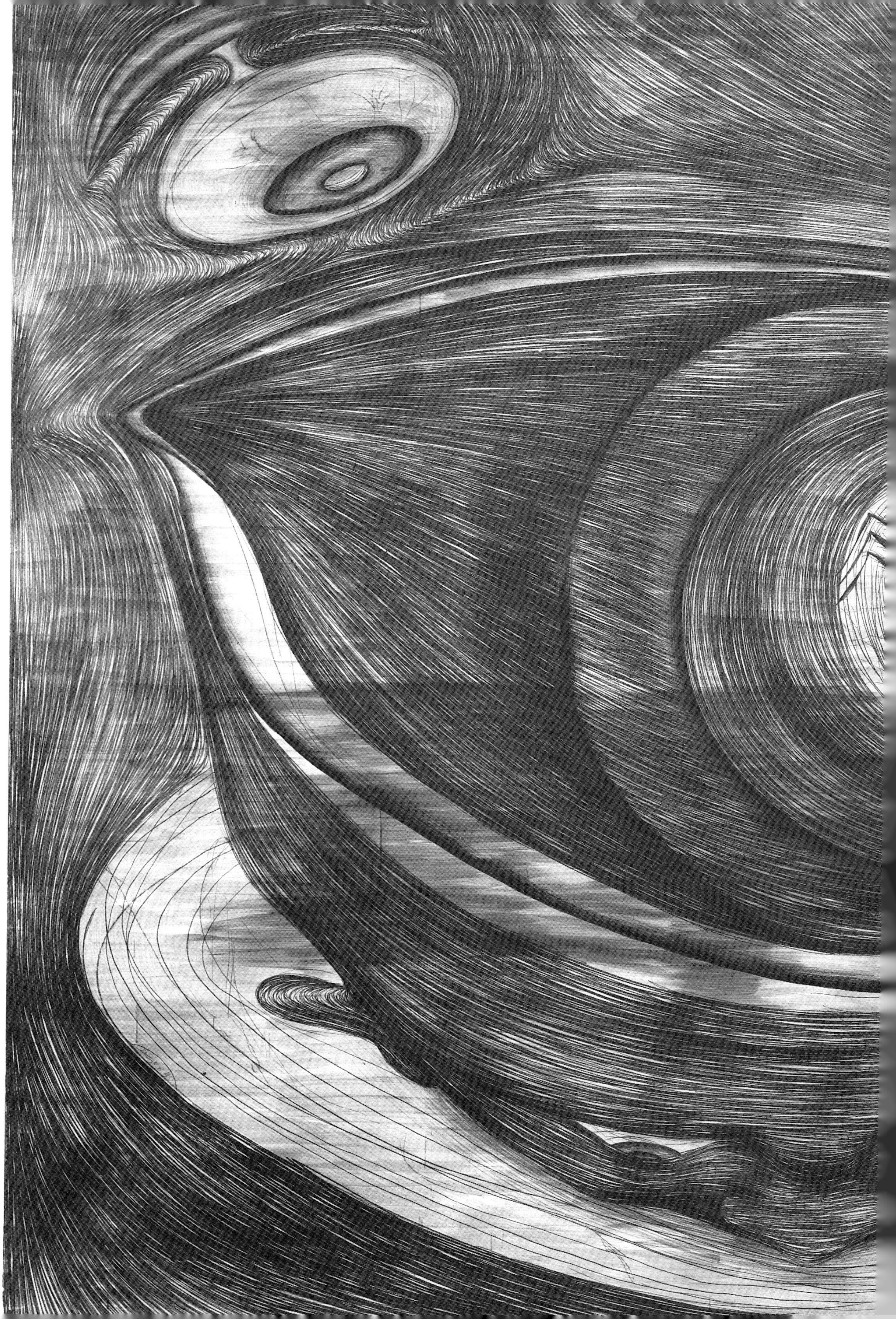

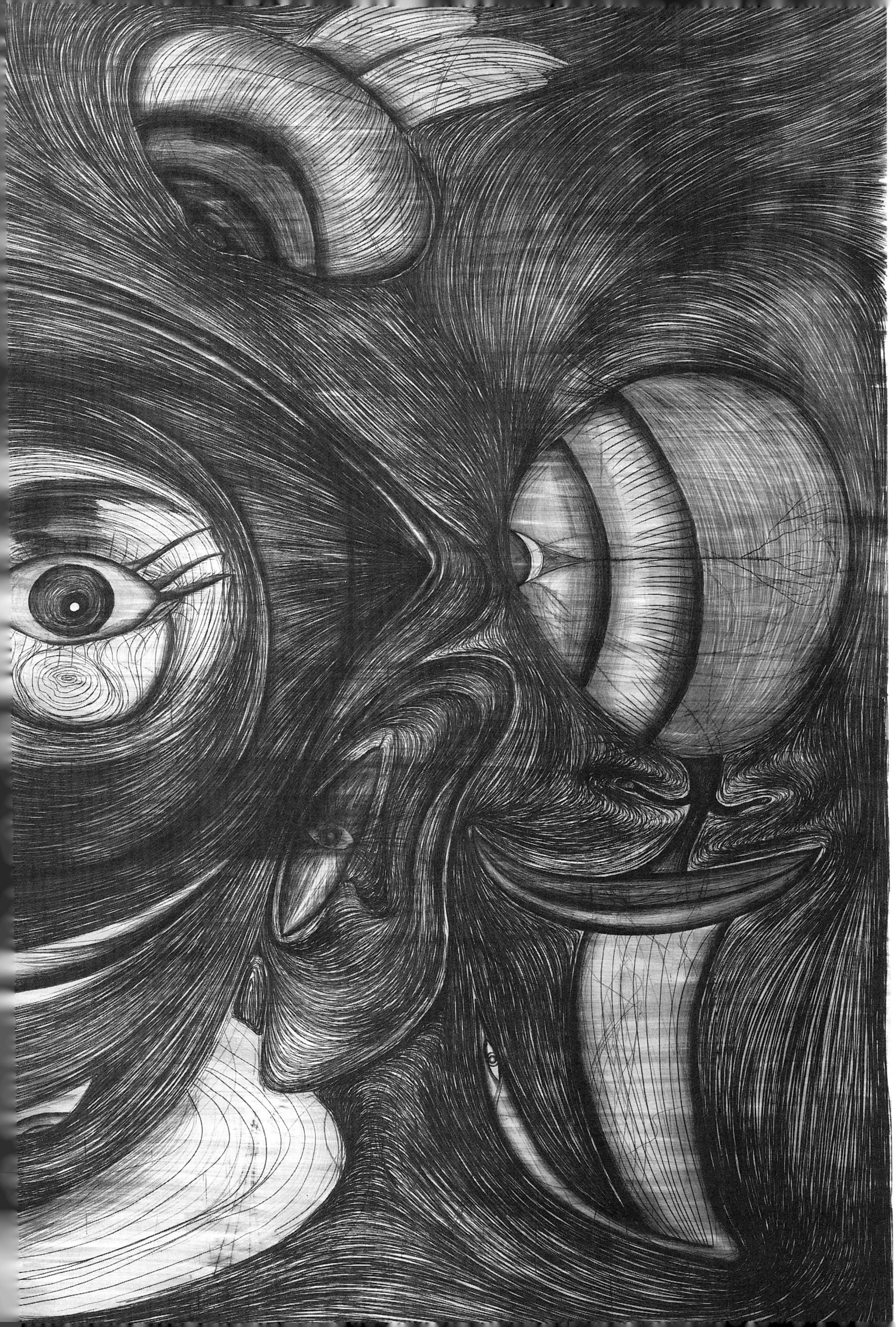

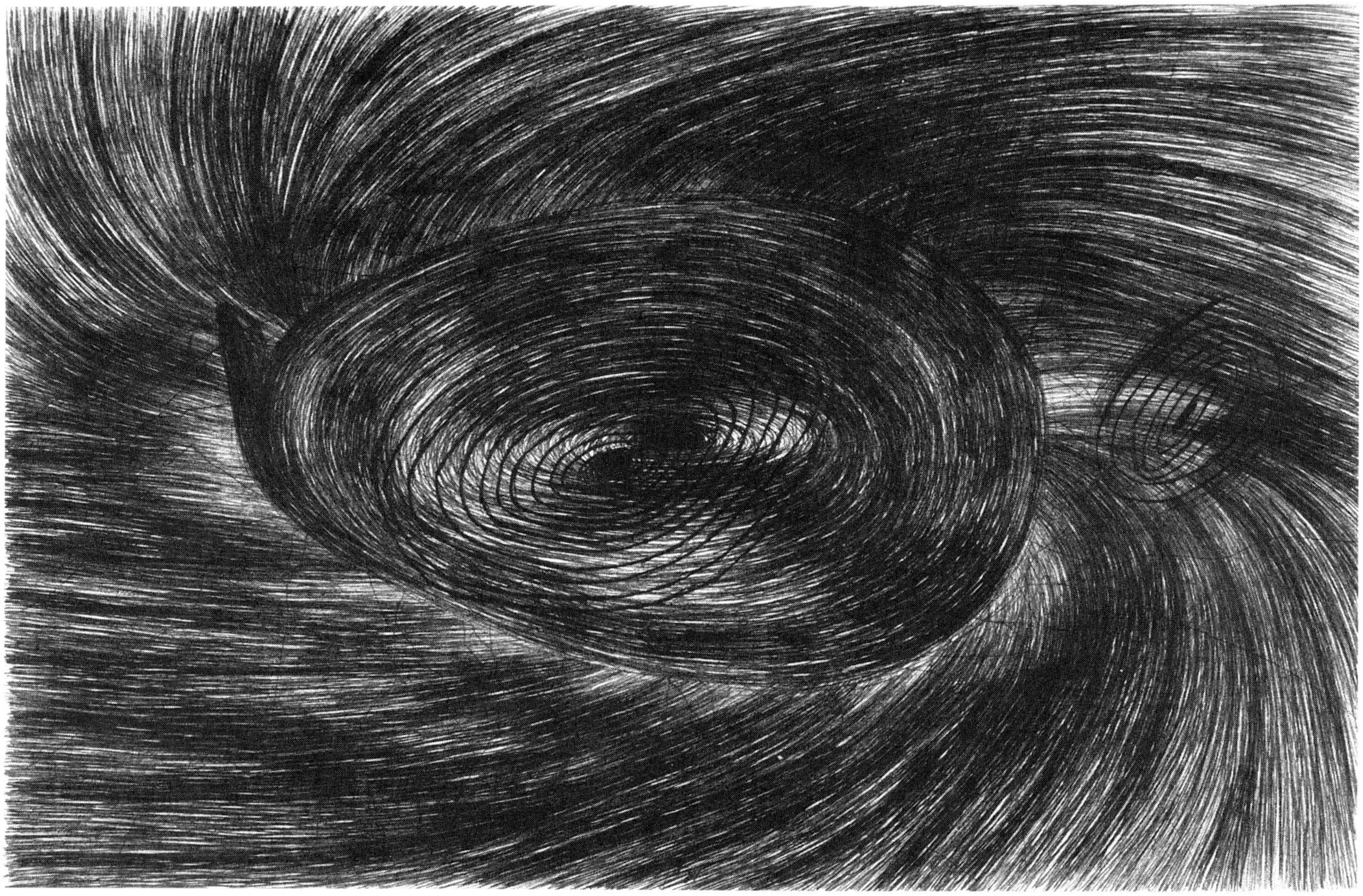

Figure 24
At All at Least a Mountain Tradition
Pencil on paper
130 x 200 cm
1981
Private collection, Bologna, Italy

Previous page:
Figure 23
Self-Portrait with the Spider's Itch in the Mind's Eye for the Baboon's Dinner where the I's have it (Self- Portrait with the Future)
Pencil, acrylic wash, on paper
369 x 279 cm
1985

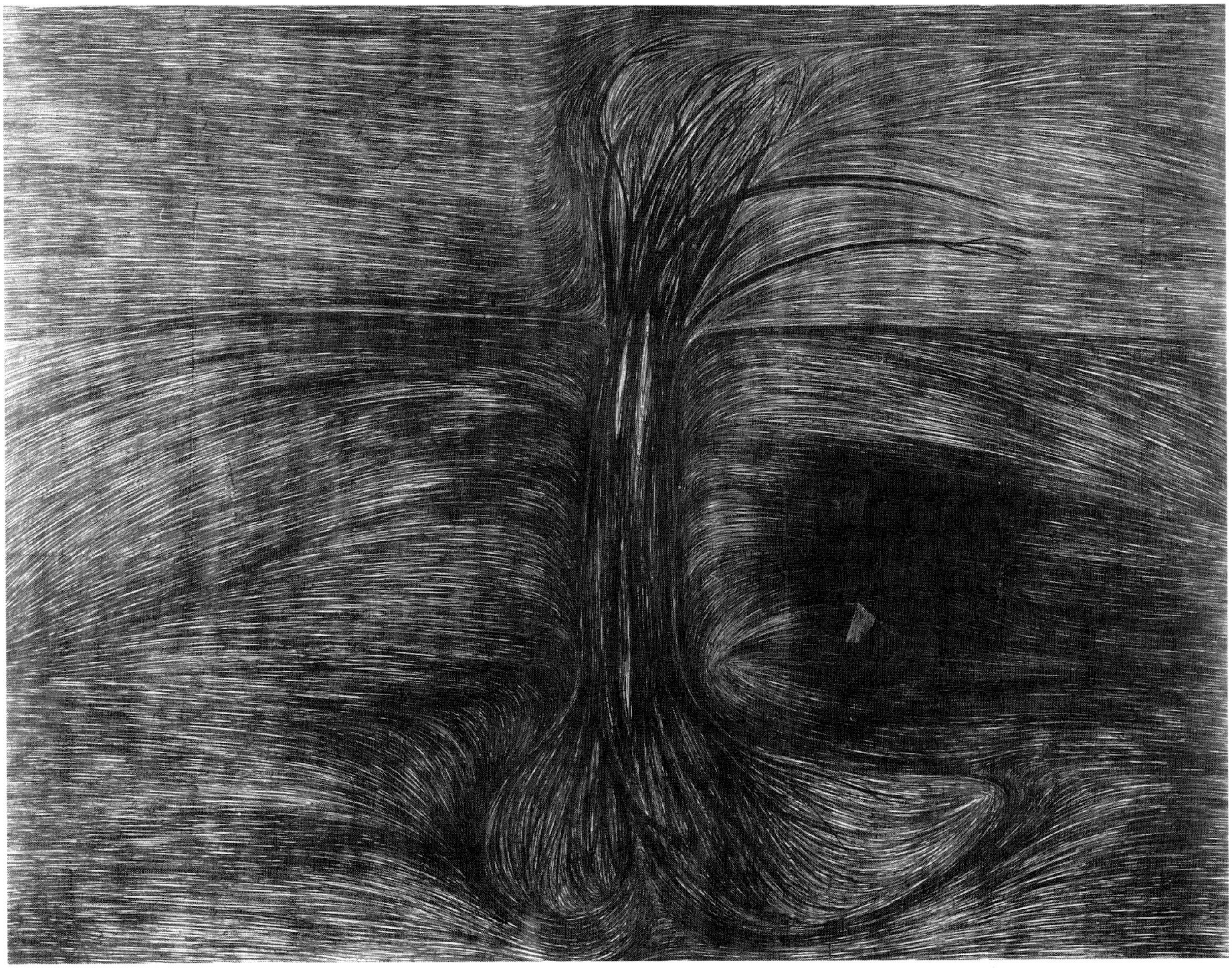

Figure 25
Intrusion and Facial Shock of the Tree
Pencil on paper
217 x 268 cm
1982

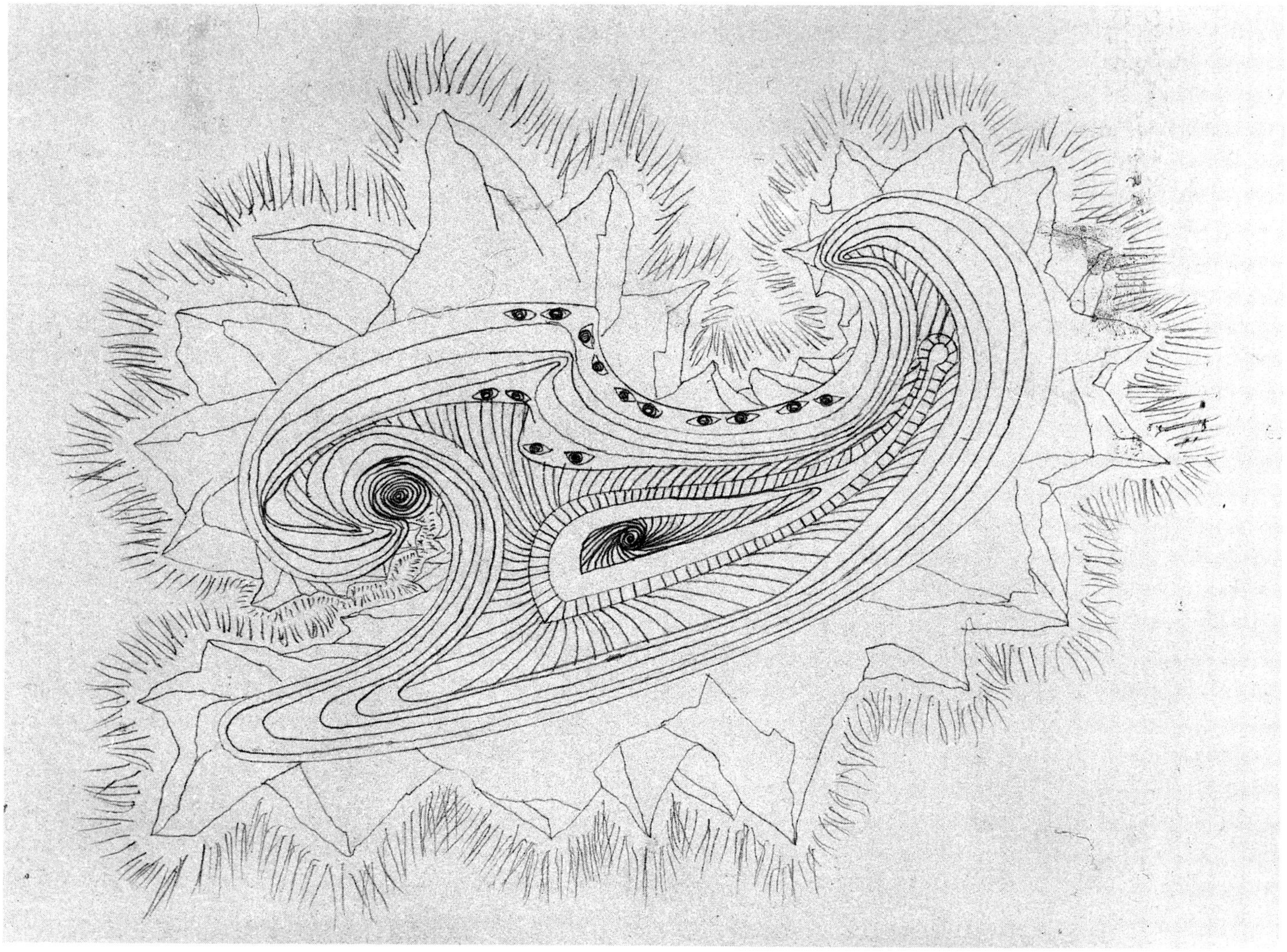

Figure 26
The Failure and Fear of Swimming Pools in Relation to the Artist's Lost Anus
Pencil on paper
32 x 35 cm
1981
Private collection, Munich, Germany

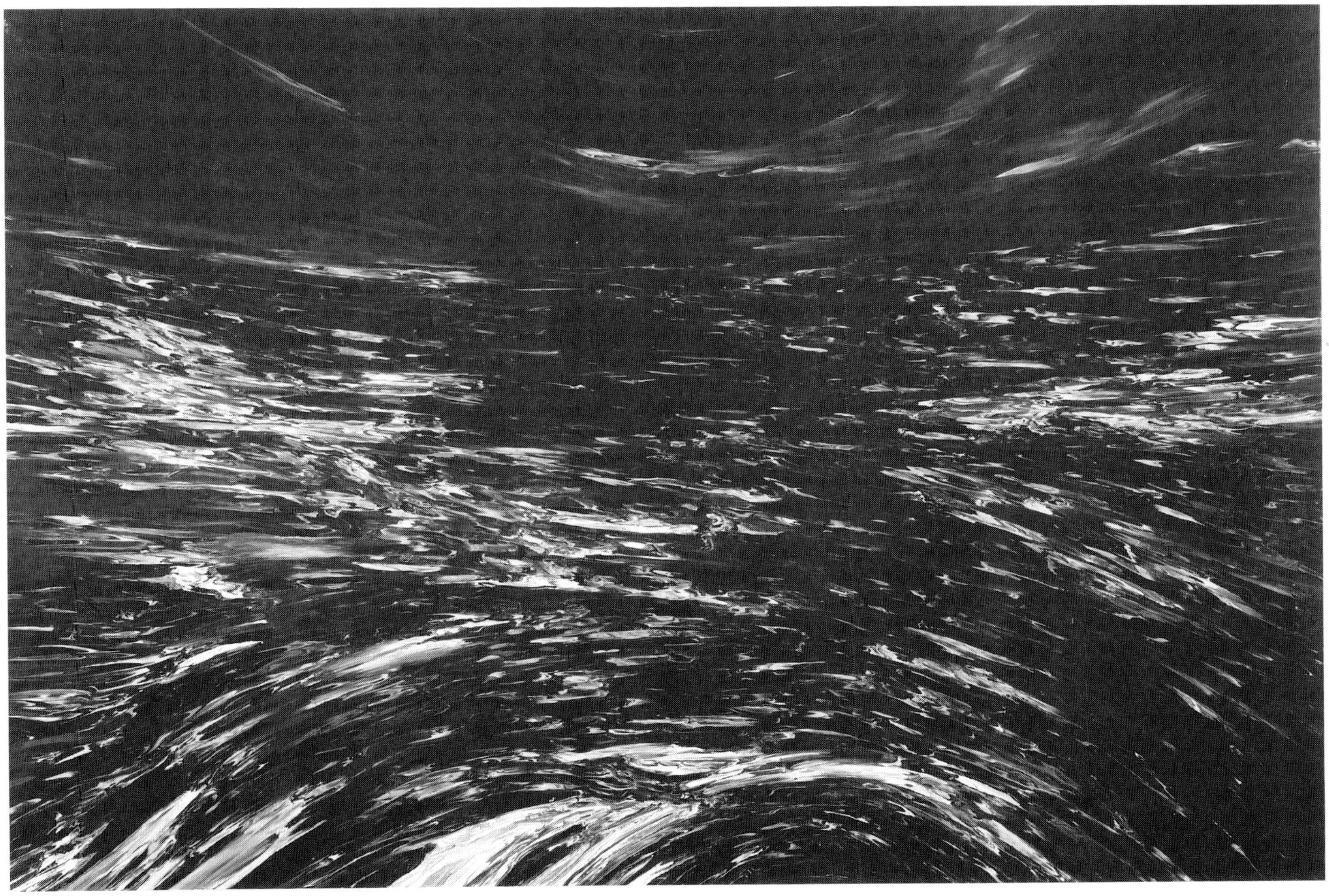

Figure 27
The Swimmer in the Flooded Studio and the Drowning at the End of the Pier. The Swimmer — The Flooded Studio
Acrylic paint on canvas
199 x 299 cm
1984
Private collection, Amsterdam

Bibliography

1982 Wystan Curnow, 'Christchurch ANZART', (review), *Artforum*, New York, April
Terence Maloon, 'Dale Frank rides the crest of a wave like an experienced surfer', *The Sydney Morning Herald*, 4 September
Bernice Murphy, 'Some Recent Painting in Australia', in Archille Bonito Oliva (ed), *Transavantgarde International*, Milan, Giarcarlo Politi, p. 275
Roberto Daolio, 'Dale Frank, Artista', *Lapis Arte*, Salerno, June, pp. 8–10
Bari Epo Arte, Art Fair, (review), *Domus*, Milan, No. 629, June, p. 74
Helena Kontova, 'From Performance to Painting', *Flash Art*, No. 106, Milan, February, pp. 16–21
Mike Parr, 'Vision in Disbelief, 4th Biennale of Sydney', (review), *Flash Art*, No. 108, Milan, June, pp. 71–72
William Wright, *Vision in Disbelief, 4th Biennale of Sydney*, (catalogue), Art Gallery of New South Wales, Sydney
Marcia Tucker, 'An Iconography of Recent Figurative Painting: Sex, Death, Violence and the Apocalypse', *Artforum*, Vol. XX, No. 10, New York, June
Roberto Daolia, 'Dale Frank Artiste', *Lapis Arte*, Salerno, Italy, June, pp. 8–9
Editorial, Review of Bari Expo Arts, *Domus*, No. 629, Milan, June, p. 74
Mike Parr, 'Glossolalia/Stroke: the Art of Dale Frank', *Aspect*, Sydney, Spring, pp. 60–63
Jennifer Phipps, 'Anzart', *Australian Art Review*, No. 1, Sydney, p. 81

1983 Sue Cramer, 'Masterpieces and Tall Poppies', (review), *Art Network*, Sydney, No. 10, Winter, p. 42
Elizabeth Cross, *Figures and Face Drawn from Life*, (catalogue), Melbourne, Heide Park and Art Gallery, October
Dale Frank, *Punchline*, (broadsheet), Sydney, Roslyn Oxley9 Gallery, Sydney, August
Bernice Murphy, *Australian Perspecta 1983*, (catalogue), Sydney, Art Gallery of New South Wales, May, p. 44
Jennifer Phipps, 'Paintings', in Leon Paroissien (ed), *Australian Art Review 2*, Melbourne, Warner Association, pp. 74–81
Tim McLauchlan, 'The Art Market in 1982', in Leon Paroissien (ed), *Australian Art Review 2*, Melbourne, Warner Association, pp. 122–125
Robert Rooney, 'Taylor Made to Fit a Theory', *The Australian*, Sydney, 14 May
Michael Spens, 'Australian Art Beyond the Cringe', *Studio International*, London, Vol. 196, No. 1002, pp. 13–15
Paul Taylor, 'Arts News: Artists in Paris', *Vogue Australia*, Sydney, October
Bernice Murphy, 'Recent Painting in Australia', *Flash Art*, No. 110, Milan, February, p. 56–59
Helen Kontova, 'Anselm Kiefer, Thomas Lawson, Dale Frank' in Achille Bonito Oliva (ed), *Critica ad Arte: Panorama della Post—Critica*, (catalogue), Musei Palazzo Lanfranchi, Pisa, Italy, March, pp. 138–142
Paul Taylor, *Tall Poppies*, (catalogue), Melbourne University Gallery, Melbourne, April
Mathew Collings, 'Place at Gimpel Fils', (review), *Artscribe*, London, No. 42, September, pp. 61–62
Helen Kontova, 'La Peinture issue de la performance', *Flash Art*, (edition Francaise), No. 1, Milan, Autumn, pp. 12–17
G. Galantai, 'New Painting', *Artpool*, No. 3, Budapest, Winter
Leon Paroissien and Suzanne Page, *D'un Autre Continent: L'Australia*, (catalogue), Musée d'Arte Modern de la ville de Paris, September, pp. 29–107
Robert Lindsay, *Vox Pop*, (catalogue), National Gallery of Victoria, Melbourne, December, pp. 24–25, p. 27
Ashley Crawford, 'Dale Frank', *Tension*, No. 2, Melbourne, October, pp. 28–30
Michael Spens, 'Dreams and Reality', *Studio International*, Vol. 196, No. 1002, London, November, pp. 13–14
Bill Wright, 'Australian Perspecta', *Studio International*, Vol. 196, No. 1002, London, November, pp. 36–39
Paul Groot, *The Divine Comedy*, (catalogue), Rotterdamse Kunststichting, Rotterdam, October
Peter Haynes, 'ACT 3: Ten Performance Artists', *Australian Art Review*, No. 2, Sydney, pp. 49–54
Robert Rooney, 'Tall Poppies', (review), *Flash Art*, No. 115, Milan, November, p. 74

1984 Cathy Peake, 'Tiber to Lilliput—and back again', (review), Sydney, *The Financial Review*, 29 June
Arthur McIntyre, 'Slow down, young man', (review), *The Age*, Melbourne, 10 July
Gertrude Langer, 'Young Artist's Images, Eerie, Disturbing', (review), *The Courier Mail*, Brisbane, 19 September
Grant Hannan, 'Effective, original', (review), *The Herald*, Melbourne, 16 August, p. 26
Robert Rooney, 'Bygone era meets "new wave"', (review), *The Weekend Australian*, Sydney, Magazine 13, 11 August
Vivienne Shark LeWitt, 'The End of Civilisation Part II: Love Among the Ruins', *Art and Text*, Melbourne, No. 10, Winter, pp. 1–6
Ron Radford, *Recent Australian Painting—A Survey 1970 to 1983*, (catalogue), Adelaide, Art Gallery of South Australia, p. 17, 53, 93
Sue Cramer, 'A change of place, a change of meaning', (review), *The Age*, Melbourne, 17 August

Eric Gibson, 'Australian in Manhattan', *Studio International*, London, Vol. 197, No. 1007, p. 45
Stuart Morgan, *The journey from the Tiber to Lilliput and back, again, Dale Frank — Death*, (broadsheet), Sydney, Roslyn Oxley9 Gallery, June
Jennifer Phipps, *Symbols, Emblems, Signatures: Australian Drawing 1984*, (exhibition catalogue), New Plymouth, Govett-Brewster Gallery
Diane Waldman, *Australian Visions: 1984 Exxon International Exhibition*, (exhibition catalogue), New York, Solomon R. Guggenheim Museum, September, pp. 19–20, 32–40
Susanna Short, 'Seascape surge ahead of the narrow, cosy view', (review), *The Sydney Morning Herald*, 29 June, p. 10
Elwyn Lynn, 'Still Life: delusion to the didactic', (review), Sydney, *The Weekend Australian*, 28 April
Tony Bond, *Form>Image>Sign: Survey of Contemporary Australian Art*, No. 3, (catalogue), Perth, Art Gallery of Western Australia, February
Paul Taylor, 'Tall Poppies', *Art and Text*, No. 12–13, Melbourne, January, p. 52
Sue Cramer, 'Vox Pop', (review), *Art and Text*, No. 12–13, Melbourne, January, p. 136–142
Jenny Watson, 'Urgent Images', *Art and Text*, No. 14, Melbourne, June, pp. 69–74
Flavio Caroli, *Aperto 84: XLI La Biennale di Venezia 1984*, (catalogue), Venice, June, p. 201, 207
Helena Kontova, 'Dale Frank', (interview), *Flash Art*, (Edizione Italiana), No. 122, Milan, July, (Estate), pp. 22–23
Flavio Caroli, 'La Biennale di Venezia', (review), *Flash Art*, (Edizione Italiana), No. 122, Milan, July, (Estate), p. 67
Judy Annear, 'Us in the US', *Vogue Australia*, Vol. XXVIII, No. 8, Sydney, August, pp. 160–163, 193
Paul Groot, *Dale Frank*, (catalogue), Melbourne University Art Gallery, Melbourne, August
Memory Holloway, *Recent Australian Art — An American Perspective*, (catalogue), *Bleak Romantics*, Solomon R. Guggenheim Museum, New York, September, pp. 11–21, 32–41
Paul Groot, 'Closed Quotes', (review — Venice Biennale), *Artforum*, Vol. XXIII, No. 1, New York, September, p. 107
Stuart Morgan, 'Dale Frank', (review), *Artforum*, Vol. XXIII, No. 2, New York, October, p. 101
Paul Groot, 'Dale Frank', *Artists*, No. 22–23, Paris, October, p. 116–119
Elio Graziolo, 'Dale Frank', (review), *Flash Art*, (International), No. 11, Milan, November, p. 49
Ken Sofer, 'Views from Downunder', *Art News*, Vol. 83, No. 10, New York, December, p. 157

1985 Helena Kontova, 'Dale Frank', (interview), *Flash Art*, (International), No. 120, Milan, January, pp. 70–71
Michael Kohn, 'Dale Frank', (review), *Flash Art*, (International), No. 120, January, pp. 43–44
Paul Groot, *Dale Frank*, (catalogue), 9e Foire d'Art Actual, (Galerie Albert Baronian), Palais Des Beaux-Arts Brussels, January
Gerrit Henry, 'Dale Frank', (review), *Art in America*, 1985, No. 2, New York, February, pp. 140–141
Paul Groot, 'De Surrealistiche Variaties van Dale Frank', *Museumjournal*, No. 1, Amsterdam, March, p. 49
'Dale Frank', Artists Pages, *Museumjournal*, No. 1, Amsterdam, March, pp. 50–51
Donald B. Kuspit, 'Australian Visions at the Guggenheim', (review), *Art in America*, No. 3, New York, March, pp. 153–154
Angela Vettasi, 'Europe and America: Two Aspects of the New Surreal', *Flash Art*, (International), No. 122, Milan, May, pp. 20–21
Paul Groot, 'Cover/Doppelganger', (catalogue), *Aorta*, Amsterdam, May, p. 95
Arthur McIntyre, 'Freudian Imagery Abounds' (review), *The Age*, Melbourne, 25 May, p. 44
Elwyn Lynn, 'View of Chaos, Malignity', (review), *Weekend Australian*, Sydney, May 25, p. 14
Achille Bonito Oliva, *Nuove Trame Dell'Arte*, (catalogue), Castello Gennazzano, Italy, July, pp. 68–69
Antonio d'Avossa, 'Le trame del Castello', *Flash Art*, (Italia), No. 128, Milan, Summer, pp. 62-63
Helena Kontova and Giancarlo Politi, 'From New York with Love', *Flash Art*, No. 123, Milan, Summer, pp. 46–47, (reprinted, *Flash Art* [Italia]), No. 128, Milan, Summer, pp. 26–27
Lucia Spadano and Achille Bonito Oliva, 'Nuove Trame Dell'Arte', *Segno*, No. 47, Rome, June, pp. 8–15
Ashley Crawford, 'Dale Frank: Dionysus versus Apollo', *Stilletto*, No. 24, Melbourne, June, p. 4
Alida Militello, 'Tanti Modi Di Essere Blouson', *EpocaModa*, No. 11, Verona, October, pp. 66–67
Silvia Zangheri, 'Espressione, Spirito Selvaggio e neoprimitivo', (catalogue), *Anniottanta*, (Flavio Caroli and Renalto Barilli), Bologna, July, pp. 163–169, 195–196, 223
Lucia Spadano, 'Fall Out', *Segno*, No. 48, Rome, September, pp. 30–32
Gregorio Magnani, 'Dale Frank', (review), *Flash Art*, (Italia), No. 130, Milan, December, p. 46
Francesca Alfano Miglietti, 'Provisioni de Tempo', *Flash Art*, (Italia), No. 130, Milan, December, pp. 62–64
Megan Cronly, 'Mastering the Art', *Follow Me*, No. 19, Sydney, October, pp. 136–141
Rondo, (catalogue), Antichi Arsenali, Amalfi, December, pp. 50–51, 90–91
Camille Sbrissa, 'Milan', *Artline*, London, Vol. 2, No. 10, Winter, p. 18
Peter Haynes, *Dale Frank*, (catalogue), Canberra, Canberra School of Art Gallery
'Bold and Provocative', (review), *Canberra Times*, 18 June
Paul Goodwin, 'Dale Frank', (review), *Flash Art*, (Italian edition), Milan, No. 126, January
John McDonald, 'Dale Frank/Mike Parr', *Art Network*, Sydney, No. 17, Spring, p. 53
Terence Maloon, 'Australia, emotionally unbuttoned', *The Sydney Morning Herald*, 16 March
Ronald Miller, 'Neurotic vision fits the bill', *The Herald*, Melbourne, 20 June
Giulio Ciavoliello, 'Dale Frank', *Juliet*, Trieste, No. 23, December, p. 9
Paul Groot, 'Dale Frank: With the eye if you are quick enough to turn on the light you can see what the dark looks like', *Art and Text*, Melbourne, No. 17, April, pp. 29–30, 81–83

1986 Gregorio Magnani, 'Dale Frank', (review), *Flash Art*, (International), No. 126, Milan, February, pp. 60–61
Gregorio Magnani, 'Dale Frank', (interview), *Westuff*, No. 3, Florence, March, pp. 16–17
Pier Luigi Tazzi, 'Dale Frank', (review), *Artforum*, Vol. 24, No. 8, New York, April, p. 118
Timothy Morrell, 'Big Drawings', *Art and Australia*, Vol. 23, No. 3, March, p. 366
Francesco Alfano Miglietti, 'Che Tempo Fara?', *Flash Art*, (Italia), No. 133, April, pp. 72–73
Paul Groot, 'Die Malerei im Dienste eines anatomisdhen Projects. Einige Bermerkungen zum jinger europaischer Maler', in *Europe — America: 1940 to the Present*, (catalogue), Cologne, Museum Ludwig, September, pp. 407–418
3rd International Triennale der Zeichnung, (catalogue), Nurnberg, Nationalmuseum, Nurnberg
Leo Loomans, *Dale Frank*, (unpublished interview for undergraduate history thesis), Sydney, August
Hannah Fink, 'Art Stars: Dale Frank', *X-Press*, Sydney, Vol. 1, No. 6, December, p. 12
Ted Gott, *Backlash: The Australian Drawing Revival 1976–1986*, (catalogue), Melbourne, National Gallery of Victoria, pp. 38–41, 83, 95

1987 Naomi Cass (ed), *What Is This Thing Called Science?*, (catalogue), Melbourne, The University Gallery
Daniela Salvioni, 'Combustible Demarcations: The Art of Dale Frank', in Tony Bond (ed), *The Australian Bicentennial Perspecta*, (catalogue), Sydney, Art Gallery of New South Wales, October, pp. 28–35
Dale Frank, (catalogue), Realities Gallery, June
Luisa Somaini, 'tuttoarte', *La Republica*, Milan, 16 January
Gian Petro Vincenzo, 'Neo Geo', *Per Lui Vogue*, Milan, 16 January
Arturo Carlo Quintavalle, 'Dale Frank: Quadri come apparizioni', (review), *Panorama*, March, p. 26
Adriano Antolini, 'E l'arte trovo casa a Milano', *Il Giornale Nuovo*, Milan, 8 February
Luciano Caprile, 'Da Schlichter a Frank e Pardi', (review), *Il Sole 24 Ore*, Milan, 8 February
Giancinto di Pietrantonio, 'Dale Frank/Alfredo Pirri', (review), *Flash Art*, (Italia), Milan, March, pp. 50–51
'Thronging The Canvases', *Follow Me*, Sydney, August, p. 140
Pamela Hansford, 'Dale Frank', *Art and Australia*, Vol. 25, No. 2, Summer, pp. 240–243
Terry Smith, 'Frank Explores the Heights of Bad Taste', (review), *Times on Sunday*, 11 October, p. 30
Elwyn Lynn, 'From the Hall of Fame ...', (review), *The Weekend Australian*, 10 October
Robert Rooney, 'A Return to Cosmic Abstraction', (review), *The Weekend Australian*, 27 June
Shona Martyn, 'Why Dale Frank can buy Gaultier', *Vogue Australia*, No. 4, April, p. 101
Robert Rooney, 'Marvelling at this thing called science', (review), *The Weekend Australian*, Sydney, 5 December
Dale Frank, *The Story of a Crime — for Want of a Better Title*, (unpublished manuscript), Murrurundi, March, pp. 1–16

1988 Andrew Bogle, *Advance Australia Painting*, (catalogue), Auckland, Auckland City Gallery
Dan Cameron, 'Showdown at Southern Cross', Notes on the 1988 Australian Biennale, *Artlink*, Adelaide, Vol. 8, No. 3, pp. 10–14
Betsy Brennan, 'Avant Gaga', *Vogue Living*, June–July, pp. 114, 117–118, 152
Graham Coulter-Smith, 'Dale Frank', (interview), *Eyeline*, No. 6, September, pp. 10–11
Robert Rooney, 'Dale Frank', (review), *The Weekend Australian*, 14 May
Dale Frank — Trusting in the Pipe-Dream, (catalogue), Melbourne, Realities Gallery, April
Dale Frank — Drawing Survey, (catalogue), Sydney, EMR Gallery in association with Mori Gallery, May
15 Years Galerie Albert Baronian in ICC, (catalogue), Antwerp/Brussels, Galerie Albert Baronian, November, pp. 34–35
Jennifer McCamley, 'A Storm in a Teacup? — Dale Frank', *Tension*, No. 14, September, pp. 12–18
Arthur McIntyre, *Australian Contemporary Drawing*, Boolarong Publishers, Brisbane

1989 Jane Magon, 'Dale Frank', (review), *Eyeline*, No. 5, pp. 32–33
A selection of 19th and 20th Century Art, (catalogue), Deutscher Fine Art, Melbourne, November, p. 109, illustrated
Paul Groot, 'De kunstgeschiedenis is dood. Leve de kunstgeschdenis!: Pittoresk II', *Museumjournal*, Amsterdam, Vol. 34, No. 2 and 3, pp. 97–103
Dale Frank, (catalogue), Sydney, Roslyn Oxley9 Gallery, July
Ashley Crawford (ed), 'The 1980s: From Leantime to Dreamtime', *Tension*, No. 19, January
Bill Wright and Robert Lindsay, *ICI Contemporary Art Collection*, (catalogue), Melbourne
Michael Richards, 'Europia from the Abstract', (review), *The Courier Mail*, Brisbane, 5 April
'Around Brisbane', (review), *MOCA Bulletin*, Brisbane, May/June, No. 21, p. 4
Carolyn Barnes, 'Cosmic Resistance, *Agenda Contemporary Art*, No. 5, June, pp. 3–5
Bob Linguard and Sue Cramer, *Institute of Modern Art — 1975 to 1989: A Documentary History*, Institute of Modern Art, pp. 84, 121
Annette Cyr, 'Dale Frank', (review), *108 Review*, New York, No. 10, January, p. 9
Elwyn Lynn, 'Carving Out Skill's Domain', (review), *The Weekend Australian*, 19 August, p. 113
Christopher Allen, 'Satirising surfaces beneath face value', (review), *The Sydney Morning Herald*, 25 August, p. 14

1990 Ashley Crawford, 'A Chronicle of Australian Art 1980–1989', *Tension*, No. 19, January
Arthur McIntyre, *Contemporary Australian Collage and its Origins*, Craftsman House, Sydney
Anna Johnson, 'Dale Frank', *Interior Architecture and Design*, No. 22, pp. 152–157
Catherine Lumby, 'Dale Frank — Fed-up with Art', (review), *Art and Text*, No. 25, Summer, pp. 139–141
Jay Younger, 'Post Modernism — The Baby and the Bathwater', *Broadsheet*, Adelaide, Vol. 19, No. 1, March, p. 10

Rene Block, *The Readymade Boomerang: Certain Relations in 20th Century Art*, (catalogue), Sydney, 8th Biennale of Sydney, April, pp. 458–459, 475
Jane Magon, 'Fame and the Art of Dale Frank', *Dale Frank: Adieu*, Melbourne, Deutscher Brunswick Street, June
Catharine Lumby, *Dale Frank Adieu*, (catalogue introduction), Deutscher Brunswick Street, June
Louise Neri, 'Block's Buster: Eros, C'est la vie, Cumulus From Australia', *Parkett*, Zurich, No. 25, September, pp. 143–149
Paul Groot, 'Sydney Biennale', (review), *Flash Art*, Milan, No. 154, October
Shona Harford, 'Art's bad boy takes on the system', (review), *Sunday Herald*, Melbourne, 24 June
Ronald Miller, 'Go south for gentle pleasures', (review), *The Herald*, Melbourne, 20 June

1991 Elwyn Lynn, 'In or out of Race, it's a minefield', (review), *The Weekend Australian*, Sydney, 5 January, p. 8
Jo Saurin, 'Reward of Sensual Pleasures', (review), *The Sydney Morning Herald*, Sydney, 22 March, p. 12
Christopher Allen, 'Artist truth before the altar of the market', (review), *The Sydney Morning Herald*, Sydney, 23 March, p. 50
Elwyn Lynn, 'Champs canvass art with punch', (review), *The Weekend Australian*, Sydney, 23 March, p. 8
Michael Richards, 'Explosion of Paints Combines the Classical and Chaotic', (review), *The Courier-Mail*, Brisbane, 25 June, p. 20
Adam Geczy, 'Banal Art', (review), *Agenda*, No. 18, Melbourne, July, p. 16
Peter Hutchings, 'Banal Art', (review), *Art and Text*, Sydney, No. 39, May, p. 74
Bernard Smith and Terry Smith, *Australian Painting 1788–1990*, Oxford University Press, p. 531, 539
Graham Forsyth, 'Dale Frank', (review), *Art and Text*, Sydney, No. 40, September, p. 86, 87
Wayne Hudson, *Chiliasm*, (catalogue), Institute of Modern Art, Brisbane, June, Bulletin
Rex Butler, *Banal Art*, (catalogue), Artspace, Sydney
Roslyn Oxley9 Gallery, *Dale Frank*, (catalogue), Koln Art Fair, November
Felicity Fenner, 'A more than frank exchange of views', (review), *The Sydney Morning Herald*, 26 October, p. 47
Rex Butler, *The Hypothesis of Imitation*, (catalogue), Bellas Gallery, Brisbane, October, pp. 5–7
Bernice Murphy, 'The Power Collection: Development in the 1980s', *Art and Australia*, Vol. 29, No. 2, Summer, Sydney, p. 211
Robert Rooney, 'Bad Boy Ages Tastefully', *The Australian*, 23–24 November, 1991, p. 6

Individual Exhibitions

1979	Experimental Art Foundation, Adelaide
1980	Project Art Gallery, Dublin Young Artists Club, (FMK), Budapest Galerie Sixto Notes, Milan
1981	Acme Art Gallery, London PS1 Gallery (Project Studio One), New York Praxis Gallery, Perth Fernando Pellegrino Galerie, Bologna
1982	Galerie Tanit, Munich Perspective 12/82, International Kunstmesse, Basel Roslyn Oxley9 Gallery, Sydney Severina Teucher Galerie, Zurich
1983	Museum Fodor, Amsterdam Roslyn Oxley9 Gallery, Sydney
1984	Studio d'Art Cannaviello, Milan Roslyn Oxley9 Gallery, Sydney University Gallery, Melbourne Institute of Modern Art, Brisbane Monique Knowlton Gallery, New York
1985	Palais Des Beaux-Arts (Galerie Albert Baronian), Brussels Galerie Barbara Farber, Amsterdam Roslyn Oxley9 Gallery, Sydney Canberra School of Art Gallery, Canberra Studio d'Art Cannaviello, Milan
1986	Massimo Audiello Gallery, New York Galerie Polynero, Antwerp Galerie Albert Baronian, Brussels Triagono Modern Arte, Nola (Naples) Roslyn Oxley9 Gallery, Sydney
1987	Studio Marconi, Milan Musee de Ville Liege, Liege; curated by Albert Baronian Marianne Deson Gallery, Chicago Realities Gallery, Melbourne Mori Gallery, Sydney
1988	Jack Shainman Gallery, New York Milburn + Arte, Brisbane Mori Gallery, Sydney Realities Gallery, Melbourne E.M.R. Gallery, Sydney
1989	Milburn + Arte, Brisbane Roslyn Oxley9 Gallery, Sydney
1990	Milburn + Arte, Brisbane Deutscher Brunswick Street, Melbourne Roslyn Oxley9 Gallery, Sydney Sculptures and Constructions, Milburn, Brisbane
1991	Roslyn Oxley9 Gallery, Sydney Institute of Modern Art, Brisbane (collaboration with John Coburn) Tamworth City Gallery, Tamworth Deutscher Brunswick Street, Melbourne
1992	Newcastle Region Gallery, Newcastle (collaboration with John Coburn) Roslyn Oxley9 Gallery, Sydney Contemporary Art Centre of South Australia, Adelaide Nolan Gallery, Canberra (collaboration with John Coburn) Peter Bellas Gallery, Brisbane Karyn Lovegrove Gallery, Melbourne The Villa of Count Vladimir Svareff, Kuala Lipis (Kuala Lumpur), Malaysia, (touring Europe 1993/1994) Roslyn Oxley9 Gallery, Sydney

Group Exhibitions

1974 'Red Cross Art Prize', Sydney, (winning entry — John Olsen, Judge)

1975 'Wynne Exhibition', Art Gallery of New South Wales, Sydney
'Maitland Bradmill Painting Prize', Maitland, Australia (Syd Ball, Judge)
'Contemporary Art Society Exhibition', Hogarth Gallery, Sydney

1976 'Four Painters', Cooks Hill Gallery, Newcastle

1977 'Mildura Sculpture Triennale', Mildura Arts Centre, Mildura
'Contemporary Art Society Exhibition', Paddington Town Hall, Sydney

1978 'Ten Contemporary Sculptors', State Office Block, Sydney
'La Trobe University Sculpture Festival', La Trobe University Art Centre, Melbourne

1979 'Sydney Biennale "Alternatives"', Sculpture Centre, Sydney
'Nexus: Four Artists', Triskel Art Gallery, Cork

1980 'Post '80s Video', Action Space Gallery, London
Project Art Gallery, (Spring Program), Dublin

1981 'Les Oeuvres Plastiques Exposition', Espace Lyonnais d'Arte Contemporain, Lyon, France; curated by Marie Claude-Jeune
'April Show', PS1 (Project Studies One), New York
'Anzart', Robert McDougall Art Gallery, Christchurch; curated by Ian Hunter

1982 '4th Biennale of Sydney', Art Gallery of New South Wales, Sydney; curated by William Wright
'Muswellbrook Art Prize', Muswellbrook, (winning entry, Bernice Murphy, Judge)
'White and Black Drawings', Willard Gallery, New York

1983 'Panorama della Post — Critica', Musei Palazzo Lanfranchi, Pisa, Italy; curated by Achille Bonito Oliva (with Thomas Lawson and Anselm Kiefer, invited by Helena Kontova)
'Tall Poppies', Melbourne University Gallery, Melbourne; curated by Paul Taylor
'Perspecta '83', Art Gallery of New South Wales, Sydney; curated by Bernice Murphy
'Pirates and Mutineers', Roslyn Oxley9 Gallery, Sydney
'End of Civilisation, Part II', Ewing Gallery, Melbourne; curated by Caryn Faure-Walker
'De Goddelijk Komedie (The Divine Comedy)', Galerie t'Venster, Rotterdam and Bonnefantan Museum, Maastricht; curated by Paul Groot
'Faces and Portraits from Life', Heide Park Gallery, Melbourne
'D'un Autre Continent', ARC2, Musee d'Art Modern de la ville de Paris; curated by Suzanne Page
'Recent Australian Painting', Art Gallery of South Australia, Adelaide Drawings, Art Projects, Melbourne
'Vox Pop', National Gallery of Victoria, Melbourne
Michelle Foundation Collection, National Gallery of Victoria, Melbourne

1984 'Fremantle Drawing Exhibition', Fremantle Arts Centre, Fremantle; curated by Christa Johannes
'Form>Image>Sign', Art Gallery of Western Australia, Perth; curated by Tony Bond
'Dreams and Nightmares', Roslyn Oxley9 Gallery, Sydney
'Aperto '84', Arte e Arti: Attualita e Storia', Biennale of Venice; curated by Flavio Caroli and John Roberts
'Symbol, Emblem and Signature', Govett-Brewster Gallery, New Plymouth; curated by Jennifer Phipps
'L'Occhio Sull Imagine', Carla Feishci, Sestri Levante
'Recent Australian Art — An American Perspective', Solomon R. Guggenheim Museum, New York; curated by Diane Waldman
'Inspirit', Monique Knowlton Gallery, New York; curated by Garry Nichols

1985 'Dale Frank/Roberto Agus', Unimedia Galerie, Genova
'Australian Visions', Queensland Art Gallery, Brisbane, Art Gallery of New South Wales, Sydney, Art Gallery of Western Australia, Perth; curated by Diane Waldman
'Doppelgänger/cover', Aorta Gallery, Amsterdam; curated by Paul Groot
'Nuove Trame dell'Arte', Castello Genazzano, Rome; curated by Achille Bonito Oliva
'Anniottanta', Chiostri di San Domenico, Imola (Museum of Modern Art, Bologna); curated by Renato Barilli, Flavio Caroli
'Master Drawings', Galerie Barbara Farber, Amsterdam
'Rondo', 2nd Rassenga Internazionale d'Arte, Antichi Arsenali, Amalfi; curated by Gaspare Russo

1986 'Everyman, Zurich Forum', (Barbara Farber Gallery), Zurich
'New Generation, Five Painters from New York', Segal-Steinberg Gallery, Montreal
'New Purchases — Recent European Art', Museum of Modern Art, Chicago
'Forbidden Objects', Roslyn Oxley9 Gallery, Sydney

1987 'Primal Painting', Heide Park Art Gallery, Melbourne
'Nature Re-defined', Galerie Segal-Steinberg, Montreal
'Documentation', Danial Newburg Gallery, New York

'Drawings', 56 Bleeker Street, New York
'The Australian Bicentennial Perspecta', Art Gallery of New South Wales, Sydney; Art Gallery of Western Australia, Perth
'The Australian Exhibition', Frankfurter Kunstverein, Frankfurt; Wuttembergische Kunstverein, Stuttgart
'What Is This Thing Called Science?', The University Gallery, University of Melbourne, Melbourne
'Australian Contemporary Drawing', Heide Park and Art Gallery, Melbourne
'Group Show', Jack Shainman Gallery, New York
'Backlash: Australian Drawing Revival 1976–1986', National Gallery of Victoria, Melbourne
'Milano + 12', OSAON Centro di Arte Contemporanea, Milan

1988 '15 Years Galerie Albert Baronian', Museum International Cultureel Centru, Antwerp
'Advance Australian Painting', Auckland City Art Gallery, Auckland; Robert McDougall Art Gallery, Christchurch
'Australian Drawing', Australian National Gallery, Canberra
'The New Generation (1983–1988) Phillip Morris Arts Grant Purchase', Australian National Gallery, Canberra
'Irony, Humour and Dissent', Manly Art Gallery and Museum, Sydney; curated by Alison Carroll

1989 'ICI Contemporary Art Collection', Australian Centre For Contemporary Art, Melbourne; Ballarat Fine Art Gallery (touring)
'Group Show', The University of South East Queensland, Toowoomba
'Australian Art Post 1960', Deutscher Gertrude Street, Melbourne
'Cosmos', City Gallery, Melbourne

1990 'Group Show', Roslyn Oxley9 Gallery, Sydney
'8th Biennale of Sydney', Art Gallery of New South Wales, Sydney; curated by Rene Block
'Australian Contemporary Art Fair 2', Royal Exhibitions Buildings, Melbourne
'Greenpeace Benefit Exhibition', Linden Gallery, Melbourne; curated by Patrick Hoppe
'100 Artists Against Animal Experimentation', Deutscher Brunswick Street, Melbourne
'Vache', Site Gallery, Brisbane

1991 'Selected Contemporary Australian Artists', Deutscher Brunswick Street, Melbourne
'Banal Art', Artspace, Sydney; curated by Rex Butler
'The Hypothesis of Imitation', Bellas Gallery, Brisbane; curated by Rex Butler
'The History of the Electronic Page', Institute of Contemporary Art (ICA), Amsterdam; curated by Paul Groot

1992 'The Hypothesis of Imitation', Sutton Gallery, Melbourne; curated by Rex Butler
'Drawings', Gow/Langsford Gallery, Auckland
'Courts and Jesters', Ars Multiplacata Gallery, Sydney; curated by Jeff Gibson

Public Collections

Solomon R. Guggenheim Museum, New York
Zurich Kunsthalle, Zurich
Musée de Ville de Leige, Leige
Trans-Art Collection, Milan
Ball State University Collection, Indiana
First National Bank of Chicago Collection, Chicago
Westpac Collection, New York
Exxon Collection, New York
Allen Allen and Hemsley Collection, Sydney
University of Melbourne Collection, Melbourne
Tamworth City Gallery Collection, Tamworth
National Gallery of Victoria, Melbourne
Australian National Gallery, Canberra
Art Gallery of South Australia, Adelaide
Art Gallery of Western Australia, Perth
Queensland Art Gallery, Brisbane
National Gallery of New Zealand, Wellington
Auckland City Gallery, Auckland
Perc Tucker Regional Art Gallery, Townsville
Wollongong City Art Gallery, Wollongong
Burnie Municipal Gallery, Burnie
Griffith University Collection, Brisbane
Darwin Institute of Technology Collection, Darwin
Newcastle Region Art Gallery, Newcastle
Museum of Contemporary Art, Sydney
ICI Collection, Sydney
Philip Morris Collection, Canberra

Private Collections

Hugh Jamieson Collection, Sydney
Smorgon Family Collection, Melbourne
Jim Wolfensohn Collection, New York
Clayton Press Jnr Collection, Los Angeles
Chartwell Collection, Christchurch
as well as numerous private collections in:
Amsterdam, Antwerp, Brescia, Brisbane, Brussels, Budapest, Chicago, Cologne, Dallas, Dublin, Dusseldorf, Haarlem, Houston, Leige, London, Los Angeles, Melbourne, Milan, Montreal, Munich, Naples, New York, Palermo, St Gallen

List of Colour Plates

38 *Saddam Saddam He's My Man*, Acrylic paint on canvas, 260 x 200 cm, 1991

39 *Venture Venture Nothing Gained, into the Artist's Arms without Refrain. With only Disgust Disgust, it is only Me you can Trust. Listen Hard, Listen Long, Listen Listen, but not too Long*, Acrylic paint on canvas, 260 x 200 cm, 1991

40 *The Artist's Fairy Floss Sold on the Merry-Go-Round of Life, (Sucker Dealer), Sucker Dealer and the Righteous Anus*, Acrylic paint on canvas, 240 x 200 cm, 1991

41 *Cilla Black*, Acrylic paint on canvas, 240 x 200 cm, 1991

42 *The Beached Sperm Whale and his Affection to the Disinfected Onlooker, an Art Moral*, Pencil, acrylic wash on paper, 182 x 356 cm, 1985

43 *I*, Pencil, acrylic wash, on paper, 182 x 248 cm, 1985

44 *The Demon Artist's Portrait with a Question of Siamese Success*, Pencil, acrylic wash on paper, 182 x 320 cm, 1984, Private collection, New York

45 *The Deformed Artist with no Excuse — the Creature from Self-Portraits — the Clam*, Pencil, acrylic wash, on paper, 182 x 343 cm, 1985

List of Black and White Figures

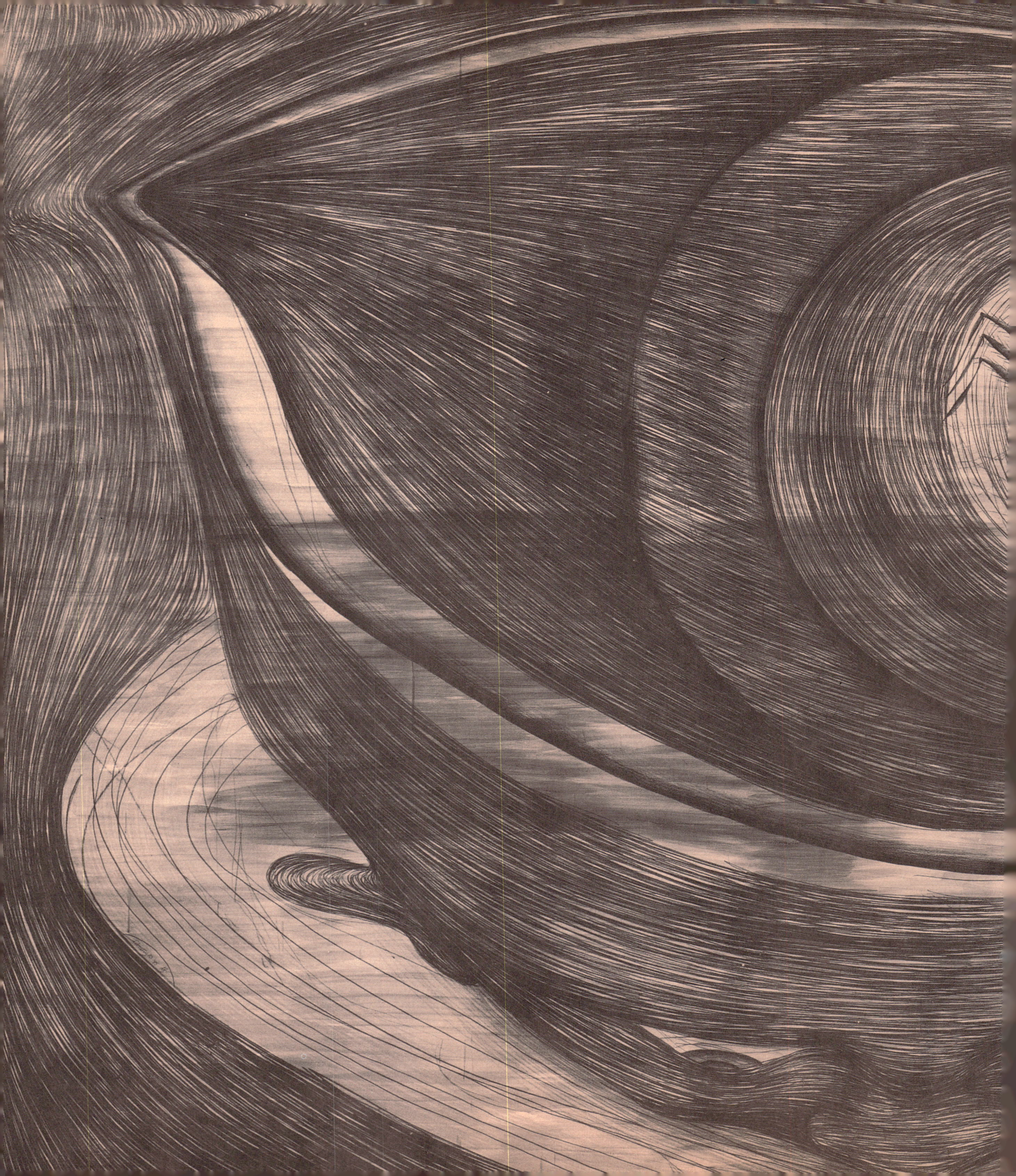